MY BROTHER'S FAITH

MY BROTHER'S FAITH

UNDERSTANDING THE BELIEFS OF OTHERS
WITHOUT COMPROMISING YOUR OWN

CARLTON FISHER

PEACE FISH

Wetumpka, AL

To My Beloved Soul Mate
Lisa Jane Peace Fisher

CONTENTS

Introduction

It is understanding that gives us an ability to have peace.
When we understand the other fellow's viewpoint,
and he understands ours, then we can sit down
and work out our differences.

Harry S. Truman

A few hours after Islamist terrorists killed nearly 3,000 people on September 11, 2001, I was called on to defend Muslim inmates in a prison. The following Sunday I felt obligated to defend Islam in my home church. These were not customary duties for a Baptist minister, but as a chaplain in the Federal Bureau of Prisons, I knew the character of most of the Muslim men in the prison where I worked, and I had learned at least the basics tenets of Islam. I could not just sit back and see the Muslim inmates get railroaded or listen quietly to my Christian brothers and sisters say absurd things about Islam.

Within hours after the attack, the Federal Bureau of Prisons ordered inmates affiliated with any type of Islamic belief to be segregated from the rest of the inmate general prison population. At the minimum security Federal prison where I worked, the warden directed me to help identify suspected Islamist terrorists at our prison. I knew our Muslim inmates. Sure, there were a few knuckleheads in the group, just like there were knuckleheads in the inmate Christian community and other religious groups, but none of these guys were terrorists, at least as far as I knew. So I informed our warden, in my opinion, none of our Muslim inmates were terrorists, and in fact, a number of them were positive role models for other prisoners on the compound.

The following Sunday when attending my local Baptist Church, several church members, knowing I worked with Muslim inmates, rushed to me to confirm their suspicions that all Muslims were like Al-Qaeda and the Taliban. While I did not agree with all the theological tenets of Islam, I could not silently stand by and confirm their suspicions.

As a chaplain in the Army Reserve, I was called to active duty soon after 9-11 and later for two other tours. I spent a total of two and a half years away from my family in support of the war effort, to include service in Afghanistan, Qatar, and twice in Iraq. I was privileged to practice the Chaplain Corps core competencies of nurturing the living, caring for the wounded, and honoring the dead. As a Christian chaplain, I led Christian services and guided fellow Christians in their Christian journeys. As a chaplain for people of all faiths, I helped U.S. and Coalition Muslim personnel and those from other faith traditions to have what they needed to practice their faiths. I also worked in humanitarian operations that included the combined efforts of Christians and Muslims.

In these environments I witnessed how U.S. personnel viewed or reacted to Islam and Muslims. Generally speaking, the Army did a great job in training soldiers in pre-deployment briefings with a general knowledge of Islam and the cultures of Iraq or Afghanistan. Some soldiers took the time to study Islam on their own, and while in Muslim countries, they developed deep relationships with Muslim people and tried to better understand what Muslims believe and why.

Still others, to include a few top leaders in the military and State Department, avoided or disregarded the importance and influence of complex religious beliefs in Iraq and Afghanistan. There are generally three reasons for this kind of negligence.

First, some people disparage the religion of those who believe differently than they do. Some who hold exclusive truths about their religion do not want to cloud their minds with the "ignorance" of other belief systems, so they lump all believers of another faith into one general category. On the other hand, some secularists who hold exclusive views about their worldview judge religious people in a similar way, lumping them into stereotypes as naïve and superstitious people.

Second, some are simply naïve about the impact of religion and have no desire to learn because any major religion, like Islam, is heavily nuanced with many differences among its various sects and cultures. Some people simply don't have the desire to learn all this.

Third and probably the most important factor is that Americans champion freedom of religion and prize separation of church and state. Some leaders believe they are respecting the religion of the other by not talking about it. After all, in the United States we often say, "It's not polite to talk about religion in public." In a Muslim country this polite practice can be offensive. Most Muslim people would never think of separating mosque and state. To ignore their faith is to ignore them.

Thankfully, leaders such as General David Petraeus, former Commander of the Multi-National Force in Iraq, recognized the need to understand indigenous faith and co-opted local religious leaders into the peacemaking and peace keeping process. Some leaders were too late to recognize this need. Take for instance former Secretary of State Madeleine Albright's honest assessment.

> One of my premises was that, whereas before, as a practical diplomat we tried to keep God and religion out of foreign policy, it was evident to me even as I was completing my time as Secretary of State that religion was playing a larger and larger part in what was going on in the world. And when you look at the issues we're dealing with today that have to do with the Muslim world, for instance, we absolutely do not understand Islam per se.... And as Secretary of State you have all kinds of advisers – economic advisers and arms control advisers and climate

change advisers – and the point I want to make is that it would be good to have some religious advisers too.[1]

Perhaps with the best of intentions, some Western world leaders have made mistakes in the Middle East by not acknowledging and exploring significant religious factors. Western leaders drew borders across broad landscapes to separate groups into imaginary cultures. They often funded the rich at the expense of the poor, backed alleged friends who would later become enemies, and often exported democratic values while ignoring existing Muslim values.[2] The wars in Afghanistan, Iraq, and Syria, the conflict between Israel and Palestine, the Arab Spring, ongoing conflicts with Iran, and the war with the so-called Islamic State (ISIS) are examples of conflicts jam-packed with religious ramifications. We cannot afford to ignore the impact of religious beliefs and practices in these global issues.

We cannot resolve religious conflicts with exclusively secular solutions. Military might and economic sanctions cannot defeat an ideology. Ideology must be fought by another ideology. We have certainly learned over the last two decades that killing a few terrorists doesn't mean their organizations go away. Miscalculated kills, especially when grave collateral damage is caused and innocents are killed, only makes others want to join such organizations. The key to defeating religious terrorists is understanding why young people join terror organizations in the first place and then influence social, cultural, and religious changes to make such organizations look foolish to join. Granted, we cannot and should not invite everybody or just anybody to the peace table, but with a little bit of common sense and foresight, we can influence emotionally and spiritually mature religious leaders to be part of the solutions.

In spite of our many religious differences, there are common patterns in how people of all faiths grow in their faith and love. These patterns are

---

[1] Romesh Ratnesar, from an interview with Madeleine Albright. "Albright Opens Up,"
[2] For examples, see the Sykes-Pikot Agreement, funding of the Suez Canal, and funding to various Mujahedeen fighters who later joined the Taliban. Ask any imam about the conflict of Western values versus Islamic values.

central to helping us understand our own faith, the faith of others, and inviting the right people to the peace table at the right time.

Globalization also impacts the way we react to the beliefs of others. As globalization continues to bring cultures together, fundamentalist leaders on the far right are worried their young people will slide down the "slippery slope" of secularism. They react with a fortress mentality, becoming more exclusive and typically avoid any overtures to inter-faith dialogue. On the extreme side are those, like the Islamic State, who opt for terrorism to stop their perception of globalization corruption.

On the other end of the continuum are those who welcome the new evolution of merging cultures. Many liberal religious leaders find commonality with other faiths, claiming everyone worships the same God, regardless of differences in religious faith. These leaders often play a large role in inter-faith dialogue, particularly as they relate to world peace issues. Some, claiming to be inclusive, in reality hold to a new politically correct form of exclusivism because they typically disparage or ignore fundamentalism, particularly in their own faith traditions.

The pathway to understanding is not making the other person see it your or my way. The path to understanding is finding safe common ground to discuss our differences. Genuine inter-faith dialogue takes into account the person on the far right with exclusive beliefs and the person on the far left who claims to hold inclusive beliefs.

Mad Dog Maddox, one of my prison flock, once told me, "Chaplain you can preach the best sermons in the world, and a fellow will agree with you and like you, but if he looks down and doesn't like the color of your shoes, he will write you off and never come back to church again." Mad Dog was in prison for selling meth, but he was one of the smartest prison chapel clerks I ever had. He was referring to the judgmental attitudes of self-righteous prisoners, yet his observation can certainly be applied beyond the prison walls. Self-righteousness is not unique to prison or religious people.

In over three decades as a Baptist minister and over a quarter of a century in ecumenical ministry and inter-faith work, I have learned many differences among various faith traditions. I also discovered many commonalities. While belief systems vary, people tend to share a similar process in getting to their beliefs. In this book I share what I have learned in hopes of helping people, whether religious or secular, to better get along.

For my Christian brothers and sisters, particularly for those who are more to the right, please don't put this book back on the shelf and judge me as some liberal Christian attempting to water-down Christianity and create a politically correct religion. I realize our differences in religion are much more complicated than the color of a pair of shoes. You more likely compare differences in faith to wearing entirely different clothes. If you need to know up front, I am a follower of Christ, committed to orthodox Christianity,[3] and I consider the Bible as my ultimate source of written authority.

For my brothers and sisters from other worldviews, please don't place this book back on the shelf and judge me as someone trying to manipulate you into my faith. If you come from a secular perspective, you may see religious differences as petty, like the color of a pair of shoes. If you need to know up front, I have studied the faith traditions and worldviews of others, have come to appreciate the rich stories and lessons from these views, and have applied many of these lessons in my own life.

I use the word "beliefs" in the title of this book in the broadest sense of the word. All people, whether religious or secular, have belief or faith in something. Religious people have faith to varying degrees in God or gods and their religious system. Atheists and humanists have faith to varying degrees in their worldview. In this sense, I often interchange the words "belief," "faith" and "worldview."

What this Book is about

This book has three parts. In the first part, I tell two stories. One story is about what happens when we fail to understand the faith of the other

---

[3] By orthodox here, I refer to commitment to the tenets of the Nicene Creed.

person. The second story is about the transformation that takes place when we do understand.

In the second part, we will explore struggles and stages that shape the way we believe. When we understand the similarities in our respective journeys to find meaning and purpose in life, we will get along far better, even if we arrive at different destinations. To understand a person's worldview, we must take into account more than a belief system. We must understand how culture, individual personality, and emotional and spiritual development impact worldviews.

In the third part, I outline some of the heady religious and political issues of our day, particularly as I see them in the Deep South, but I think our issues in the South are a microcosm of other issues in other parts of the United States and the world. We still fuss over separation of church and state. The Church is split over Democratic and Republican issues. Racial issues between blacks and whites are still hot. I still meet Baptists who believe Catholics are "lost," and Catholics who believe Baptists belong to a cult. Many Southerners are unfamiliar with other major religions of the world and have an outright fear of Islam. In this part of the book, I try to look at both sides of these issues. I admit our impasses, but also suggest ways for better understanding and reconciliation.

If you are struggling in your own faith, this book will help you better understand your personal struggle and perhaps restore confidence in your faith. If you are wondering why others believe so differently, this book will help you walk in their shoes and understand why they believe what they believe. If you are finding yourself in religious and political feuds at home, work, or in your own faith community, it will help you navigate through those feuds to healthier dialogue. If you are in the military or other government service and work with people in other lands who have different views, this book will help you better understand why you cannot ignore their faith. Their faith may not be part of the problem. It may be part of the solution.

I now realize when I first started making notes for this book a few years ago from a remote mountain in Afghanistan and subsequently writing the draft in my home in Wetumpka, Alabama, I was reacting to theological snobbery. When I was a young adult, I often felt stifled by the judgmental views of so many people from my own faith tradition. It's not that I disagreed with their theology. I just did not like the close-minded way of judging others without any attempt at trying to understand why others believe differently.

I've always had a need for people to get along. When I was 17 years old and decades before this became the modern mantra, I used to say, "The only thing I'm intolerant about is intolerance," but I never figured tolerance would become a new religion.

About halfway through this book project and particularly while living in the Washington, D.C. area, I became equally frustrated with intellectual snobbery. I noticed that many who champion liberal views look down on those who dare to question their new religion of tolerance. While I agree with the basic suppositions of tolerance, I found that many so-called liberals are more judging than any fundamentalist I've ever known.

I don't claim to solve all the issues between conservative and liberal worldviews, but I hope this book will serve as a bridge where people can meet in the middle and at least get a better view of the other side and grow in understanding.

Why Listen to a Chaplain?

Why listen to some preacher from Wetumpka, Alabama? My wife and kids will tell you I'm a decent husband and dad. I have a good beginner's knowledge about gardening, and I can name the constellations in the night sky, but I am forgetful, trip over details, and cuss at the computer when it won't act right. I still fight bouts of doubt, have impure thoughts, and sometimes don't delay my gratification well. However, I do have:

- First-hand experience from years of ministry in multi-cultural and multi-denominational churches and working with people from many different faiths and worldviews to ensure their freedom of religion. These groups include:

- o Christians from Catholic, Orthodox, Eastern Rite, Protestant, and Non-Denominational traditions
- o Messianics, Mormons, Jehovah's Witnesses, and Rastafarians
- o Jews from Orthodox, Conservative, and Reformed traditions
- o Muslims from Sunni and Shia traditions
- o Native American spiritual adherents from many American Indian traditions
- o Hindus from various traditions
- o Buddhists from various traditions
- o Santerians and Yorubans
- o Wiccans and other pagan adherents
- o Nation of Islam adherents
- o Moorish Science Temple of America followers

  The list also includes humanists, atheists, and agnostics who often express their desire to have freedom from religion.

- Two decades of chaplaincy experience with the Federal Bureau of Prisons, having served in maximum, medium, and minimum-security level prisons.

- Served over a quarter of a century in the Army Reserve with six mobilizations, including two deployments to Iraq and one to Afghanistan. Served as a battalion, group, brigade, major support command chaplain, and marriage and family chaplain. Also served as the advisor to the Chief of the Army Reserve regarding the individual readiness of our Army Reserve soldiers and families and building private public partnerships to increase that readiness. Currently serve in the rank of brigadier general as the senior chaplain for the Army Reserve.

- Served three years as a Director of Church and Community Ministries, leading Baptist churches in Christian social ministries and ecumenical ministries in a five-county area.

- Designed and wrote (in the context of a doctoral project) a course entitled *For God and Country: Enabling Chaplains of Various Faiths to Work Together.* Taught this course to Christian, Jewish, and Muslim chaplains in the Army. Later used the material to help inmates from various faiths get along in prison and prepare them to leave prison and return to their communities as productive citizens.

My Brother's Faith comes from my experiences in denominational, ecumenical, and inter-faith ministries. I don't claim to be writing on behalf of my denomination, the Federal Bureau of Prisons, or the U.S. Army, or to be vetting all my observations with metrics. I freely admit to wearing my own colored lenses, but I do use commonsense. Occasionally, you will find me hinting toward my preference on various issues, but my intent in this book is not to convince you of my side on controversial issues. Rather, my intent is to invite you and others to meet me at the middle of the bridge and have honest dialogue about our spiritual and emotional formations and how these formations impact our understanding on race, religion, power, and politics and our ability to get along. If you meet me at the middle of the bridge, I ask that you admit to wearing your own colored lenses as well. I've made my share of mistakes along the way, and no doubt, will continue to do so, but I've also been blessed with numerous successes in conflict resolution and reconciliation. I will share a few of those successes as well as some of the failures. The following two stories are examples of both.

Part 1

Getting Along

*When we become old and look back on life,
we will discover the only things that mattered
were the relationships we had.*
Carlton Fisher Sr. (author's Dad)

Chapter 1

Bad Assumptions in A'bad

Everything that irritates us about others
can lead us to an understanding of ourselves.

Carl Jung

T he Army Chaplain Corps was short on active duty chaplains when I got a call from the Chief of Chaplain's office in the summer of 2005. Joint Special Operations Command (JSOC) needed a base-hopping chaplain to minister to Special Operations personnel at remote bases in Afghanistan along the border of Pakistan. I met the minimum requirements: held the rank of major, was physically fit to deploy, and held a top-secret clearance (gained working a few years earlier with Central Command). It probably helped that I was Airborne qualified, but in reality, I was just a five-jump chump. I had made just enough jumps to qualify for my Airborne wings. I answered yes to the call, and a few weeks later I was working with the same outfit that would five years later, kill Osama bin Laden.

Whenever I called SOF (Special Operation Forces) guys on the phone to tell them I was coming for a visit, I sensed their eyes rolling on the other end of the phone and could filter their thoughts – "A chaplain?

What are we going to do with him? We'll have to hide the beer." Nevertheless, I smooth-talked my way to seeing them.

My favorite forward operating base, commonly called a FOB, was located in A'bad (short for Asadabad). A'bad is nestled in a mountain valley through which the Pek and Kunar rivers flow. Whether coming in from a Black Hawk or trekking up an adjacent mountain and looking down, the scenery was breathtaking.

While in A'bad I joined a few SOF guys on mountainous hikes. As we approached the top of one of the mountains, we watched our steps cautiously as we passed through the Claymore minefield to reach the observation post. The squad of marines waiting on top was surprised to see a chaplain at such a lonely place and welcomed our company. It wasn't long before these tough marines were telling me about their combat stress and challenges with family and girlfriends back home.

One marine had a brutal prayer request for me. "Chaplain, pray for me. When I fire my weapon at the enemy, I want my bullet to hit its mark." I kept my game face, but inside I wrestled for a few seconds with everything I had been taught about war and peace, and then I placed my hand on his shoulder and said something like this:

> Lord, we thank and praise you for the natural beauty of this place and the wonder of your creation. I thank you for my brother who you have placed on this mountaintop to defend this ground, the people of Afghanistan, and our nation. Use him as your peacekeeper. When the time comes, make his aim true. For those who need your justice, help my brother to use his weapon in an honorable way. May the deaths of our enemies be swift and without prolonged suffering. We trust you for their eternal safekeeping. For those who need your mercy, show my brother restraint, and for all innocent people caught in the middle of conflict, protect them from harm. Guide my brother and his comrades with your Holy Spirit, and protect them with your ministering angels. In Christ's name. Amen.

The young marine's request helped me to understand the lethality of our mission and the enormous responsibility that came along with it. That prayer evolved over the years into what would later become my combat prayer for our troops.

On one recon mission, an operator and I climbed past a lone, elderly Afghan man perched on a precipice overlooking the FOB. We suspected he was a spotter. Later that evening the main guard tower at the FOB was rocketed. Fortunately, no one was in the direct vicinity of the explosion.

At different times every night, our field artillery unit placed indirect fire on the enemy's area of operation. The likelihood that enemy combatants would be killed with sporadic firing was remote, but it did shake them up and prevented them from hunkering down in any particular place. One night when visiting the artillery soldiers, the battery commander asked me if I wanted to pull the lanyard on the Howitzer. The idea of firing a big cannon appealed to me, but I declined the offer. Chaplains are called to be symbols of peace, albeit very imperfect symbols, among warriors who bear arms. We are noncombatants and are not permitted to carry weapons, or in this case, fire a cannon on the enemy. Individual chaplains have their own ideas about what they would do if caught in a moral dilemma and had to defend themselves or others, and I know of several chaplains who have fired back, but pulling the lanyard at that moment did not fall into that moral category. With such sporadic firing, no one was likely to get killed if I pulled the lanyard, but how would I really know? As I walked away, I wondered if the young commander really saw me as a symbol of peace or a self-righteous preacher who wasn't willing to get his hands dirty. Killing is dirty business, and our nation calls its warriors to dirty their hands, often without regard for what happens to these warriors after they do the business of killing.

There were days our troops were not so fortunate. On one visit to the FOB, I paid a call to a young, unconscious marine in the combat area support hospital. His left leg was mangled from an IED explosion, and it had to be amputated. He died a few weeks later. Marines, traveling up

15

and down the road between Asadabad and Jalabad, were attacked almost daily.

The FOB contained a motley group of American SOF guys, soldiers, sailors, airmen, marines, other clandestine operators, and State Department workers along with Afghan soldiers and civilians and the occasional U.N. visitor. The clandestine operators and SOF guys rarely told me their real names.

I led general Christian worship services for anyone in the motley group who wanted to attend. Some attended out of boredom. One night in a service when I was asking the participants if they had any prayer requests, one marine who was bored and just looking for something to do that night, said, "Sure, I need you to pray for my "f***ing Commander." Later he interrupted me in the middle of Communion to ask, "What are you doing?" I told him about the bread and wine and how they symbolized the body and blood of Christ, that I would offer bread and wine to those who wanted to receive the elements as reminders of God's atoning sacrifice and Christ's presence, and those who participated could choose to dip or sip from the cup. Perhaps I should have better explained this at the beginning of Communion. He bluntly replied, "You can do that, but I don't want to." I said "Okay" and continued with the service. He sat back and seemed to enjoy the remainder of what he observed.

While in A'bad, I also led a seminar called "Keeping the Home Fires Burning." Deployments can be rough on marriages, and many single soldiers make unwise decisions in their dating relationships that lead to disastrous marriages. So I designed this seminar to help married soldiers strengthen their marriages and to help single soldiers prepare for marriages.

On one visit I tented with a Navy SEAL operator and two Afghan interpreters. The SEAL told me about his personal and family challenges. We prayed together – even climbed a mountain together, just the two of us. Even then, he never told me his real name. I knew the interpreters by their real names, Gholam and Zia. They were in their mid-forties. They grew up in Afghanistan during the Russian invasion and fled to the

United States before the rise of the Taliban. They became successful American citizens and raised families in San Francisco. They were back in Afghanistan to serve as linguists and take advantage of lucrative American contracts.

Mihr visited us often in the tent. Mihr was a young Afghan man, also a linguist, but he had never traveled past Afghanistan or Pakistan, and he was paid a much lower wage than the two older Afghan Americans. Mihr was born near the end of the defeated Russian regime and grew up under Taliban rule. He learned to speak English in one of the few colleges across the border in Pakistan. He was desperate to emigrate to the United States and hoped to become an American soldier or win a yearly Afghan lottery that offered a one-in-two-hundred chance of going to the United States. He solicited my help to find a church in the United States to sponsor him.

These three Muslim men took advantage of the Christian chaplain's knowledge on Christianity and eagerly asked me questions about Christianity, particularly about the history of Christianity and specific beliefs about Jesus. On a marker board in the tent, I drew time lines that traced the history of Judaism through early Christianity. Likewise, I asked them about Islam, concentrating in areas where I was still confused. They drew time lines on the board to help me better understand the differences between Sunnis and Shias.

Their knowledge of Christianity was peripheral, and they pushed me to clarify what Christians believe about Jesus. It came as a shock to them when I told them that Christians believe Jesus is God. I had to tell them twice. They tried to hide their disappointment and changed the subject. Nevertheless, their friendship with me did not change when we encountered this impasse.

Gholam, Zia, and Mihr stopped their work routine during the day to make *salat* (the daily prayers), but they were not religiously committed to keeping a tight prayer schedule. If they missed a few of the five required daily prayers, they had an "oh-well" attitude. They smoked cigarettes and watched Bollywood DVDs on their laptop computers, glued to the choreographed dance scenes of scantily clad, beautiful Indian women.

They drank beer, perused *Maxim* magazines, and told dirty jokes. They also showed me photos of their families and talked about how much they missed their wives and children. They extended to me genuine Afghan hospitality and revealed to me their dreams of a new Afghanistan and their commitment to Allah. I admired these earthy, honest Muslim men.

In true Afghan hospitality, Gholam and Zia hosted me as if I were a visiting dignitary. They respected my rank as an officer and my position as "imam" within my religion, but my titles had nothing to do with their desire to show hospitality. As I was to learn from them, they showed hospitality because I was a foreigner in their country, helping them to build a new Afghanistan, and hospitality is something Afghans simply do. When I awoke in the morning, they had hot chai prepared for me. They arranged a tour for me in the adjacent village, and when I told them I wanted to purchase a *kamiz shalwar* (traditional Afghan male blouse and trousers), they arranged for me to meet the local tailor. When the tailor completed his work, the suit was hand delivered to me at no charge. When I pleaded to pay, they would not accept my money. When I invited Gholam to get a haircut with me at the village barbershop, he and the Afghan barber had already made a deal under the table. My haircut was paid for. I was embarrassed by my lack of knowledge in their hospitality protocol and would have never asked about a couple of things had I known they intended to pay. When they noticed my interest in a corral of Arabian horses, they tried to arrange a trail riding adventure, but after I learned the horses had not been ridden for some while, they seemed relieved when I told them we could forgo that little adventure.

Gholam and Zia invited me to the tent of another Afghan man for supper. We sat barefoot on a carpet where they lavished me with local cuisine. Not in Muslim form, but in Afghan hospitality, they offered me beer. It was wintertime. I sat next to a space heater. The combination of a filling meal, reclining and relaxing after a long day's hike up and down a mountain, the warmth of the heater, the effects of the beer, and a lengthy discussion in Pashto (of which I heard but understood nothing) mesmerized me into a trancelike state. When they offered me another beer, I declined, remembering I had a marriage seminar to teach in less than an hour.

I bid them good evening and walked contentedly to the chow hall to conduct a session on "Keeping the Home Fires Burning." Without knowing it, my Afghan tentmates had advertised the seminar to other interpreters in the camp, and when I arrived to hold the first session, I was surprised to find that half of the seminar participants were Muslim interpreters. They were spellbound when I talked to them about understanding a woman's heart and the link between good communication and good sex. Some of them were shocked to hear a man could have a good relationship with his wife without using a stick or fist to beat her. Even the most educated Afghan men I talked with about marriage had no issue with the use of physical force to gain a woman's compliance in marital matters. While we may look aghast at their old-world ways, by contrast, I think they would have been just as stunned to discover the high divorce rates in the United States. They lined up after the seminar to ask for additional advice on boyfriend-girlfriend relationships and marriage relationships. When some of the young Afghan men asked me for advice about relationships with potential second, third, or fourth wives in their marriages, I had to remind them I was from a Christian culture where only one wife, at least one at a time, was permitted in a marriage. I encouraged them to consult their imams for advice on second, third, or fourth wives.

At lunch one day, I met the imam who served as the chaplain for the Afghan soldiers in the area, and we hit it off rather well. From a strategic point of view, I was working with Americans and Coalition Forces to win the hearts and minds of the local people. Since my meeting with the imam for the soldiers went so well, I wondered what it would be like to meet the local mullah for the civilian community. I expressed my thoughts to Gholam and Zia. I knew that American soldiers were prohibited from entering mosques without explicit permission from the command; however, Gholam and Zia were not aware of the rule. Wanting to be great hosts, and without my knowledge, Gholam and Zia sent Mihr to see the mullah to request permission for me to visit the local mosque and meet him. The mullah declined Mihr's request for me to visit the mosque, but he told Mihr he would like to meet me. So Miihr arranged for a meeting in the local market.

On a sunny, winter afternoon, I walked with Gholam, Zia, and Mihr to the meeting. The mullah was not much older than Mihr, perhaps in his mid-twenties. He claimed to have memorized the entire Quran. To Westerners this may seem an impossible feat, but to many Muslims, memorizing the entire Quran is seen as a pinnacle of devotion to Allah. In Sunni Islam there is no place for clergy. Imams are not ordained like priests and pastors in Christianity. They are elected by the *ulma,* the local body of Muslim believers. The man who has the greatest knowledge of the Quran is customarily elected as imam by the ulma. No doubt the young mullah had been selected for just such a reason.

Mihr served as my Pashto interpreter. The mullah and I greeted one another in the familiar Arabic *As-Salam Alaikum* and *Wa Alaikum Assalam* ("Peace be upon you" and "Peace to you"). Muslims from non-Arabic cultures (as the Pashto in Afghanistan) have enormous respect for the Arabic language, as Muslims believe the Word of God was given to Muhammad in the Arabic language. I have read an English translation of the Quran, but any serious student of Islam would challenge my claim to have read the real Quran. It must be read and understood in Arabic to capture its full meaning and application. Therefore, some Muslims who do not speak Arabic covet those who do. Most Afghans along the eastern border cannot read or write in their own language of Pashto, much less Arabic. As a result, they rely heavily on their madrasa-trained imams to tell them what they are to believe about Islam.

We also exchanged greetings in Pashto, *Sanga ye* and *Khushaal una* ("How are you" and "fine"). Beyond that I completely relied on Mihr to translate our conversation. The mullah, Mihr, and I sat around a small table in the open market place, and about ten other young Afghan men pulled up chairs and encircled us, eager to hear the dialogue between their mullah and the Christian soldier-minister from America. Though winter, it was a picture-perfect afternoon: the sun shining on us, about 60 degrees Fahrenheit, crisp and cool. The village looked as it would have been centuries ago, and the snow-covered mountains in the background completed the idyllic setting. The older interpreters, Gholam and Zia, stood outside the circle, smoking cigarettes, giving Mihr his chance to shine. The only thing that gave our setting away as the 21st century were posters of beautiful Bollywood actresses, accenting a wall on one of the local shops next to us. The women seemed to be smiling sensuously on our meeting. Everything was perfect. Then…

After the mullah and I completed our greetings, the mullah glanced over to Gholam and Zia and said something to them in Pashto. They replied in Pashto in an angry tone. They turned to me in English and said, "Let's go."

Mihr, embarrassed by the exchange, motioned for me to stay seated and continue the visit as if nothing happened. I could hear Gholam and Zia talking to each other in Pashto, cursing sporadically in English. Their sidebar and the difficulty of language translation made my concentration difficult. Gholam and Zia broke into my conversation with the mullah a couple of times to interject some heated statement in Pashto to the mullah. The mullah rolled his eyes at them, made a brief comment in Pashto and went back to talking with me, ignoring the two older men.

Feeling the tension rise, I thought I might try a little humor to calm things down, so I told the mullah that I sometimes bored my parishioners with my sermons and wondered if that ever happened to him when he gave his weekly *kutbah* (sermon).

I was hoping he might laugh and say something like, "Yes, it's a common problem," giving us the opportunity to engage in safe conversation about a common challenge for all preachers.

Instead, he said in Pashto, Mihr translating, "Oh no. That never happens. When I preach from the Quran, the power of Allah fills the mosque, making it impossible for the people to be bored. They are enlivened by the power of Allah."

I kept a smile on my poker face but silently thought, "That's a load of *BS*." It's not that I doubt the power of Allah, but I do doubt that rare ability in any preacher, Christian or Muslim, to thoroughly engage an audience every moment of every sermon. No preacher is that good.

Gholam and Zia were thinking exactly was I was thinking, but they made no attempt to keep a poker face. They fired back at the mullah with curt statements and then looked at me and pleaded, "Let's go!" Mihr, extremely uncomfortable now, motioned for me to get up, but the mullah motioned for me to stay seated and asked one of his eager followers to bring us some chai.

Gholam and Zia exploded in English, "Oh, now you're going to bring him tea... After he's getting ready to leave!" Then they turned to me and said, "Don't let him insult you like that. Let's go."

Not understanding what had caused any of this mess, I apologized to the mullah through Mihr, and the mullah and I bid each other awkward farewells.

For the next three hours, I wrung my hands with the three linguists trying to understand what caused the meeting to fall apart. It took another day for Gholam and Zia to cool down.

After lengthy conversations I came to understand what caused the breakdown. As soon as we arrived for the meeting, the young mullah told Gholam and Zia to extinguish their cigarettes. Feeling insulted, they wanted to know what gave him the right to be so sanctimonious and insult them while he was leering at the posters of scantily clad Indian women across the street. The mullah told them he was not leering and had nothing to do with the posters on the wall.

While the mullah and I continued our attempts at pleasantries, Gholam and Zia discussed their perception of the mullah's hypocrisy. When the mullah told me that his sermons were never boring, this further enflamed their perception of the mullah's hypocrisy and arrogance.

The final insult to injury was when the mullah offered me tea at the end of a meeting. In a country where hospitality is paramount, the tea should have been offered right away, not at the end of a meeting.

Gholam and Zia continued to berate the mullah. "He doesn't know anything. He can't even read and write. He can't even read the Quran in Arabic. The only education he ever received was at a madrasa under the direction of the Wahhabi Taliban. He doesn't know math. He doesn't even know about the history of his own country. All he knows is what they taught him about Islam... and another thing, if he doesn't like women, he must be a pervert. He probably goes to man dances and keeps a little boy on the side."

When I asked them what they planned to do for *Juma* (the Friday prayer service) since the young mullah was the only show in town, they said they would not dare attend any mosque where he was leading Juma. I asked, "But what about the ulma?" They told me the Quran taught them they didn't have to sit under the teaching of a hypocrite.

In hindsight, everyone arrived at the marketplace table with different agendas and expectations, and we all heard one another's comments through our own biased filters. Not to mention, we didn't even speak the same language.

Gholam and Zia wanted to be perfect hosts. They felt honor-bound to show me hospitality, and I added a little excitement to their daily routine. I think they were hoping I might make the mullah look like a simpleton in front of the mullah's fan club. They saw the young mullah as the epitome of what needed changing in Afghanistan. They were thrilled to be back in Afghanistan and hoped the meeting would be another small step in an education revolution. The young mullah came from the Wahhabi-style tradition of Islam. This tradition is deeply rooted in the faith of the majority of Muslims from Saudi Arabia and the Gulf States, but it was hijacked and twisted by the Taliban and Al Qaeda. Gholam and Zia were only familiar with the Taliban version of it, so they labeled all "Wahhabis" as backward and ignorant.

Educated in a madrasa during the Taliban days, the mullah probably wanted to keep Afghanistan under the Taliban's version of Sharia. From the looks of his adoring fans, the mullah probably wanted me to look like a theological simpleton in the presence of his superior knowledge of the Quran.

Perhaps the only motivation any of us had in common was our excitement about the gathering and our anticipation of what might come from such an experience.

I had hoped to win hearts and minds. I wanted the mullah and his buddies to know I respected them and their culture. I thought that if he saw me attempting to take one brick out of the ideological wall on my side, he might remove a brick from his side as well.

Lessons

When I look back on my experiences in A'bad, I believe the marriage retreats and worship services were a blessing for those who attended. I appreciate the friendships made there, and I sincerely hope my one-on-one counseling was beneficial. However, I did several things wrong during my visit with the young mullah. First lesson, my attempt at humor failed. Jokes rarely work in such a situation. Something gets lost in translation. Second lesson, I should have been better prepared for the meeting by learning more about the mullah. Third lesson, I could have better informed the chain of command. Fourth lesson, I was naïve. I was relying on my experiences with incarcerated Muslims in the Federal prison system and was virtually untrained regarding the finer nuances of Afghan Muslim culture. I could have walked into a trap, endangering the lives of the interpreters and others. I think everyone involved in that meeting did a poor job of sizing-up each other, and each of us left the meeting with poorer perceptions of each other.

When it comes to the faith of others, we often size-up people too quickly. To truly understand what people believe and why, we have to understand their unique personalities, cultures, and the way they approach faith and love.

Back at the prison, when I explained the Chaplain's role to new prisoners at the new-prisoner orientation, I could tell the new prisoners were sizing me up. To be honest, I was sizing them up as well. Whenever I walked down a village path in Afghanistan or later when I walked down a busy street in Baghdad, I could tell the local nationals were sizing me up. When they saw the cross insignia on my body armor and asked me what the insignia symbolized, I could sense their minds going into overdrive. I normally had to explain what a chaplain was, "I'm sort of like an imam for our soldiers. Only I'm a Christian imam." Almost always they responded with a smile and said something like, "Oh, we worship the same God."

We all compartmentalize information. When we compartmentalize information based solely on race, gender, or religion, we call this "profiling." Many states have laws to prevent law enforcement officers from detaining a person based on these profiles alone, yet we all profile to some extent. This is something our brains do naturally. We categorize sights, sounds, and touches in our mind: short or tall, skinny or fat, dark or light, loud or quiet, Southern drawl or Jersey accent, rough or smooth... the list goes on. Sometimes we have to profile quickly to avoid danger. If I am walking across the street and see a bus headed straight toward me, my brain will not take the time to calculate the weight of the bus, its trajectory, or speed. My brain will simply tell me, "Jump back. That bus will kill you." Likewise, law enforcement officers sometimes have to make quick life-and-death decisions, and they may not have the time to discern complex information.

When it comes to religious issues, the problem is not compartmentalizing information. The problem is we do not compartmentalize enough. The more compartments we have in our minds from which to draw information, the better we are able to make complex decisions. I could give a few, quick, dogmatic profiles and get this book over with now, and some people would be happier for it, but human beings and their beliefs deserve more than wide sweeping statements. We are complex.

Chapter 2

Love and Fear in Prison

Perfect love drives out fear
I John 4:18

In a Federal prison correctional workers can activate a prison-wide emergency response call by pressing the number "two" three times on any phone. This is known as "calling deuces." Correctional workers carry radios, so when the alarm message is sounded on their radios, staff members throughout the prison run to the site of the emergency. I began my career as a young chaplain with the Federal Bureau of Prisons at the United States Penitentiary (USP), a maximum-security prison, in Lompoc, California. At USP Lompoc there was a reason to call deuces nearly every hour.

Whenever I heard deuces at USP Lompoc, it seemed I was always working alongside Chaplain John Burke, the institution's Roman Catholic chaplain. I remember well my first emergency response to the prison infirmary. Chaplain Burke and I were some of the first staff to respond. As we entered the infirmary, we heard a prisoner moaning in the examination room. Entering the room we saw him writhing on the metal examination table, blood gushing from a gash on the back of his head and running down the silver-gray table and dripping onto the white linoleum floor. The doctor yelled at us, "Hold him down!" We did our best while the prisoner wailed and thrashed, and the doctor frantically sutured the gash.

The prisoner had been a long-time member of the Aryan Brotherhood, but he had fallen from grace with the racist gang, and his days had been numbered. The gang had placed a hit on him. One of the younger members of the gang, seeking to impress other gang members, volunteered for the job. While the older man was curling a set of weights on the exercise yard, the young man grabbed a weight bar. Gripping it like a baseball bat, the young man snuck up behind and took at swing at the back of the old Aryan's head.

I turned a little green from the sight of red spurts and the smell of copper and was relieved when another staff member offered to take my place at holding him down on the table. I left the room, sat on the hallway floor and tucked my head between my knees to get my color back. The doctor stitched him up, but the poor fellow's brain continued to swell. He slipped into a coma and died a few days later.

A few weeks later as Chaplain Burke and I walked down the main corridor, we noticed a trail of red drops on the gray concrete floor. We followed the trail into the same prison infirmary and discovered a big, tough African American inmate, pacing back and forth and saying, "Don't let me die. Please don't let me die." The same doctor ordered the prisoner to sit down on the metal examination table. The prisoner complied for a split-second, then jumped off the table and paced and pleaded again, "Please don't let me die. Don't let me die."

The doctor repeated the order, "Sit down so I can examine you."

He sat for maybe two seconds, jumped up again and pleaded, "Please don't let me die. Don't let me die."

The trail of blood in the hallway was not gruesome; just a few splatters here and there. There was not a sufficient amount of blood on the prisoner's white T-shirt to make us believe the wound was fatal. Touching his arm and coaxing him, Chaplain Burke said, "We only want to help. Please sit down so the doctor can take a look."

He sat one last time. His eyes glazed over, and he did not speak again. We took turns at CPR. We could hear the blood gurgle with each chest compression. We noticed a pinhole-size puncture on his chest, just over the heart. The doctor ordered us to continue CPR but rolled his eyes. Other staff members arrived and took their turns at CPR as well. About an hour later, the doctor told us to stop and pronounced the prisoner dead. We went back to our office. Chaplain Burke called the prisoner's counselor, got the phone number for the next of kin, then telephoned the prisoner's mom and notified her that her son had died in prison. Even from where I sat away from the phone, I heard her screams.

In a maximum-security penitentiary, inmates and staff have an ever-present fear of getting killed, but there is a fear that runs deeper. It is fear of dying in a prison. There is a difference. The inmate who fears being killed hopes to get out one day. The prisoner who fears dying – knows he will never leave.

Chaplain Burke and I often teamed up to help inmates. We had a common interest in Tony, a 50-something Italian American inmate. Tony had decided to turn his life around and started taking every rehabilitative class the prison had to offer. Shortly after making his life changing decision, he found out he had terminal cancer.

The prison infirmary was not prepared to handle stage-four cancer patients. Tony did leave the prison but only to go to the local community hospital. Lying unconscious and dying, he remained shackled to a hospital bed, guarded by three correctional officers. There is no room for grace in a prison sentence, even at death. Tony was unshackled only after he was pronounced dead by a physician.

There were five of us at Tony's funeral. Really, there were only two. Chaplain Burke and I led the service over a pauper's gravesite while three gravediggers leaned on shovels and waited for us to finish. Out of Tony's 50-plus years of living, the only two people who came to honor him were two prison chaplains. Many inmates fear that they will die like this, with no one left who gives a damn.

I was not with Chaplain Burke on another day when the deuces sounded from K unit, commonly called Killer unit. Correctional officers ran up two flights of stairs to the third tier in K unit to the cell door of an Australian prisoner named Mick. As officers ran to his cell, inmates scurried away like roaches. No prisoner wants to be caught near a shanking. Prisoners also fear being blamed for something they did not do. When the first officer reached Mick's cell, he saw blood splattered on the cell walls and Mick kneeling on the floor with a shank stuck in his back. A few seconds later, Mick fell over, face forward on the concrete floor.

One of the correctional workers who responded to the scene was a guy named Mack. No kidding, this is a story about two guys named Mick and Mack. Mack had the respect of staff and inmates, a rare combination in an us-against-them prison environment. After Mack raced up the stairs and reached the third floor, he suffered a massive heart attack, and he too fell unconscious on the concrete floor.

The prison infirmary was not equipped to handle trauma like this. Prison staff hurried to get the two unconscious men through seven sets of slow moving, bar-jangling doors. It took longer to get them out of the prison than it did to get them from the prison to the community hospital. Both men were pronounced dead on arrival at the local Lompoc hospital.

I did not go to the funeral home two days later. I was tending to the aftermath of another emergency. Chaplain Burke, however, was able to go and told me what happened.

After Chaplain Burke had given condolences to Mack's grieving widow, the funeral home director approached Chaplain Burke and whispered, "I don't know whether you know this or not, but the inmate – the one that Mack attempted to rescue – Well, his body is in the room next door."

No prison official was aware of this. Mick's body had been sent to the coroner's office in Santa Barbara, about an hour away. We figured the next-of-kin would have made arrangements from there to ship the body home. Prison officials would not have consented to this situation. It just didn't seem proper to honor a fallen correctional worker and a convict in the same place at the same time, especially when Mack's running to rescue Mick may have tipped off the heart attack that killed Mack.

Chaplain Burke left Mack's family and slipped into the other room. He was the only living soul in the room, and it appeared that once again a convict had died with no one to grieve him, except for a lone chaplain. Chaplain Burke leaned over the open casket and prayed for Mick's eternal safekeeping. A few minutes later an elderly woman with an Australian accent walked into the room. She looked into the casket and cried over her son. Chaplain Burke steadied her. As she regained her composure, she told Chaplain Burke how much she loved her son.

When the timing was right, Chaplain Burke said, "I don't know whether you know this or not, but the correctional worker who died racing up a flight of stairs to try to save your son – Well, his body and his family are in the room next door.

For a few seconds, she stared at Chaplain Burke, and then she asked, "Do you think it would be alright if I were to pay my respects?" Chaplain Burke told her he thought it would be just fine.

While other correctional workers looked on, Chaplain Burke introduced Mick's mom to Mack's wife. In the funeral home in the small town of Lompoc, near an us-against-them penitentiary; the wife of a correctional worker and the mother of a convict held one another and wept in their common grief.

That same week Lisa, my wife, and I were handling our own emergency. Two weeks earlier during recess at the elementary school, our son, Travis, and a large boy fell from the top of a set of monkey bars. The larger boy landed on Travis' leg, completely severing Travis' femur from the kneecap.

Travis emerged later that day from the emergency room with a cast covering the full length of his broken leg. Travis was small and thin for his age. When outfitted with crutches, he resembled a little waif from a Charles Dickens novel.

Two weeks later when we took Travis, outfitted in his cast, back to school, two girls from his second-grade class ran to meet him in the parking lot as he hobbled along, leaning on a pair or crutches. One girl was African American, tall and mature looking for her age. The other girl was Latino and looked every bit of her eight years. They made a fuss over Travis and mothered him. Lisa and I winked at each other, realizing we did not need to escort Travis to class. He was in good hands. We said goodbye to Travis, slipped away and left him in the charms of the two girls.

Lompoc is a small town. I knew something about the two girls I am not sure they knew about each other. Or if they did know, it didn't seem to matter. The tall African American girl was the daughter of one our correctional officers. The Latino girl was the granddaughter of one of our prisoners. And here they were: the African American daughter of a correctional officer and the Latino granddaughter of a convict, taking care of the little white son of a prison preacher. If they knew their social distinctions, the distinctions made no difference to them.

A few days later as I led an inter-faith prayer service for the inmates to honor Mick and Mack, I told the prisoners about the two grieving women from opposite sides of the world and the two girls from opposite sides of town. The two women let go of their distinctions to embrace one another in their shared grief. The two girls dismissed their distinctions to embrace a little boy in their shared compassion. Amidst such grief and compassion, they did not see an us-against-them world. They did not see any classification of "us and them," or "me and them," or "them and us." In each story, they saw only "us." It was just about "us."

Both religious and non-religious men attended the memorial service. The religious men included those from several different faith groups. Over the years I have given many sermons where I struck out, but on that night I sensed a homerun. I could see the tension of incarceration release from their faces. One Muslim inmate came to me afterward and expressed his hopes and prayers that people of all faiths could lay aside their fears, whether in a prison or the free world – and where we could imagine the power of "us."

God is Wooing Us

The Lakota (Sioux) Indian prisoners used to tell me, "We are a pitiful people." They were referring to humanity's broken relationship with the Creator, to one another, and even to the other people of the earth. By "other people," they meant the animal people, the plant people, and the rock people. The Lakota, as do most First Nation people, believe humans have a responsibility for all the earth. The Lakotas have a saying, *Mitakuye oyasin,* which means "All my relations." They often use this phrase in their greetings and partings and in sweat lodge ceremonies. The phrase expresses their inner longing to be rightly connected to the Creator, to all people, and to God's good earth.

From Judeo Christian tradition, when God created the Heavens and the Earth, God said his creation was very good. God told the humans to produce children and tend the earth. He placed them in charge of his good earth and made them responsible for the way they treated each other and the other creatures of the earth.

The subsequent stories of Genesis tell of humanity's failure to fulfill this responsibility. There were three major failures or "falls." In the first fall, Adam and Eve ate the forbidden fruit. This is the first story of a person or persons rebelling against God. In the next generation, there was a second fall, when Cain murdered Abel. This is the first story of a person rebelling against another person and God. By the time of Noah's day, the third fall occurred. Humans lived by violence and rebellion. This is the first story of a collective rebellion against God and a rebellion within the community itself. These falls symbolize the human condition – the yearning to "have it my way" and to shirk individual and community responsibility.

The rest of the Bible is about God wooing humanity back to God's self, to one another, and to community. This theme can be found in the remaining stories of Genesis through the lives of the patriarchs and in the rest of the Old Testament through the stories of the kings and prophets. The New Testament refers to all three falls. Paul recounts Adam's fall.[4] John recalls Cain's fall,[5] and Peter recounts the people of Noah's day.[6]

---

[4] Romans 5:12-30
[5] I John 3:11-18
[6] I Peter 3:18-20

Gabriel Yanez, a wise man from one of my previous prison flocks, summed it up this way.

> Astronomers say that our sun is just an ordinary-sized star among billions of other stars in the Milky Way Galaxy, and that our solar system is located on an outer spiral of the galaxy, far away from its center. The Milky Way Galaxy is an ordinary-sized galaxy, among billions of other galaxies, located far away from the center of the universe. That's the reason God sent the patriarchs, later the prophets, and why ultimately, God sent Christ – to draw us back to the center of the universe.

We have a long way to go to reach the center of the universe and to mend the divisions that separate us. Granted, there are many issues today that cannot be settled by consensus or compromise. There simply is no common ground in certain areas. Someone has to be right, and someone has to be wrong. However, much of the turmoil in the world boils down to a fear of what we do not understand.

Fear Versus Love

There are basically only two thoughts or emotions that motivate us in life. They are opposing forces. One is love. The other is fear. Some say hate is the opposite of love. Some say apathy, but according to John the Apostle, theologically speaking, the opposite of love is fear. When John was an old man, he taught that love and fear were the great mitigating forces of life. He declared, "God is love" and "perfect love drives out fear."[7]

We are not talking about healthy fear, the kind of fear that enables us to respect danger and is necessary for self-preservation, but the kind of fear that leads to worry, anger, depression, and bad choices in life.

Nor are we talking about unhealthy love, the kind of love where we love one person (perhaps ourselves), one group, or a cause so much that we neglect or harm others. Sure, love is often accompanied with feelings,

[7] I John 4

but feelings wax and wane. Genuine love is hard work and requires commitment and sacrifice.

Authentic love is an expression of thoughts or actions that engender the physical, mental, emotional, and spiritual growth of others and promotes healthy relationships. As we discuss love as it relates to emotional and spiritual maturity in this book, this is the kind of love we are discussing. Admittedly, I have my own biases, so as we explore worldviews, this is the definition I apply to any ideology as to whether that ideology is bad or good.

Consciously or unconsciously, we are motived by fear or love in nearly everything we do every day. We get out of the bed in the morning, either dreading forthcoming events or looking forward to the day's opportunities. When we eat breakfast with family members or eat lunch with colleagues, we sit next to those we trust and avoid those who get on our nerves. Fear and love guide us through our table talk. We give or withhold information, based on what we think or feel people will do with the information.

Even our personal hygiene reflects the way we love or fear. If we love ourselves, we tend to take care of our bodies. We brush our teeth, eat right, exercise right, get enough sleep, and wear clothes that complement our features. Yet if we love others, we balance our need to love ourselves with others' needs. We do not become so self-absorbed with our own needs that we neglect others.

Fear, on the other hand, tends to shut down our bodily maintenance. When we worry, we do not get enough sleep, or we may sleep too much. We may not eat right. We may self-medicate with drugs and alcohol or run to inappropriate relationships. When our appearance becomes haggard, we may withdraw into our frumpy clothes and stay cooped up in our house or private office, afraid to face the world. Or we may dress smartly and put on our best face as a defense mechanism, hoping others won't notice our insecurities. This self-absorbing fear causes us to neglect the needs of others. When they react to us out of their own fear, we strike back or run away in fear, continuing a destructive cycle of confrontation and/or avoidance.

Take a moment right now. Analyze your plans for today or tomorrow. You will discover that everything you plan to do or avoid is based at some level on what you love and/or fear.

Fear and love do not always act independently of one another. They often interact in our decision-making processes. The way we react to and express fear or love greatly impacts our quality of life and the quality of life of those who depend on us. The more mature we become in life, the less we are motivated by fear and the more we are motivated by love.

Too many people go to bed every night, worn out from the anxieties of their day and the worries of tomorrow. They are depressed. They are angry. Many of these fearful people are deeply religious. Unfortunately, nonreligious people often judge an entire religion based on their experiences of fearful religious people.

I hope this book will be helpful in showing the tensions of fear and love in any belief system or worldview. I've still got a long way to go myself. I wish I could tell you that I live by love every moment of the day, but from time to time, I slip back into a fearful way of looking at life. I have discovered this however: the more I let go of fears in my life and the more I let God's love empower my life, the freer I feel and think. I encourage you, especially as you continue in this book, to assess your own fears. The more you allow love to "drive out your fear," the more you will improve your own readiness and resilience and your ability to understand and help others, without compromising your own beliefs.

Part 2

Understanding Our Spiritual Journey

Our wisdom… consists almost entirely of two parts:
the knowledge of God and of ourselves.
As these are closely connected,
it is not easy to decide which comes first.
John Calvin, *Institutes of the Christian Religion*

Chapter 3

Our Soul's History

If from there you seek the Lord our God,

you will find him if you look for him

with all your heart and all your soul.

Deuteronomy 4:29

T here are two extreme types of counselors I generally warn people to avoid: the psychologist who views religion as a crutch and the pastor who ignores the relevance of the behavioral sciences. The field of psychology was born alongside other behavioral sciences in the 1800s in the new era of scientific methodology. Prior to that era, shamans or priests from various cultures often combined a prescription for herbal treatments (medicine) with common sense counseling, spiritual guidance, and prayer.

The word "psychology" itself is religious in nature. It is a combination of two Greek words that when combined, means "study of the soul." Some of the greatest classical works on spirituality and religion are rich in psychological nuances. Check out *The Spiritual Exercises* of Saint Ignatius of Loyola written in the 16th century, *The Cloud of the Unknowing* written in the 14th century, *Job* written approximately 2000

BCE, or even further back to one of the first known written works, *The Epic of Gilgamesh*, dating back to approximately 2700 BCE. In a very broad generalization, many of the tools of the trade of psychology are not new. If we were to go back 2,000 years, we would find Jesus doing what today we might call active listening, psychoanalysis, and behavior modification.

In the last two centuries, a wall was built between psychology and religion. When God and miracles allegedly did not measure up to new scientific litmus tests, some of the early neurologists, like Sigmund Freud, threw religion overboard. Many clergy then reacted in a fortress mentality and threw great counseling techniques overboard because these techniques were linked to the new "worldly" behavioral sciences. Both sides of the spiritual-scientific divide threw out the proverbial baby with the bath water.

In the last few decades, many professional psychologists and ministers have been tearing down the wall to rediscover common ground. Psychologists often weave spirituality into the therapeutic process and encourage religious faith. Ministers often blend psychological counseling techniques with Biblical guidance and prayer.[8]

If you want to understand your soul or the soul of another person, then consider the best of what both fields have to offer. In any thorough counseling process, a good counselor, whether psychologist or pastor will take into account the following information of the counselee.

- Age
- Ethnicity and culture
- Socio-economic background
- Financial and basic needs (food, clothing, and shelter), stability, and comfort level
- Past and present family relationships and demographics
- Patterns in family relationships

---

[8] For examples, see Carl Jung's *Answer to Job*; William James, James Fowler, and Scott Peck's work on stages of spiritual development; Wayne Oates and John Drakeford's work on the integration of psychology and pastoral counseling; and James Dobson's work on child psychology.

- Health history and hereditary factors
- Major failures and successes
- Past and current crises
- Significant losses and important blessings
- Unresolved issues
- Personality temperament
- Quality of love received from parents and other family members
- Ways of expressing and receiving love
- Work history
- Academic background
- Physical maturity and ability
- Rational maturity and ability
- Emotional maturity and ability
- Spiritual maturity and ability
- Religious/worldview background

There are plenty of books on these subjects, so it is not my intent in this book to review all of these factors but to acknowledge all these factors have tremendous impact on the way a person sees the world.

Take for example the quality and quantity of love parents give to their children. The right balance of nurture and discipline, or the lack thereof, or an imbalance of the two, has tremendous impact on how children grow up. In my years of being a chaplain I have seen few issues more catastrophic than the absence of a parent's love in the life of a child. I often wonder what life would have been like for many prisoners had they had a loving father in their lives. I have counseled many women who had difficulty in relating with men and ended up in disastrous marriages or exhausting relationships because they did not have a loving father in their lives. And God help those who did not have a loving mother in their lives. Every child needs a trusted mother and father figure. Without the blessing of parental affirmation, many people spend a lifetime looking for this blessing and never find it. This deep yearning greatly impacts a person's worldview.

I've heard it said, "You are who you are because of where you were when you were ten years old." There is some merit to this. A person raised with ten other siblings in a two-room shack in the country during the Depression sees the world differently than a person raised in a luxurious townhouse in an uptown area during the age of globalization.

Look at tragedies and stages of grief. When we lose a loved one, feel betrayed or exploited, experience a shattered dream, or fail an important mission, we go through grief. Elizabeth Kubler-Ross names the natural stages of grief: denial, anger, bargaining, depression, and acceptance. These feelings significantly impact the way we approach or respond to matters of faith.

Our unique personality temperaments shape us as well. If you have never taken the Myers-Briggs Personality Instrument or the Keirsey Temperament Sorter, or another personality-type indicator, you can take one of these indicators on-line in about 20 minutes. These indicators basically address four questions concerning your likes and dislikes:

Do you get most of your energy from other people or from within yourself? (Extroversion versus Introversion)

Are you a detail person or a big picture person? (Sensing versus Intuitive)

Do you generally make decisions on how you think or how you feel? (Thinking versus Feeling)

Do you generally make decisions quickly or do you prefer to take your time and explore options before making decisions? (Judging versus Perceptive)

Your answers can be categorized into one of four major personality types with the possibility of 16 variants. People are often shocked at how accurate these indicators reflect their personalities. These personality indicators are often used to help people find jobs to match their personalities, identify specific leadership skills, resolve marital conflict, or find a suitable mate. Personality temperament has a major impact on preferences in religious beliefs and practices. People tend to go to churches, synagogues, or mosques that suit their personality preferences within their respective faith traditions. Conversely, they are often uncomfortable in religious settings that conflict with their temperaments.

Our individual personalities also affect the way we express love. Gary Chapman has written a series of books on the "five love languages." He says people express love in five different ways; by giving words of affirmation, appropriate physical touch, quality time, acts of service, or gifts. According to Chapman, we may like all of these ways to express affection, but we generally make one of them a primary way to express love, another secondary, and so on. Marriage relationships often begin to fail when spouses no longer express the primary love language of their partners. Chapman has saved countless marriages by helping couples recognize the need to meet and speak each other's love language. Keeping this in mind, imagine all the different ways we express love and how this impacts what we like or don't like in religion, or how we want to relate to God.

Spirituality

We began Part Two with a quote from John Calvin, "Our wisdom... consists almost entirely of two parts: the knowledge of God and of ourselves. As these are closely connected, it is not easy to decide which comes first."[9] To understand why we believe the way we do, we must be self-reflective and examine hereditary and environmental factors that shape us. To fully understand others, we must take into account the factors that shape them as well.

If Calvin were with us today, he would probably agree that self-reflection is an important part of the process of understanding one's soul. However, self-reflection for self-reflection's sake can become narcissistic. Calvin's real intent was to help people realize their need for God. And what is a soul anyway?

As already noted, the word "psychology" gives us a hint. In the English translation of the New Testament, the Greek word *psyche* is translated as soul.

With the exception of one writer, all the writers of the New Testament documents were Jewish and wrote in the popular Greek

---

[9] John Calvin, *The Institutes of Christian Religion*, ed. Tony Lane and Hilary Osborne, (Grand Rapids, MI: Baker House, 1986), 1.1.1, p. 21.

language of their day. A mixture of Jewish and Greek culture impacted their worldviews. In the Greek thinking of that day, many people believed the soul was a part of the human spirit that continued to live on when a person dies. The Jewish religious leaders of their time differed with this Greek thinking. In the Hebrew Bible, the word used for soul is *nephesh*. This Hebrew word is not a general reference to a spirit that lives on beyond the grave. The nephesh comprised a person's complete self – a person's body, thoughts, and character. The same word nephesh is used in Genesis when God created animals as living souls. Animals too, in this sense, have a soul. Another word often used in connection to the soul is *ruach*, the same word used for wind or the breath of God. In this sense, the soul is created by the breath of God and uniquely desires to be connected to God.

The Jews of Jesus' day differed on their opinions about the afterlife. The Sadducees did not believe in an afterlife. The Pharisees did believe in the afterlife. Yet even the Pharisees did not necessarily accept the Greek belief in some unseen spirit that departed the body immediately at the point of death. They generally believed that when a person died, that was it. The person was dead – no spirit leaving the body to go somewhere else. The nepesh or soul remained dead in the grave, awaiting the resurrection. At the resurrection, the soul would be restored.

Even today, Christians still debate issues about the soul. Do animals have souls like people? Does the soul immediately depart at the moment of death to the afterlife, or does the soul await the resurrection? Regardless, most Christians and Jews would agree today that the soul is something created by God and there is an inner longing in the human soul to be connected with something greater than one's self.

We often associate this desire with another word, "spirituality." Some see spirituality and religion as totally separate. People often say to me, "Well, I don't consider myself religious, but I'm spiritual." I get what they are saying, but others consider such comments as foolish. They see spirituality and religion as fundamentally connected. On the other hand, some religious people view modern-day spirituality as being too esoteric, a little spooky, and a threat to orthodox faith. Some non-religious people see spirituality as silly and superstitious, something associated with séances or "naïve" religious people praying to their imaginary, heavenly friend.

Here is a basic working definition of spirituality. Spirituality is a connection with a cause or force greater than one's self that compels a person to love life, love others, and find meaning and purpose in life.

This cause or greater force, depending on the person, may be religious faith, a worldview, or a guiding principle. In this sense every person has a spiritual life, whether he or she is a devout religious person, committed humanist, or somewhere in between.

As you think about your own spiritual life, here are four questions to consider. How well do you generally...

- Love instead of fear?
- Trust instead of despair?
- Forgive instead of resent?
- Choose right instead of wrong?

Love instead of fear

Almost everything you do today or tomorrow is based at some level on how much you love what you are doing, or fear it, and how much you love the ones you are with or mistrust them. Healthy fear (a respect for danger) is necessary for self-preservation. However, unhealthy and unrealistic fear can lead to worry, anger, and depression. Love is the only real antidote – not narcissistic, syrupy, or obsessive love – but the kind of genuine love that requires commitment, faithfulness, and hard work. This kind of love promotes health, and purpose and meaning in life.

Trust instead of despair

Do you generally trust that life will go well for you when you do your part to love well and live well? This is to some extent, faith. Without faith we will go through life seeing the glass half-empty and miss many opportunities to find joy and make a difference in the world. Faith does not remove or ignore difficult times, but it carries us through such times and empowers us to believe in others and ourselves.

Forgive instead of resent

Forgiveness is hard work. It is difficult to forgive others for their sins, let alone forgive ourselves for our own failures. Please hear me. I am not suggesting we excuse horrible behaviors or let others off the hook for their personal responsibility. But there is no better medicine than forgiveness. Bitterness is self-consuming and destructive. Forgiveness is freeing and healing, and can often lead to reconciliation.

Choose right instead of wrong

We all mess up from time to time. It is part of being human. Most of us do not have issues in moral areas that are clearly black and white. Rather, we get in trouble in the shades of gray. Without good moral character, we are prone to make poor decisions that not only adversely impact our own lives but negatively impact our relationships and commitments with family members, friends, co-workers, and even our enemies. A strong spiritual fortitude enables us to set strong boundaries to make the right decisions when we land in these gray areas.

Summary and Way Ahead

Environment and heredity shape our worldviews. I know that is an obvious statement, but when we become angry or fearful, we tend to forget the obvious and are often shocked or overreact to people who see the world differently than we do. Our level of spiritual and emotional development contributes immensely to the level of satisfaction in our relationships, our meaning and purpose in life, and our individual ways of seeing the world and reacting to it. This will be the subject of the remainder of this book.

Chapter 4

Stages of Spiritual Growth

If you realize that all things change,

There is nothing you will try to hold on to.

If you aren't afraid of dying,

There is nothing you can't achieve.

Tao Te Ching 74

W hen I was a 12-year-old boy in the last of an era of hellfire-and-brimstone preaching, the fear of going to Hell gripped me for months. I had reached what Baptists call "the age of accountability" and realized I was "lost." In evangelical language, that meant I was on the wrong road regarding my eternal destination. Take a pubescent kid with self-esteem issues and mix in a fear of going to Hell, and you've got a nervous wreck. I was jumpy anytime I got into a vehicle, fearful I might get killed in a car wreck down the road and initiate my journey to Hell. My life was in **disorder.**

On September 13, 1970, just a few minutes before noon while our congregation was singing the second line of the first stanza of "Just As I Am," I got up from my pew and walked down the aisle of our Baptist church. There in front of the altar, the pastor awaited with an outstretched hand. I shook his hand and told him, "Preacher I need to be baptized and let Jesus in my heart."

Instantly, a burden fell from my shoulders. I was baptized that evening and fell more in love with God as each day passed. My fear of Hell disappeared. I sensed God believed in me, and because of that, for the first time in my life, I believed in myself. I attended church every time the door was open, paid attention to every word the preacher said, and signed up for every available church program. Some of the kids at my high school dreaded to see me coming because they knew I would whip out my Bible and tell them about the Lord. I became known as the "Reverend" and maintained that title all the way through high school. I had a great sense of **duty**.

As I continued my Christian journey, my zeal began to wane as competing feelings and doubts toyed with my Christian faith. As a pubescent kid, not all of my thoughts were holy. I thought about sex... a lot, and I also secretly wondered about the religious beliefs I had been taught. I dared not mention my doubts to anyone, but I wondered if I was really saved. Was Jesus really God? Was there really life after death? Was there really a God at all? Or had I just worked myself up into some religious hysteria? This was a time of **doubting**.

In spite of the doubts, I never gave up on my lifelong commitment to follow the Lord. In time, the more I studied the Bible, the more I realized how little I knew the Bible. The more I loved the Lord, the more I realized how incomprehensible God was. But after a while, the doubts did not matter as much anymore. I just enjoyed the mystery. This was a time of **discovery**.

Generally speaking, as we mature in our spiritual growth, we go through four stages. These stages of spiritual growth can be compared to our stages in human growth development. Let's take a look at them.

Stages of Spiritual Growth

1. Disorder
2. Duty
3. Doubting
4. Discovery[10]

Disorder

Newborn babies are precious. We have great hopes for their future and want them to be blessed and be a blessing to the world, but let's face it. Babies are clueless about the world. They can't name the President of the United States, don't know how much a gallon of gasoline costs, and they do not know how hard their parents work to keep them healthy and happy. Their cries typically mean, "I'm hungry, so feed me. I'm thirsty, so give me something to drink. I'm bored, so rock me or let me suck on a nipple. I'm wet or there is gooey stuff on my bottom, so get me out of this nasty diaper." It is natural for them to act this way. After all, they are infants. If they could express their worldview, it would be something like: "It's all about me!"

We too are infantile in our first stage of spiritual growth. We are unconcerned or unaware of the spiritual world around us. We are lost. In this stage of spiritual development, we are normally concerned with only our basic needs, and once those basic needs are met, the search for happiness consumes us. Who doesn't want to be happy? But happiness is based on happenstance, and we cannot always control our circumstances.

When happiness becomes our primary goal in life, we burden ourselves with an unachievable goal, and the more we strive for happiness, the more miserable we become. Finding it hard to delay our gratification, we become angry. Some people in this stage of disorder turn to food, drugs, alcohol, sex, or material possessions to fill the void. While these behaviors and things may offer a temporary sense of

---

[10] For modern works in this area, see James Fowler and Scott Peck on stages of spiritual development. See the works of Lawrence Kohlberg and Jean Piaget on stages of moral development. I credit Chaplain Dallas Speight with helping me to coin the four stages as they are named here.

gratification, if we end up abusing our body or crossing inappropriate intimacy boundaries, we only feel worse later on. Then our self-esteem suffers. In this stage of disorder, people are prone to depression. Often, people give up in this stage, thinking, "School is hard, so I'll quit… This job stinks, so I'll quit… This marriage isn't working, so I'll get a divorce." To get happy, they start looking for the high again. Some think, "If only I had more money, more sex, more status, or more toys," and the lost cycle begins again. This is a stage of disorder.

Duty

If environment and heredity are kind, infants ordinarily grow to become well-adjusted children, respecting their parents or guardians and the rules their parents or guardians set for them. As they transform from toddlers to preschoolers, they soon realize they are not the center of the universe and normally adjust their desires, albeit with struggle, to meet the needs of their authority figures and to fit in with other siblings and peers.

Provided we are given good emotional and spiritual support, we too outgrow the stage of disorder and become well-adjusted spiritual children and enter our duty stage of spirituality. We realize life is not about us. We discover God (or in other worldviews, a spiritual or transcendent force). In this new stage, we seek to please God or find contentment in this new transcendent force. With this new awakening, we also sense the needs of others. Our quest for personal happiness becomes a lower priority, and our need to please God and others becomes a higher priority.

We enter this stage in childlikeness. Jesus said, "Unless you change and become like little children, you will never enter the kingdom of heaven."[11] When a father tells his child to leap off a wall into his arms, the child leaps without fear, knowing her father will catch her. The child dutifully obeys her parents' rules and boundaries and finds bliss in pleasing her parents. Likewise, this stage of spirituality is filled with awe and first love of God.

---

[11] Matthew 18:3

This phase can also be filled with legalism. When a parent tells a seven-year-old child to stay out of the neighborhood street, the child dutifully obeys the command. He does not wonder, "Well, what about after dinner when there is little or no traffic?" Just as young children rarely question parental authority, new converts rarely question their new religious authority. They want their ethics and theology explained in tidy little packages. The new believer has an organized image of God in his mind that permits little room for change. He needs God in a box and is not comfortable with mystery. In this stage of spiritual development, the faithful person diligently seeks to follow the rules of the religion, rarely questioning his faith.

I clearly remember the duty stage in my own development. When I realized how much God loved me, I fell in love with God. I was at church every time the door was open. Every week I dutifully placed my tithe of dollar bills into the weekly offering envelope and faithfully checked off each block on the front of the envelope:

- ✓ Offering
- ✓ Studied Sunday School Lesson
- ✓ Read the Bible Daily
- ✓ Attended Sunday School
- ✓ Attended Worship
- ✓ Contacts (the number of people we had invited to church)

If by chance we visited my grandmother over the weekend, and I had not read my Bible by the time we got back home late Saturday night, I would rush to my room to read the Bible before the clock struck midnight. That way I could faithfully check the box, indicating I read my Bible every day of the week and proudly submit my weekly report, showing I completed 100% of the essential tasks for weekly Christian living.

When we are in the duty stage, we are also prone to quickly judge others who do not follow our rules and beliefs. I found this to be a common challenge with many prisoners who became new converts. Having lived a hedonistic lifestyle and being judged by others for such a long time, they felt empowered by their new righteousness. Sometimes it went to their heads, and I encountered many who seemed to be telling me, "I know the truth and I'm the only one who knows the truth." This is one of the down sides to the duty stage.

The transition from disorder to duty may happen instantaneous as often happens in a passionate conversion. This quick transition was the case in my conversion. Or it may take months or years through careful evaluation in an intellectual process. We may passionately arrive at this stage out of guilt and shame, or we may intellectually approach this stage, realizing it as the next practical step to take. Others who recognize it is the right time may carry us to this stage through religious teaching and ritual. This happens when a Catholic goes through confirmation, a Baptist walks down the aisle, a Muslim takes the *shahada*, or when a Jewish person goes through a bar mitzvah. Rituals do not necessarily guarantee our entrance into this new stage of spirituality. During a ritual, a person may just be going through the motions. For transformation to truly take place, the person must understand and apply the meaning of the ritual to his or her life.

Doubting

Little children eventually become teenagers. The teen years are awkward for budding young adults. Their bodies are caught between childhood and adulthood, and their emotions constantly change. Sometimes they act like children, and other times they act grownup. In their quest for personal independence, they may question the authority of their parents regarding curfews and other limitations. They may also doubt themselves as they struggle to build self-confidence. Normally, the more loving and understanding the parents are, the better the child will transition through this stage, but even the best of parents cannot stop such doubts from arising.

Just as teens go through a doubting or searching stage, we pass through a doubting phase in our spiritual lives. Some may doubt the authority of their religious leaders. Others may doubt the essence of their faith. The Christian may wonder, "Is Jesus really God? The Muslim may wonder, "Is Muhammad really the last and final prophet?" The Jewish person may question, "Did God really hand the Ten Commandments to Moses?" The Hindu may wonder, "Will we really be reincarnated?" Even the atheist might doubt his worldview, wondering, "Maybe there really is a god."

Some people remain confident in their belief system, but they may doubt the personal decisions they made during the duty stage of faith. They may wonder if they will be able to live up to the tenets of their faith, or in an evangelical sense, wonder if they are still saved.

However, the doubting stage is simply another normal phase in spiritual growth. When some people enter this phase, they are naturally frightened by it. They feel they are losing their faith; however, when nurtured in a good way, they will actually mature in their faith.

There are various ways a parent might react to a child who challenges parental authority. Some parents react harshly to their children. If so, children may rebel or leave home before they are ready, believing they have outgrown the primitive notions of their parents. Others, too afraid to question their parents, might live in emotionally suppressed relationships for years. Other parents are good listeners and encourage their children to ask the "why" questions. These parents don't tell their children, "Just because." They see the questioning phase as a new opportunity to nurture their children and encourage them to adulthood.

When religious people become aware of their own doubts, they react similarly, depending on the response of their religious authorities. My Christian denomination does a great job of bringing people from disorder to duty, but I think in the past we often failed in nurturing people through their doubts. I remember when I went through this phase. I do not recall any sermons informing me that doubts were a normal part of spiritual growth. I did not know who to trust in my church. So I suppressed my doubts, wondering, "Suppose they find out?" But the more I suppressed my doubts, thinking, "Oh no, you cannot think this way. It's wrong. Just believe," the worse my doubts became. In hindsight there were people in my church who would have understood and helped me, but I was simply naïve at the time. So I remained silent about my doubts, afraid I was losing my faith and feeling I would be condemned if others found out.

In some religious traditions it is taboo to express doubt. This is not healthy. If people cannot express doubt in a safe environment, they will likely eventually leave that faith tradition. Those who continue in their tradition but hide their true feelings and thoughts will do so with great emotional anxiety and possibly resentment.

Most parents understand the difference between a child shaking his fist in defiance and simply asking a question. The same is true for mature religious leaders. They know how to listen to the doubts of their faith tradition's followers and can nurture and guide them through this difficult time.

Discovery

Generally, young people reach adulthood when they take responsibility for their own lives and are able to live independently from their parents. Mature young adults typically take the values their parents gave them, perhaps tweak them a bit to fit their new environment, and make those values their own. They do so, not because their parents forced their values on them but because they believe the values are right for them. They come to realize, as did their parents, they do not have all the answers to life. Yet they will discover fulfillment and meaning in life. If they grew up in a home devoid of good parenting skills or a home without spiritual guidance, they will probably strive even harder to find and take ownership of a worldview that works for them.

When we reach the discovery stage of our spiritual quest, we look back on our faith journey and the disciplines and values we were taught. Unless we grew up in an unhealthy religious environment, we normally take these disciplines and values, perhaps tweak them a bit, and then make them our own. Our faith is no longer just the faith of our mothers and fathers. It now belongs to us. If we grew up in a home that was spiritually empty, we will probably work hard to find a spiritual path that works for us.

The discovery stage is a stage of exploration. We enjoy reading our sacred texts, but the more we read them, the more we realize how little we really know. The more we love the Lord (or supernatural power or some intrinsic cause – depending on your worldview), the more we realize how incomprehensible this God is. Yet, our doubts do not matter as much anymore. We enjoy the mystery.

Biblical Examples of the Stages

There are hundreds of examples of biblical characters in the different stages. Here are my favorites.

King Herod represents disorder. While he was responsible for building the great temple in Jerusalem, he never spiritually comprehended what the temple represented. He was so driven by power and ambition that he killed his own wife and son. He had all the male infants in Bethlehem killed in order to kill the one who would grow up to challenge his power.

Zacchaeus is the classic example of duty. Zacchaeus was a small man who probably suffered from short man's syndrome (I can say this. I'm a short man). He focused on making money to find happiness, and as a tax collector, he had the perfect job to make money in his culture. He cheated people, and as a consequence, he was not a well-liked person in the community. When Zacchaeus accepted Jesus as his savior, his life was immediately transformed. He paid back fourfold all he had stolen, gave half of his possessions to the needy, and transformed his home life.[12]

Nicodemus is the quintessential example of doubting. He was a Pharisee and a distinguished member of the Sanhedrin court. He came to see Jesus at night, possibly using the cover of darkness to prevent anyone from discovering his doubts. When Jesus told him about spiritual birth, Nicodemus struggled intellectually with the idea of being "born again" or being "born from above."[13] There is no written record that tells us of

---

[12] Luke 19:1-10

[13] Story found in John 3:1-21. Some Christians prefer the *born-again* translation as this fits with their theology of a time-sensitive conversion. Others prefer the *born-from-above* translation as this fits with their theology of a spiritual process.

Nicodemus' conversion experience. He probably did not have a sudden conversion experience, but we know he became a courageous follower of Jesus. When Jesus died, Nicodemus took a stand with Joseph of Arimathea and facilitated the funeral arrangements for the body of Jesus.[14] This certainly cost him his reputation in front of the religious leaders who were stuck in the duty stage of their own spirituality. Unlike Zacchaeus who had a sudden transformative experience, Nicodemus was a thinker and a doubter. He needed time to intellectually process his decision about following Jesus.

We can see all four stages in the life of the Apostle Paul: his life of disorder when hate consumed him, his life of duty right after his conversion on the road to Damascus, his life of doubting when he struggled with own personal issues, and his life of discovery, described this way:

> When I was a child, my speech, feelings, and thinking were all those of a child; now that I am an adult, I have no more use for childish ways. What we see now is like an image in a mirror; then we shall see face to face. What I know now is only partial; then it will be complete – as complete as God's knowledge of me. Meanwhile these three remain: faith, hope, and love; and the greatest of these is love.[15]

In this stage of discovery, Paul realized he did not have all of the answers to life. He was still struggling to understand himself, let alone God. Yet at this point in Paul's life, he was awestruck by God's love, and this love was enough.

Transitions Between the Stages

Conversion can be emotionally charged or a mental process. My conversion experience was similar to the conversions of Zacchaeus and Paul. In my own stage of disorder, it dawned on me that I needed the Lord. My emotional need for God was so great that when I finally gave

---

[14] John 19:38-42
[15] I Corinthians 13:11-13, Good News Translation

my life to Christ, I experienced an emotional rush. I was on a spiritual high for weeks. However, not all conversions, even among evangelicals, are filled with passion. In my children's cases, all three professed Jesus as Lord and were baptized, but they did not have earth-shattering conversion experiences. In our home my wife and I gave our children a biblical education, and we raised our children to have a relationship with God. They cannot recall a time without Christ and hence did not feel an impending need to repent. When I baptized them, the ritual of baptism affirmed a faith they had been living for quite some time.

The same processes occur in all religions. For those who grew up in homes without deep religious faith and particularly if they lived hedonistic lifestyles, their transformation to initial faith is likely to be a dramatic event or dramatic process. For those who were nurtured in deep faith and who followed the guidelines of that faith, the process of taking ownership of the faith is normally more subdued.

This is one of the reasons the early Church began baptizing infants. In the earliest days of the Church when many adult men and women were baptized, the ritual of baptism symbolized, in part, their dramatic change from pagan faith to Christianity. After several generations of passing along the Christian faith, people were no longer influenced by paganism. They were raised in Christian faith, and from this perspective, they had no need to convert to Christianity since they were already following Christian faith. Thus, baptism changed from a ritual that represented conversion to a ritual that represented a child's initiation into the Church and the lifestyle of their parents.

The Anabaptists, Mennonites, and Baptists brought the old style of baptism back to the Church. For them, being raised in the Church did not necessarily make a person a Christian. Ultimately, Christian faith was the result of one's choice. Once that choice was made, baptism then followed as a natural response to the person's new faith.

Conversion can take place instantaneously or over a period of time. Look at Paul's conversion experience on the road to Damascus[16] as

---

[16] Acts 9

compared with Jesus' companions on the road to Emmaus.[17] In Paul's journey on the road to Damascus, he experienced a blinding, sudden conversion. On the road to Emmaus, the two disciples did not recognize Jesus as the Christ as they walked along with him. They only recognized Jesus as the Christ when they reached their house and Jesus vanished from their sight. In that moment their spiritual eyes were opened. The house experience did not diminish their commitment along the road. The house experience confirmed their commitment on the road.

All religious cultures have half-hearted adherents in their ranks. They may participate in religious services and rituals, but they are just going through the motions. If children notice this hollow spirituality in their parents, the children may react in several ways. Out of a sense of guilt or duty, they may carry on the same mundane faith as their parents. Or their parent's hollow spirituality may stir within them a passionate need to rediscover a meaningful faith. Or they may jettison what they perceive as an empty faith and turn to another worldview. If they rediscover the faith, they are likely to be passionate about their religion. If they force this new passion on their children, their children are likely to rebel against the faith or dutifully go through the motions, and the same generational cycle begins again.

I have discovered that religious people entrenched in a sense of duty are often better at bringing people out of the disorder stage, and those in the discovery stage are normally better at bringing people out of the doubting stage. Once a person in disorder has come to his senses, he craves order and discipline. Many in my evangelical faith are masterful at convincing sinners to repent. Conversely, so-called liberal churches tend to be more open to entertaining doubt and encouraging people through the doubting stage.

Cautions

The dangers of disorder are normally recognizable, and we have rules and prisons to assist us in dealing with those who take their disorder too far. However, disorder can be disguised in religious institutions, and some

---

[17] Luke 24:13-35

unscrupulous people know how to use religion to exploit vulnerable religious people. When I was in Iraq and Afghanistan, *Maxim* was a popular men's magazine among male soldiers. It was nearly impossible to go to a latrine, guard station, or workstation without finding a *Maxim* in easy reach. I admit, in my own relapses of disorder, I occasionally perused through a few *Maxims* and glanced at the photos of gorgeous women. The women were clothed just enough to accommodate the Muslim laws on banning pornography. On one occasion I read a *Maxim* article that shared the secrets on how to "score" with church girls. I was surprised at how well the author of this article knew church jargon and was shocked to see how he used spiritual language to lure vulnerable women into a false sense of intimacy. He was making money, and he did not care about the women who would be victimized by his manipulative techniques. He was a person in disorder, a wolf in sheep's clothing, completely capable of sneaking into religious institutions to scam naïve people, especially those in a stage of doubting.

However, the people most vulnerable to manipulating religion for their own selfish gain are those stuck in a stage of duty. People of faith still entrenched in the stage of duty may have great moral character, but they are not necessarily ready for leadership in our religious institutions. Yet congregations fooled by religious jargon and magnetic personalities often place these personalities in positions of power. When self-righteous leaders fall or fail, and they often do, congregations are shocked and wonder how it could have happened. The "world" judges religion based on the way religious people act. Mahatma Gandhi said, "I like your Christ. I do not like your Christians. Your Christians are so unlike your Christ." No wonder many government leaders avoid working with religious people. They often judge a religion based on their experiences or observations of the failures of leaders still entrenched in the duty stage.

Jesus took more pity on those in the disorder stage than he did those stuck in the legalistic mindset of duty. As long as people were willing to admit their disorder, Jesus encouraged them and welcomed them. He said, "It is not the healthy who need a doctor, but the sick... For I have not come to call the righteous, but sinners" (Matthew 9:12-13). Jesus framed his ministry around those in disorder. He brought to them a message of God's love and forgiveness. Jesus often healed their physical, emotional, and spiritual disorders, but he was tough on religious people who were stuck in a self-righteous worldview.

Jesus operated in the stage of discovery. When people reach the stage of discovery, they often lose interest in the ways of the world and with organized religion. Jesus was tempted by power, but he resisted it. Discoverers may be tempted by power, but they typically refuse it. They refuse it because they are keenly aware of power's addictive nature. They have also discovered the joys of a simple life.

However, discovery spirituality has its own narcissistic temptation. People can become so self-absorbed in inner-reflective spirituality that they ignore responsibilities to family and community, or they may devalue all the good that comes from institutional religion. Frankly, it is difficult to lead a simplistic, contemplative life and lead a religious congregation or institution at the same time. There are too many distractions, but more discoverers need to take on this challenge. We need their leadership.

Another reason discoverers do not take leadership positions is because people in the duty stage often label those in the discovery stage as heretics. After all, discoverers listen to doubters, and discoverers often have a different way of understanding and applying religious and spiritual training. This can be threatening to those in the disorder stage who think they are the only ones who know the truth.

Discovery spirituality cannot be rushed, particularly in an age of globalization. Parents who desire their children to be open-minded often make the mistake of teaching the importance of tolerance to their children before teaching them other important ethical and religious boundaries. On top of that, many parents allow their children to watch unmonitored television and social media. The combination of an understanding of tolerance at such a young age and unmonitored news media and entertainment is a dangerous combination. Kids will be wired to accept anything as normal and will likely adopt a worldview far different than their parents. Young children are not normally wired to understand abstract thoughts, but with appropriate nurture and discipline, they can learn appropriate behaviors early in life.

On the other hand, parents with a strong sense of duty, if they are not careful, can exacerbate their children with an overdose of boundaries. They too risk losing their children to other worldviews. Every child is different, but each one needs the right balance of boundaries and tolerance.

While we may associate the stage of duty with dogma and rules and the stage of discovery with ideas and relationships, we need a balance of both duty and discovery. Out of harmony, duty leaders promote fear and suppression in their parishioners. Discovers, left to their own egos, will promote an anything-goes attitude, losing touch with important boundaries.

Summary

Generally, as we grow in our spiritual development, we go through four stages: disorder, duty, doubting, and discovery. While in the infantile stage of disorder, our main priority in life is seeking personal happiness. When we realize such a priority does not produce a meaningful life, we search for meaning through religion or another worldview. Through a sudden conversion or a gradual transformation over time, our lives are transformed. In a new stage of duty, we surrender to a power greater than ourselves and are quick to follow the system in our new worldview or faith. Over time we may begin to doubt some of the stories or beliefs in this new worldview. But if we stay committed to the worldview long enough, our anxiety over the doubts begins to diminish. We may tweak our worldview a bit, but we finally accept it as our own in a new stage of discovery. In the discovery stage, the more we learn about the stories and tenets of our worldview, the more we realize how little we really know. Yet we come to a point where we simply enjoy the mystery. We find meaning and purpose as our love grows for God (or the higher power) and others, and we even find a new way of loving ourselves.

The stages are not phases in the sense that we finally arrive at one stage and leave behind the previous one. It would be great if we could, but we do not arrive at discovery and stay there. When challenges, boredom, and tragedies come our way, we may react in a disorderly way. We may call upon duty. We may doubt. Or we may draw upon discovery. It's possible to go through all four phases in one day or even within a matter of minutes.

Chapter 5

Levels of Love

If I speak with the tongues of men and of angels
and have not love...

I Corinthians 13:1a

C ommunion took us to a deeper level of spiritual intimacy in the prison. I have led and participated in diverse styles of Communion to include Baptist style where we pass the plate around and liturgical style where we dip or sip from the cup. I have used loaf bread, leaven bread, unleavened bread, little Baptist crackers, round liturgical hosts, matzos, and grape juice and wine. I prefer wine when we dip or sip. The wine supposedly kills any germs deposited in the Communion chalice. When I worked in the prison system, the alcohol in the wine eased my fears about drinking prison doorknob and toilet germs deposited by prisoners who did not wash their hands. During flu season I watched many guys wipe their noses on their sleeves and hands just before tearing off a piece of bread and dipping the bread in the cup.

The second reason I prefer wine is because Jesus used wine in the Passover, and I feel it adds authenticity to a Communion service. However, I typically did not let my prisoner parishioners sip from the cup when wine was served. For a few prisoners, the temptation to gulp the entire contents was too much of a temptation, and the thought of standing in front of the warden and explaining the condition of tipsy inmates did not appeal to me.

In small group settings where Communion was more intimate, I typically led Common Cup Communion, but I went back to using grape juice toward the end of my career in the Bureau. Several of my parishioners complained about the wine. They thought it made the service "too Catholic," or they were alcoholics and did not want to be reminded of their temptation, or they came from a Protestant tradition that mandated abstinence from alcohol. So I found it less controversial just to use grape juice.

Some complained about the little, round, white hosts, claiming they were "too Catholic" as well. Having already given up the authenticity of wine, I decided not to relent on the bread. If I could not use the liturgical hosts, I was not going to use the even smaller little bitty evangelical wafers. So I normally used matzo (kosher unleavened bread) from the stash of matzos that our Jewish inmates used for Sabbath services. This was closer to the type of bread Jesus would have used.

That said, I typically led Common Cup Communion with grape juice and pieces of matzo and gave my parishioners the choice to dip or sip from the cup. However, that presented another challenge. The juice had no alcohol and did nothing to kill germs. Secondly, matzo crumbles like a cracker. As the servant figure, I always felt obligated to drink last from the cup. By the time the cup got back to me, it had the potential to be loaded with soggy matzo residue at the bottom of the cup, not to mention the backwash from the sippers. Knowing all this, I customarily began Communion with a reminder to my guys that it was not necessary to insert their fingers down into the juice to get the matzo entirely wet.

In smaller Communion groups, we typically sat in a circle on the floor. I began by passing the bread and the cup to the person on my right and saying to him, "the body of Christ, the bread of Heaven... the blood of Christ, the cup of salvation." He then drew a piece of matzo from the plate and dipped it into the juice or ate the piece of matzo and then sipped from the cup. After dipping or sipping, he then passed the elements to the person to his right, saying the sacred words to that person. This process continued until the cup and any remaining bread made its way around the circle to the person on my left. That person would pronounce the sacred words to me, and I would drink the remaining contents of the cup.

One night, Richard arrived late and did not hear the reminder about not inserting fingers in the cup. Richard had annoyed me. He missed the prayers and singing in the service and showed up just in time to participate in the sacred meal. Richard was a grey-haired man, about 50 years old. His wrinkled prison uniform was too large, and his shirttail was hanging out. He was missing two front teeth, and his yellowed fingernails were grimy and long. I don't think he had showered in days, and he smelled like urine. The prisoners in our Communion circle rolled their eyes at Richard and scooted away from him, making a place for him to sit next to me on my left.

A few months earlier I had helped Richard make phone calls to a county social services office. I became involved in a conversation with the social worker handling his case. Richard's drug-addict wife was the primary care taker of his children, so he had good reason to be concerned about his children's welfare.

A few days later, he came back with a new concern. He couldn't remember how many times he had been baptized in the past, but he wanted to be baptized again, this time hoping it would stick. Under the persuasion of one of our community volunteers, a Holiness minister, Richard was convinced he needed to be baptized by her and that the words had to be said just right as he was immersed in the water; not by the traditional formula of "I baptize you in the name of the Father, Son, and Holy Spirit," but by a nuanced Pentecostal "Jesus-only" formula, "I baptize you in the name of Jesus Christ." The Holiness minister and I got along fine, often leading services together, so I wasn't going to mince words over Richard's desire to get it right, even if I allegedly didn't know how to do it, but I couldn't help feeling slighted after all I thought I had done to help him.

As prisoners passed the bread and wine around the circle, I knew it would be Richard who would give me the elements and say the sacred to me: "the body... and blood of Christ." I watched his dirty fingers with the grimy fingernails fiddle around with the matzo cracker. He tore off a piece of matzo and to make sure it was sopping wet, he stuck his dirty fingers all the way down into the juice and then decided to take a sip from the cup anyway. He wrapped his big lips around the rim of the chalice and slurped. I hate to admit it, but I joined other prisoners in my silent disgust for Richard. When it was my turn to receive the elements, I could barely understand his mumbled words. As he smacked on the cracker and mumbled the words to me, he accidently spit little moistened crumbs through the gap in his front teeth, and some of his spittle fell in the cup and the rest on my lap. I could feel the blood rushing to my head. I dreaded drinking Richard's backwash from the bottom of the cup, but I had to do it in front of the other inmates wondering how tough their chaplain really was.

Then Richard mumbled, "This is my body... This is my blood." Richard spoke the words of Jesus, and in one mystical moment, I saw Richard in a new way. I saw Christ in a new way. Richard had become Christ for me, and I could not receive the bread of Heaven and the cup of salvation without first receiving it from Richard. I saw Richard the way Christ saw him. I drank the entire contents, feeling Richard's backwash go down the back of my throat. It did not matter. The juice tasted good.

Our perspectives change when we see others the way God sees them. Few people made this clearer than Bernard of Clairvaux, a prominent leader in the Church nearly 1,000 years ago. Bernard described four levels of love. I paraphrase them here...

- First, we love self for self's sake.
- Then, we love God for self's sake.
- Next, we love God for God's sake.
- Finally, we love self for God's sake.[18]

---

[18] Paul Halsall, web editor *of On Loving God* by Bernard of Clairvaux, http://www.ccel.org/ccel/bernard/loving_god.html (version from Grand Rapids, MI: The Christian Classics Ethereal Library), 31.

One of our most basic instincts is self-preservation. We must have food, clothing, and shelter to survive. Once these needs are sated, we turn our attention to seeking happiness and being loved. In Bernard's way of thinking, this is when we love self for self's sake.

Eventually, we discover our need for God or something transcendent, but we basically love God for what we get out of the relationship. We want God to get us through tough times, bless us the rest of the time, and in anticipation of death, we want God's assurance that we will live forever. This is what Bernard would call, loving God for self's sake.

Then one day, something wondrous happens. We experience some moment of unexpected grace when we are spiritually touched by the brilliant fall colors in a forest, a baby's smile, a first kiss, or the forgiveness of sins. Somehow we release all of our anxieties, and we simply enjoy God's good company. We need nothing in return. This is when we love God for God's sake.

And then on rare moments, and Bernard said they were very rare; we actually love self for God's sake. This is the moment we look in the mirror and we see ourselves as God sees us. We feel believed in, loved, and affirmed by the Almighty Creator. At such moments we are able to look at others differently too. We see them, even our enemies, as God sees them. Fear vanishes and we are completely motivated by love. Bernard described such experiences like this, "Then in wondrous wise he will forget himself and as if delivered from self, he will grow wholly God's. Joined unto the Lord, he will then be one spirit with Him."[19]

These stages of love are similar to the stages of spiritual development. During any time in the day, we could experience all four stages within a matter of minutes. We could easily become angry or selfish and revert back to self-love and then try to manipulate God for self's sake. With a little self-soothing and prayer, we might begin to relax and enjoy God's good company, and if we are fortunate enough, we

---

[19] Ibid., 31.

might experience a sense of oneness with God and let go of all our anxieties.[20]

Altruism is like any other ability. As in mathematics, singing, or athletics, some people are simply better at these things than others. Some people are more naturally altruistic than others. Is it heredity or environment or a combination thereof? You decide. The good news is this ability or gift can be strengthened. It takes hard work, time, and courage to strengthen this ability, and some of the greatest leaps in altruism cannot be planned or measured. They come to us when we least expect them, through crisis and suffering, or through serendipitous moments of grace.

---

[20] In the spirit of full disclosure for my Muslim readers, you should know that Bernard was an inspirational leader for the Crusades, and I am doubtful that he extended his understanding of altruism to Muslims in Jerusalem. However, as misguided as we now acknowledge his bias, this does not diminish his understanding of the levels of love. This should prompt further discussion. What prevents religious leaders from extending altruism to people beyond their own cultures?

Chapter 6

Owning Our Own Faith

Doubt is a pain too lonely to know
that faith is his twin brother.
Kahlil Gibran

When I went through Army Airborne School, my fellow comrades and I made many practice jumps before we ever took our first real jump out of an airplane. We jumped out of a mock airplane door and landed on the dirt. We practiced our parachute landing falls in a sawdust pit. Harnessed to a wire, we made numerous jumps off a 34-foot training tower. I learned how a parachute worked and had enough confidence to believe my chute would enable me to land safely on the earth, but I had not tested it and did not know for certain it would work. I heard terrifying stories of soldiers who fell to their deaths or who were maimed for life due to inoperable chutes.

On my first jump, I remember looking down the crowded fuselage and seeing the unique faces of my comrades as we waited for the commands to jump. Some had confident stares. Others were stone-faced. Some had sweaty faces, and some looked as if they were going to vomit. I was a chaplain, and I was supposed to be instilling confidence in the soldiers around me. Above the noise of the engines and the wind whipping around in the fuselage from the open door, a female soldier stared at me and hollered, "Chaplain, You look white as a sheet." I yelled back, "I'm scared!"

Traveling at 140 mph, we all shuffled to the door and jumped out into the prop blasts of the roaring C-130 engines, and after four more successful jumps, we earned our airborne wings. While we all approached the door and jumped out using the techniques we were taught, we certainly had our own unique feelings and thoughts as we approached the door. The same is true with our respective worldviews. We may commit to a similar faith, but we often approach the door to that faith with our own unique feelings and thoughts.

The Synoptic Gospels reveal the story of a loving father who had a son who was possessed with an evil spirit. The boy manifested symptoms of what we would now call a seizure disorder. The desperate father asked Jesus, "If you can do anything, take pity on us and help us." Jesus responded, "If you can? Everything is possible for him who believes." Immediately the father exclaimed, "I do believe; help me overcome my unbelief!"[21]

Faith is not always easy. Some of the most committed religious people are not always so sure about God, even God's existence. Some of the heroes of Christian faith were doubters. Jesus said John the Baptist was the greatest man who ever lived.[22] Yet when John found himself in prison and did not see the kingdom of God coming about as he had anticipated, he asked Jesus, "Are you the one who was to come, or should we expect someone else?"[23]

Even non-religious people are familiar with Doubting Thomas. Thomas was away from the group of disciples when the resurrected Christ first appeared to the group in the upper room. When the disciples told Thomas they had seen the risen Lord, Thomas told them "Unless I

---

[21] Story found in Mark's Gospel, Mark 9:14-29
[22] Matthew 11:11
[23] Matthew 11:3

see the nail marks in his hands and put my finger where the nails were...I will not believe it."

A week later when Thomas was with the disciples, Jesus appeared to them again. Jesus challenged Thomas, "Put your finger here; see my hands... Stop doubting and believe."

Thomas exclaimed, "My Lord and my God!"

Jesus responded, "Because you have seen me, you have believed; blessed are those who have not seen and yet have believed."[24] Jesus corrected Thomas, but he did not condemn him because of his doubts.

Christians in subsequent generations labeled him "Doubting Thomas." We often forget that when the other disciples warned Jesus not to go back to Jerusalem for fear they would all be killed, Thomas said, "Let us go that we may die with him."[25] According to Church tradition, Thomas died a martyr's death. It is not uncommon for people of uncommon faith to have common doubt.

People from the same faith traditions often disagree over various theological positions; however, they rarely get to the root of why they disagree. Faith does not mean the same thing to every believer. Jesus spoke of the happiness of those who believe and need no physical evidence. Some people need no proof. Others do. When John the Baptist and Thomas began to follow Jesus, they had all the proof they needed, but along the way, their faith was shaken by crisis. They were no longer confident and needed additional evidence to support their faith. Still, even in the midst of doubt, they carried on in faith. Although Thomas doubted, he showed up in the upper room anyway. Although John the Baptist questioned the mission, he made a stand anyway.

People approach faith in a variety of ways based on their heredity and environment. Some people are drawn toward empirical evidence and will not commit to a faith system without evidence. They want to be certain. Faith often begins in their minds. Others are drawn to mystery. They enjoy the wonder of faith and do not require all of their questions answered. Faith often begins in their hearts.

---

[24] John 20:25-29
[25] John 11:16

In this chapter I offer a continuum of different ways people approach their supernatural beliefs. How do Muslims interpret the story of Muhammad's night flight from Mecca to Jerusalem to Heaven? How do Christians understand the resurrection of Jesus? How do Jews interpret the parting of the Red Sea? How do followers of all three Abrahamic faiths understand Heaven? Or how do Hindus understand reincarnation?

These beliefs cannot generally be proven by scientific methodology. Many from these respective religions may argue that such beliefs can be proven, but there is no consensus on the certainty of such beliefs, especially from those outside of these respective religions. By contrast, once introduced to the history of George Washington, I've never met anyone who doubted the existence of George Washington or that he was the first President of the United States. Such a person might be from another country and have no reason to care about George Washington, but once informed, he would still believe in the one-time existence of George Washington and that he was once a president. But people from all over the world have plenty of different beliefs about God, gods, the Savior, saviors, and the afterlife.

Some people approach the supernatural beliefs of their faith tradition with certainty. Others approach them with mystery, and some approach them to varying degrees with a combination of both. If we were to place these different approaches along a continuum, it would look like this.

No Certainty................All Mystery
Some Certainty.........Mostly Mystery
Mostly Certainty.........Some Mystery
All Certainty................No Mystery

By certainty, we mean that a person knows for certain the sun will rise tomorrow morning. By mystery, we mean it in two ways. One is the way a person may wonder if the sun will continue to rise ten million years from now. There is a bit of uncertainty about this. There is still another way to look at mystery. The word "mystery" has a deeply held religious connotation. What many Christians refer to as the "sacraments," "rites," or "ordinances" of the Church, Orthodox Christians refer to them as "mysteries." Various beliefs in the New Testament are also called mysteries. The apostle Paul refers to the calling of Gentiles to the Church,[26] the resurrection of the dead,[27] and the union of Christ and the Church[28] as mysteries. In this sense of the word, "mystery" does not imply the believer has doubts about supernatural beliefs; rather the beliefs are simply unexplainable in human understanding or by scientific methodology, but one has faith in them anyway.

Of course, we know the sun doesn't exactly rise in the morning. A person can believe with certainty that the sun does rise, but by scientific methodology we now know the earth actually rotates once around on its axis every 24 hours, giving us the appearance the sun is actually rising every day. There was a time when people were certain the sun orbited the earth, not the earth orbiting the sun as we now know to be true. Our point here is that a person can be certain about something, yet be wrong in his belief.

For our purposes here, we will examine the supernatural belief in the resurrection of Jesus and apply a continuum of various approaches to understanding the story and faith. If you come from another faith tradition, choose one of your supernatural stories and apply the continuum to your faith.

If you need to know up front, my faith is in the supernatural story of the resurrection of Jesus and my commitment to Christ. However, that doesn't tell you anything about my degree of certainty or mystery in the story or for that matter, my commitment to Christian faith. We will also examine how certainty, mystery, and commitment pertain to faith.

If you come from another worldview, please remember I am not attempting to manipulate you into my faith. I actually hope people of my faith will better understand why you believe the way you do. Or if you share my faith, please don't be too disappointed I am not using this book as a direct way to spread the gospel. Nevertheless, I do hope this book

---

[26] Ephesians 3:8-11; Colossians 1:25-27
[27] I Corinthians 15:51
[28] Ephesians 5:31

gives Christians a greater opportunity to learn from people of other faiths, and in turn, a greater opportunity to share the gospel.

Keep in mind belief is not necessarily the same thing as faith, nor is faith necessarily the same thing as belief. A person may believe with certainty in the dogmas and essential stories of a worldview but have no commitment to that worldview. From a religious viewpoint, genuine faith implies commitment. Likewise, a person may doubt the dogmas and essential stories of a worldview but remain very committed to that worldview.

Faithful and unfaithful people, or rather committed and uncommitted people, exist at both ends of the faith continuum. Some have certainty in their belief system. Others may wonder. When tragedies occur, belief systems may be shaken or may be strengthened, but after we own our own faith, we typically settle into either a faith of certainty or one of mystery or somewhere in between.

As we look at this continuum of certainty and mystery, these different approaches to faith are not placed in any particular order of importance. Nor are they presented in an order to suggest a person will start out on one end and end up on the other. We simply acknowledge a variance in the way people respond to the stories and dogma that constitute their worldviews.

No Certainty, All Mystery

When people follow a particular faith tradition but have no certainty in the traditional supernatural stories of that faith; they normally have one of two basic approaches to that faith. Like Rudolph Bultmann, some may reinterpret traditional beliefs to something that makes sense to them. Or like Blaise Pascal, others may place blind faith in the traditional beliefs. Some go back and forth between both approaches.

German theologian and existentialist Rudolph Bultmann could not accept the resurrection of Jesus Christ as a literal event. In his mind such an event was implausible. Nor could he accept other supernatural stories in the Bible at face value. He demythologized the supernatural stories in the Bible to strip away what he considered the husk to find the kernel or the essential message of the stories. He could not believe that a dead person could come back to life. Yet he did not dismiss the resurrection story. He proclaimed the story as one might tell the mythological resurrection stories of Osiris or the phoenix. Bultmann believed the allegorical story of the resurrection had enormous relevance for society and individuals to find meaning and purpose.[29]

Now Bultmann was certain of his version of the story or else he would have never challenged centuries of traditional theology. So this is a reminder. This chapter is about the certainty of traditional supernatural beliefs, not necessarily the certainty of one's worldview.

There are people in our churches who find it difficult to accept the resurrection story along with other biblical miracle stories at face value. They may want to believe that Jesus literally rose from the dead; however, their minds simply cannot accept a phenomenon that appears to be scientifically impossible. So they reinterpret the supernatural stories to something that makes sense for them.

They are not likely to be motivated by traditional systematic theology, but they are ordinarily motivated by the ethical and moral teachings of Jesus and the spiritual applications of the supernatural stories. Since they lack certainty in traditional faith, they tend to be open minded about the tenets of other faiths, but they would apply the same skepticism about the supernatural stories of other faiths as they would their own.

With such a rejection of the traditional resurrection story, many would say why bother with Christianity at all if one sees it as a mythology equal with other mythologies? The Apostle Paul said, "If Christ has not been raised, your faith is futile?"[30] Why have faith in something when there is no confidence in the outcome? For this reason, many Christians do not accept Bultmann-type Christianity as authentic Christianity.

Those with a Bultmann-type faith would disagree. They may want to believe that Jesus rose from the dead, but they simply cannot accept the story as fact. Their brains are not wired to accept supernatural claims.

---

[29] Ronald H. Nash, *Christian Faith and Historical Understanding* (Grand Rapids, MI: Zondervan Publishing House, 1981), 116-117.
[30] I Corinthians 15:17

However, they claim Christianity as their faith because they were raised in a Christian culture or simply want to follow the ethical teachings of Jesus. In this sense they consider themselves to be genuine followers of Christ.

They may hope the resurrection is true and that an afterlife exists, but they will not exert much energy into pie-in-the-sky theology because in their minds there is no proof for such claims. However, they will proclaim a gospel that changes lives in the here and now. They continue in a Christianity of their own understanding, not to hedge their bets against Hell (something even harder for them to believe in) or to get to Heaven but because they have discovered a path they believe works for them. Fundamentalist pastors may not know it, but these faithful people are often in their churches. These faithful people know that Christianity is better than anything they can come up with on their own. They may have studied other belief systems and simply prefer Christianity. They know the benefits, and in spite of their doubts, follow Christianity to the extent they find possible. They often sit silent in conservative churches, afraid to express their doubts for fear of being judged as not being a Christian, but they cannot imagine leaving the heritage of their faith.

Not all are content to sit silent in conservative churches. Some become a bone of contention for their churches. Others attend classical liberal or Universalist-type churches. Some are dogmatic and intolerant of those who have strong beliefs in the traditional supernatural stories.

But not all are like Bultmann. Consider the 17th century French mathematician, physicist, and philosopher Blaise Pascal. Pascal reasoned the existence of God could neither be proven nor disproven. Given the two possibilities, there is a God or there isn't, he wagered faith in God. If he chose no faith in God and it turned out there was a God, he risked losing everything. If he chose faith in God and there was no God, then he lost nothing. However, if he chose faith in God and there was a God, then he gained everything. Not certain one way or the other, he saw he had a 50/50 chance of being right, so he chose the course with the positive outcome, even if it was entirely unexplainable. Pascal looked at all the supernatural stories the same way, including the resurrection.

Many accept the resurrection story this way in blind faith. They are not certain of the story but are willing to accept it as a great mystery. They are content with wonder.

Others go back and forth between Pascal's blind faith in the traditional resurrection story and Bultmann's version or some other non-orthodox interpretation of the story. They hope the orthodox version is true. They would rather have false hope in an afterlife than make the dismal decision that there is no life beyond this one. But since they do not know if there really is an afterlife, they hold on to an allegorical version of the story as well. This backup version gives them meaning and purpose as well, if only for this life.

The faith of my mother mirrors more Pascal's approach. She has little or no certainty, but she trusts in the supernatural stories on blind faith. I doubt if she has ever heard of Rudolph Bultmann or ever considered alternative versions of the resurrection story. However, her faith is not certain to her. It is a mystery. Her father died when she was four years old. When she was seven, her mother married a drinking man. She observed an often-tumultuous relationship between her mother and stepfather. Her mother was a good woman but perhaps too busy running a large farm to notice all the emotional needs of her youngest child. Now in her eighties, my mother still has a great emotional need to know that people believe in her.

Over years of counseling, I have observed a vast difference in the faiths of those who grew up with a lack of parental blessings versus those who received all the blessings they needed as children. Often a person who lacks affirmation as a child may have challenges with religious faith later in life. While doubting their parent's love for them, they may also doubt God's love for them, or they may doubt the existence of Heaven, Hell, or even the existence of God.

Yet I would never think of calling my mother an unfaithful person to God. In her own emotional yearnings, she yearns deeply for God. She wants to believe in God and for God to believe in her. She does her best to follow the teachings of Christ. Unlike the person who does not believe in an afterlife, she follows the Lord, partly to hedge her bet against Hell but mainly because it is the right thing to do. Her faith is part of her culture. It is the belief system she was taught, and she could never imagine rejecting this faith.

While growing up in a culture that often ridiculed non-Christian worldviews, her doubts enabled her to be respectful of other faith traditions. When people doubt their own faith, it is not abnormal for them to wonder about the validity of other faiths. One of the first songs I learned from my mother was "Jesus Loves the Little Children," a song about God's love and what we would call "diversity" today.

> Jesus loves the little children,
> All the children of the world.
> Red and yellow, black and white,
> They are precious in his sight.
> Jesus loves the little children of the world.

She also taught me, "Don't ever make fun of people because they believe differently or have a different religion than yours." This was years before the era of political correctness. I think my mother's influence engendered my calling to ecumenical and multi-faith ministry.

We might say about my mother and others who have her kind of faith that they are deeply committed Christians, but their faith has little or nothing to do with certainty in their belief system. Their faith is one of wonder and mystery.

Some Certainty, Mostly Mystery

Perhaps the most noted theologian of the 20th century, Karl Barth, agreed with Bultmann that one could not scientifically substantiate the physical resurrection of Jesus; nevertheless, he did not deny the resurrection as a literal event. For Barth the proof of the resurrection was evidenced in the way believers live out the resurrection.[31]

Many Christians approach the resurrection this way. In their minds there is no way to prove the event ever happened; however, they accept

---

[31] Ibid., 120-122.

the resurrection story as a literal event because they see evidence of the resurrection in their lives and the lives of others.

Since their faith is still a very experiential faith, not centered on any solid historical evidence, they too are more open to validating the tenets of other faiths as well. They notice the transformational experiences that people of other faiths encounter in their worldviews. So in their minds, who is to say that one faith tradition is more valid than another? A person who has this kind of faith has some certainty in the supernatural story but is still motivated more by mystery.

In my father's teen years, he was ashamed of his parents. His father loved history, loved to tell stories, played the guitar, and had a great singing voice, but his addiction to alcohol wrecked his family. Had my father's mother been properly diagnosed, she would have been treated for bi-polar. She was prone to fits of rage and periods of great laughter. She was the first person to ever tell me a dirty joke. I would love to tell it here, but I'm not sure it would be appreciated.

In spite of her temper, foul language, and moodiness, she was one of the saltiest saints I ever knew. I cannot recall a time when my grandmother did not have some stranger living in the house with her. Her live-in guests were mentally ill, physically disabled, or poorer than she was. She lived Jesus' teaching, "Whatever you did for one of the least of these... you did for me,"[32] better than any person I ever knew. She daily took care of thirsty, hungry, destitute, homeless, and sick people. I remember one elderly man who lived with her for years. I assumed he was kin and called him Uncle John. It wasn't until I was nearly grown that I found out he was not my uncle at all.

Later in life my father recognized the goodness in his parents, but during his childhood and young adult years, he had little respect for them because of the public humiliation he often endured because of their actions. He left home at age 15 and moved in with his grandparents. His grandfather was one of the first adults to give him the affirmation he was seeking. Later when he married, my mother also affirmed him. He gained

---

[32] Matthew 25:39

further affirmation from superiors in his career as a soldier and later as a Georgia State Patrolman.

My father's faith mirrors one who has some certainty, but his faith is more motivated by mystery. Somewhere along my father's journey, with the affirmation of others, he began to believe in himself. My father taught Sunday school for nearly four decades. He is a Baptist deacon, and like his father before him, fancies himself a singer. He sings Gospel songs and brings a word of encouragement to old folks in the local nursing home. Every now and then, someone old enough to remember his father back in the day will tell him, "Carlton, that shore was a good song, but it ain't as good as your Daddy's sangin."

Both of my parents have strong morals and taught them to me. At the same time, they were liberal thinkers compared to the Baptist party line of their generation. My father did not react against his father's alcoholism by choosing abstinence of alcohol as a way of life but chose rather to drink rarely and when he did, to do so responsibly. In Baptist tradition the trump card used to convince people of the evils of "demon alcohol"[33] is to quote from the Apostle Paul and say, "You don't want to be a stumbling block to anyone, do you?" My father, a Baptist deacon, ignored the party line and brought his homemade scuppernong wine to the front porch of his local Baptist church and gave it away to other Baptist deacons and church members. Years ago he quit smoking on the front porch of the church, but until he totally stopped smoking, he still slipped behind the house to smoke cigarettes. Mama would not let him smoke cigarettes in the house.

My father will tell you he wonders about some of the stories in the Bible and wonders if he should take them as literally as the Baptist preachers in his community do. He wonders about the afterlife, but he trusts the story on faith. He stepped out in faith, trusting that Christ died to reconcile humanity to God, rose from the dead, ascended to Heaven, and is coming back one day to redeem the world. He recounts small and large miracles in his life, and at this stage in his life, what he cannot figure out about faith, he simply doesn't worry about. He sort of enjoys the

---

[33] I Corinthians 8:9-13

mystery. This is the kind of faith where one would say there is some certainty in the belief system, but the faith is still prompted more by wonder and mystery.

Mostly Certainty, Some Mystery

Baptist theologian George E. Ladd believed there was enough empirical evidence to substantiate the literal resurrection of Jesus, although he would probably concede parts of the story could not be proven. Given the choice of accepting the story at face value or denying its plausibility because of a few parts in the story that are difficult to substantiate, Ladd chose to trust the ample evidence he did have, especially when he considered the ramifications for not believing in the story.[34]

For Christians like Ladd, there may not be enough evidence to prove the story of the resurrection in a court of law, but there is enough evidence to make a solid commitment one way or the other. When their lives are subsequently changed because of their decision, their faith in the story is even more empowered. People with this kind of faith have much more certainty in their faith and don't spend a lot of emotional energy wondering about the supernatural stories.

This is the faith of my wife. Lisa's father was a Navy pilot during World War II and became a very successful businessman and vice president of a major company. He came from a faithful and loving church-going family. Lisa's mother, the youngest girl of eleven children, gladly traded in her country life of the 1950s to marry this successful man. What Lisa remembers most about her childhood is that her mother laughed often and her father dearly loved her.

Lisa tells me she always felt believed in by her parents, and particularly from her loving father. She dedicated her life to Christ in typical Baptist fashion when she was ten years old. Committed to a faithful and moral life, she went to a Christian College and majored in Biblical Studies. She worked for Delta Airlines as a flight attendant for seven years. As a person who gained a liberal arts education and who

---

[34] Ibid., 127-131

traveled around the world, she encountered other worldviews that deny the validity of the resurrection story. She simply doesn't accept the conclusions to these arguments.

Her faith in the resurrection is not only sustained by her personal experiences as a committed Christian and encouraged by the model of her father's faith; it is also nurtured from her deep level of satisfaction in knowing she was believed in as a little girl, and is still believed in by her aging father and middle-aged husband. Religious belief comes natural for her. She does not fret over what she does not understand. There are some things she prefers not to know. She enjoys the mystery of God. There are times she wonders about death, particularly since her own mother died at a relatively young age, but she has little reason to doubt Heaven. She dusts off the few doubts that come her way, realizing that doubts offer little in the way of comfort and prefers to believe and enjoy the mystery. We might say that her faith operates more on certainty and less on mystery.

All Certainty, No Mystery

Another German theologian, Wolfart Pannenberg, believed there is plenty of evidence to substantiate the literal resurrection of Jesus Christ. For Pannenberg, believing in the resurrection story is an act of mental ascent. Real faith and real knowledge go hand in hand. A person cannot have authentic faith without knowing that Jesus really rose from the dead.[35]

For Christians like Pannenberg, it is not only important to have faith in the gospel story, it is important to know how the resurrection occurred and to be able to defend the event. Many such Christians are familiar with Christian apologetics[36] and the cosmological,[37] teleological,[38]

---

[35] Ibid., 123-127

[36] Christian apologetics: a field of Christian study dedicated to presenting reasoned bases for Christian faith, particularly against objectives from other worldviews.

[37] Cosmological argument for God's existence: There had to be a first cause for the universe to exist. Someone had to create it. It must have been God.

[38] Teleological argument for God's existence: The universe is complex. Only a grand designer could have created such a system.

82

ontological,[39] and moral law[40] arguments for the existence of God. I have often heard preachers declaring from the pulpit, "I know that I know that I know." They are certain in their faith, and they want everyone within their hearing to have the same degree of certainty. A person with this kind of faith has maximum certainty in the supernatural stories and little or no room for wonder and mystery.

Lisa's father, Charles, possesses the last approach on our continuum. Like my wife's mother, her father was also born among 11 children and though he was not the firstborn son, he was the child honored with his father's name. He does not have a single painful childhood memory. He tells stories of working with his father in the field and wrestling with his father on the farmhouse floor. His mother was known for her kindness and strong faith and was considered a saint by her family and the community. When she died, preachers from all over the little Tennessee community came to honor her at her funeral.

Charles, now in his nineties, still does a little business consulting, plays golf twice a week, maintains a half-acre vegetable garden, and teaches Sunday School. He is a member of Atlanta's First Baptist Church and is staunchly conservative in American politics and Christianity.

If someone were to suggest to my father-in-law that there are other views regarding the resurrection story, other than the orthodox version, he would become visibly agitated. He would consider such a person naïve and would feel pity for the person and pray for the person's salvation.

With Charles there is not a lot of room left for wonder. His faith simply makes sense. He was believed in by both of his parents. He was successful in life and family. As an older man, he has few regrets in life. He believes in himself and tries to show others he believes in them as well. He has no doubts about the afterlife and is certain that when he dies, he will be with Christ in a new realm and see his family members again. We might say his faith has maximum certainty and little room left for wonder or mystery.

---

[39] Ontological argument for God's existence: Most people have an innate desire to believe in a God. So there must be a God.

[40] Moral law argument for God's existence: Most human beings are born with an inherent sense of right and wrong. The basis behind this understanding is God.

Nuances

In our continuum we are not saying that faith is solely linked to the way a person is loved when he or she is growing up, but we do underscore the importance of love's connection to faith. There are plenty of faithful people in all religions who did not experience the strong love of others when they were growing up, but they later got their affirmation needs met through religious faith.

Our personality temperaments also play an important role in belief and faith. If you have not taken a personality indicator, I recommend that you take the Myers-Briggs Personality Indicator (MBTI) or the Keirsey Sorter. These two indicators basically take Carl Jung's research on the four basic personality types and divide each one into four other types, describing a total of sixteen distinctive personality temperaments. These personality types are based on our preferences toward introversion or extroversion, sensing or intuition, thinking or feeling, and judgment or perception. Suffice it to say, Keirsey identifies four major personality types: Guardian, Artisan, Idealist, and Rational. Our preferences, natural likes and dislikes, and the way we emote and think influence the way we approach our worldviews.

Strong Guardians rarely question their belief systems and are loyal to their religious institutions. They have a need to protect their dogmas and want to make sure others are in line as well. Strong Rationals question everything and base their loyalty on the relevance and sense of a system. Artisans are resistant to institutionalization and seek individual ways to express faith. Idealists are bored by petty dogmas and details. Instead, they think in terms of the big picture, and their faith must connect them to some greater good or greater community.

I highly recommend Michael Chester's book, *Prayer and Temperament*. He draws a corollary between faith and personality. His book is extremely helpful for Christians who are struggling to find a devotional or worship style that reflects their personality temperaments.

What draws one person one way and another person the other way? Religious experience and religious education are certainly part of the equation, but our faith is a mixture of many factors. Look at the continuums below. Where would you place your preferences along these lines?

Formal Ritual Experience   or   Spontaneous Experience

←---→

Religion   Spirituality

←---→

Commandments   Principles

←---→

Certainty   Mystery

←---→

Reason   Passion

←---→

In the chapter entitled, "Our Soul's History," we listed many factors that contribute to individual faith. These factors include family background and dynamics, culture, religious education, academic education, media, age, personality temperament, emotional maturity, blessings and challenges, failures and successes, physical and emotional ability, and most importantly, the amount and kind of love we received as children. Heredity and environment shape our faith.

The way we believe and/or have faith is seminal to our understanding of one another. Why are some Christians so passionate about certain issues while others are not? Christians with maximum certainty and salesman-type personalities are normally passionate about sharing their faith. They have what the Apostle Paul called the "gift of evangelism." Others may wish for such strong belief, but they may be tamed skeptics. If such skeptics are also introverted, they will be hard-pressed to do the work of evangelism. However, they may be passionate about social programs, like serving homeless people in a soup kitchen.

The zealous evangelist should realize that guilt trips do not produce greater evangelism from a tamed skeptic. Nor will the skeptic convince the evangelist his faith could be shaken. Both have minds that are geared in different ways.

We need to affirm both of them. To the evangelist with certainty, go for it. Share your faith, but realize not everyone understands the gospel with your same degree of certainty. To the tamed skeptic, your commitment to faith may be greater than the faithful evangelist. In spite of your doubts, you choose to remain faithful to Christ and the Church. This is incredible faith. Keep going in spite of the doubts, but realize that others may not have the same need to wonder like you do.

We can apply these approaches of certainty and mystery to most any religious dogma or story. Even among atheists, there are four different approaches to the belief in the nonexistence of God. Some atheists would concede that it is impossible to prove their belief in the nonexistence of God. However, others conclude such a belief is easy to prove. Some would agree that there may be some circumstantial evidence for a god, but in their minds the case against the existence of a god is so overwhelming, they simply believe in what seems more tenable to them. Others would argue that atheism is the only rational way to believe. For them, all the evidence points to this belief, and there is never a reason to doubt their faith. Yes, I said "faith." Just as it takes faith to commit to a life with God, so it takes faith to commit to a life without God.

Summary
As a reminder, we picked a core belief of Christianity, the resurrection of Christ, to see how people from the same faith might differently understand a core belief, but the dynamics of certainty and mystery generally work the same way in all faiths. At times we have used the words "belief" and "faith" separately and at other times, interchangeably. Most of the time, belief and faith are integrally linked, but at times, they are not. Heredity and environment shape our beliefs and faith. Some people have strong certainty in the stories and tenets of a particular worldview, hardly or never doubting, while others may wonder about their sacred stories and tenets. However, belief and faith are not always

synonymous. A person can have strong beliefs in a worldview but not be committed to that worldview. Likewise, a person can have doubts about a particular belief system but have total faith in that way of life.

Chapter 7

Approaches to Other Beliefs

Education is the ability to listen to almost anything
without losing your temper or your self-confidence.
Robert Frost

I n 2003, I worked for five months as the Senior Camp Chaplain at Camp As Saliyah in Qatar. Part of my responsibilities included leading soldiers on mini-retreats on the beach near the Sea Line Resort, the southern most populated place on Qatar's Persian Gulf coast. It was a tough job, but somebody had to do it. When I received orders to go to Baghdad, I made sure I scheduled one more visit to the area before I left.

It was June. Qatar, a small peninsula country that juts out into the Persian Gulf, is one of the hottest places on earth. The heat index can be deadly when the humidity from the ocean mixes with soaring Arabian Desert temperatures. Master Sergeant Rick England, my chaplain assistant, and I made sure we brought plenty of water before heading to our favorite Qatar spot in the summer soaring heat.

When we reached the Sea Line Resort, the place looked deserted, except for a few young Qatari men. Most locals were not foolish enough to consider the place a resort in the summer, soaring heat. We drove south in our air conditioned SUV on past the Sea Line Resort, enjoying the view of the giant sand dunes to our right, some towering over 100 feet, and the emerald green ocean to our left.

There was a risk of getting stuck in the sand. We had been stuck before. No big deal. We always got out. One time the Qatari beach patrol rescued us, but on this day, we didn't see anybody as we continued traveling south. We liked it this way. Rick and I felt like we were the only ones on the planet. We felt secure with our cell phone and plenty of bottled water. We did notice one other set of tire tracks on the beach, but we couldn't decipher which way the tracks were headed. If they were headed south, we knew at some point a vehicle would turn around and come back toward us. If the tracks headed north, then Rick and I were definitely alone in this region of the world.

About five miles south of the resort, a shallow tide rushed across the sand in front of us. I told Rick, "I think we're going to have to turn back." He stopped the vehicle, and when he tried to turn the SUV around, the front left tire would not budge. We got out and dug wet sand away from the tire, but the more we dug, the more water filled the hole. The tire was stuck in a quagmire.

We devised a quick plan. Rick would stay with the vehicle and use our cell phone to contact the resort to notify the beach patrol. If he was unsuccessful, he would make the embarrassing call to my chaplain partner back at the base to contact the beach patrol, and as a last resort, he would contact the MPs at the base. I would jog back to the resort to contact the beach patrol just in case his calls proved unsuccessful.

We were wearing shorts. I took off my T-shirt and used it as a makeshift head cover. I normally maxed the Army's physical fitness test and figured I could run the whole way, but the heat overwhelmed me. I had to walk several times. My heart was pounding, both from the heat and from what I saw. The surf was splashing over our tire tracks. The tide was coming in. I lost sight of Rick and our vehicle and could only imagine how high the surf was rising around the vehicle. I kept looking back, hoping that Rick had been rescued and that he and his rescue team would be driving up any moment to rescue me. I kept thinking about the butt chewing I would get from the Colonel and how Rick and I would become the laughingstock at the base. Worst, I thought I might have to pay for a submerged vehicle.

When I reached the resort, I found the camel man, the guy who rented camels and Arabian horses to tourists to ride on the beach. He spoke very little English, but he understood my predicament and escorted me to a condo where six young Qatari men were staying.

They were smoking non-filtered cigarettes and smelled like alcohol. They grinned as the camel man explained my predicament to them. My predicament became an adventure for them in their otherwise boring, slightly inebriated day. They collected ropes and paired up into three brand-new Land Rovers and placed me in the back seat of the lead Land Rover. I could tell they had done this before.

I felt awkward. Qataris are some of the richest people on earth, and Arab men do not go around barefooted and bare-chested. I was dripping wet from sweat and sea spray and felt uncivilized sitting on the leather upholstery in the luxury SUV.

As we drove along the dunes, they played loud, Arabian disco music on the radio and offered me unfiltered cigarettes. I politely declined and encouraged them to hurry. Instead, they drove leisurely in a southwesterly direction over the giant dunes. Since the beginning of my stay in Qatar, I had wanted to trek across the dunes, but Rick and I did not have confidence in our SUV or desert-driving ability, plus the MPs forbade soldiers from cutting across the dunes. I was getting my chance to ride the dunes, but this wasn't what I had in mind. I knew the Arabic word for water and kept saying *"al mai"* and pointing to the coastline. They understood. I grew more anxious wondering just how far the tide had risen on our SUV.

When we cleared the last dune and I saw our SUV, my heart sank. The water was up to the wheel wells. When the driver stopped to assess the situation, I learned he did know some English. He turned around to face me, and with a big, toothy grin, said, "No problem!"

They jumped out of their Land Rovers and went to work. They tied a rope from the back bumper of one of their SUVs to the front bumper of our SUV and tried to pull our vehicle loose. For about 30 minutes, the rope strained and frayed. It popped loose several times. Our vehicle did not budge.

Rick had been unable to contact anyone on the cell phone except my chaplain partner. My partner called back at a moment when one of their SUVs got stuck in the surf. As I talked to him on the phone, I told him, "It doesn't look good. They're untying the rope from our vehicle to use it to save one of their SUVs. I think they have given up on us. The water is up to the wheel wells on our SUV and the tide is still coming in. I'll call you back later. You better pray."

To my surprise, they did not give up. After they saved their vehicle, they tied frayed ropes together and went right back to work on ours. One man jumped in our SUV and got behind the steering wheel. The engine still fired, and he revved it up. The vehicle exhaust coming out of the submerged muffler created a cauldron behind the vehicle and emerged from the water in noxious fumes. Rick and I got in the waist-deep cauldron and while breathing the nasty fumes, pushed on the vehicle with all our might. Two other Qataris joined in our effort to push the SUV.

Rick was a Pentecostal preacher in civilian life. He cried out, "Help us Jesus." I joined in, and for benefit of our Muslim rescuers, added "*Insha' Allah*" (if God wills it). We created a cadence that went like this: "Help us Jesus, Help us Jesus, Insha' Allah, Insha' Allah… Help us Jesus, Help us Jesus, Insha' Allah, Insha' Allah." We pushed and strained on "Help us Jesus" and relaxed our muscles momentarily on "Insha' Allah."

In one final push, with the driver's heavy foot on the accelerator and another SUV pulling with the rope, the quagmire released its grip and our SUV sprung to the dry beach. We jumped up and down, hollered, hugged, and high-fived.

After our momentary celebration, we opened the driver's door of the SUV and water poured out. I went back to the Land Rover where I had left my wallet to keep it from getting wet. I pulled out all the dollar bills and riyals I had to give to our rescuers. They deserved more, but the handful of cash was all I had. They raised their hands, motioning me to stop. I learned they knew more English. One of them said, "No! No, we're brothers" and lowered and clasped his hands as a symbol of unity. I held back tears and bear hugged them all one more time. Rick was more emotional than me. He nearly started speaking in tongues. We spent a few minutes taking pictures and enjoying handshakes. One of the young Qataris noticed a small American parade flag in the back of our vehicle. I motioned to him as if to ask, "Would you like to have it?" He smiled and accepted it right away.

Those young Qataris must have seen Rick and me as a couple of tenderfoots, definitely out of our culture and from another religion, but they helped us and accepted us as brothers.

I have called people "brothers" and "sisters" nearly all of my life. It comes natural from my Baptist upbringing – "How are you Brother Jones, and how are you Sister Smith?" I have since become aware not everyone appreciates being called "Brother" or "Sister." For some people, this endearing designation presumes a closeness that does not exist. Some Christians will not refer to Muslims as brothers or sisters since Muslims are not brothers and sisters in the context of the same, exact faith. Likewise, some Muslims will not refer to Christians as brothers or sisters for the same reason.

Occasionally, I commit a faux pas when I call someone "Brother" or "Sister," realizing too late I offended the person. On one occasion when I was visiting inmates and their families in the prison visiting room, I called one of our inmates "Brother" and learned quickly that his son did not appreciate it. The son curtly said, "You're not my uncle." Working in the prison, there were a few times when I realized too late that I had offended various Muslim inmates by calling them my brothers. They responded to me quickly as well, making sure I knew I was not a brother to them.

But the young Qatari men on the beach and many Afghan and Iraqi Muslims I would later meet did refer to me as their brother. Why the difference?

It may come down to this hot question. Do Christians and Muslims worship the same God? When someone asks me this question, they are normally asking for one of two reasons. They really do want to know. Or they are just setting me up to express their own opinion.

If you are looking for a direct answer here, you won't get it. My intent in this book is not to influence your theology but to influence the way you approach your own beliefs and the beliefs of others. There are generally three possible ways to answer this question. One, Allah and God are the same – just different language names for the same God. Two, Allah and God are not the same. Three, Muslims and Christians worship the same God, but one group has it right about Jesus and the other group has it wrong.

When we look at the worldviews of others, do we believe their worldviews have any validity? When they believe something diametrically opposed to our view, to what extent are we willing to tolerate such a polarized view? This provokes such questions as: Are those other people "saved"? Is their worldview wrong? Could part of their philosophy or religion be right? Are they as enlightened as those in our faith? Do they worship the same God?

Which of the statements below would you say best reflect the way you see your own belief system compared with the faiths and beliefs of others?

- My worldview is the only way.
- My worldview is closest to the truth.
- My worldview is more enlightened.
- All worldviews are relative.

We will place these approaches along a continuum, but let's start with a bird's eye view of Abrahamic, Eastern, and Nature-based religions and examine them in the context of tolerance of other worldviews. Before we begin a discussion on tolerance, it is extremely important to note, that in this chapter, we are not talking about tolerance of people, rather tolerance of beliefs. There is a difference. In the next chapter, we will look at tolerance of other people.

Abrahamic Faiths

Jews, Christians, and Muslims all claim Abraham as their ancestral or spiritual father. They belong to monotheistic faiths and generally have a high tolerance for one another regarding their respective monotheistic beliefs and many shared biblical stories. Bear in mind, the Christian belief of the Trinity is viewed as a polytheistic and heretical doctrine from the lenses of Judaism and Islam. Therefore, many Jews and Muslims have a zero tolerance for such a belief. That does not necessarily mean they have a low tolerance of those who hold such a view. We will get to that later.

All three faiths are linear, beginning with God's creation of the world and moving toward the fulfillment of the kingdom of God. Orthodox, Conservative, and Reformed Jews await the Messiah to usher in this fulfillment. Most Christians await a literal return of the Messiah to begin the fulfillment. Many Muslims also await the return of Jesus before the Day of Judgment, but they reject the belief that Jesus was or is divine. In many forms of Judaism and Christianity, there is a future vision of the final restoration of Israel. The whole idea of the restoration of Israel is a sore spot between Muslims and Jews. Therefore, many Muslims have a zero tolerance for the belief that Jews should govern Jerusalem or for the dispensational Christian belief that the Jewish temple must be rebuilt in Jerusalem before Christ returns. Many dispensational Christians in the United States have no idea of the strife they could spread in the Middle East by espousing beliefs about rebuilding the ancient temple. Likewise, many Jews have a zero tolerance for any kind of Islamic governance in Jerusalem.

Generally, people of all three faiths accept the idea that people will be rewarded or judged in the afterlife based on how well they lived or the kind of relationship they had with God while on earth. In the afterlife people will continue with a sense of personal identity and live in a real time and place in Heaven or Hell. Many Christians believe in Purgatory where people in the afterlife can purge themselves of any remaining sins before continuing the heavenward journey. Many Christians and Muslims make exclusive claims about the requirements to get to Heaven. These Christians and Muslims are likely to have a low tolerance level for other beliefs that they believe would prevent a person from gaining eternal salvation. This is one of the reasons they are so concerned about converting others and bringing people to the "truth." Compared to Christians and Muslims, most Jewish people do not make exclusive claims on the way to get to Heaven.

Eastern Religions

Compared to the three Abrahamic faiths, Eastern religions tend to be polytheistic or more esoteric in nature. However, Taoism, Confucianism, and various forms of Buddhism are considered more philosophies than religions. Shintoism has a great focus on ancestor worship.

Generally, Eastern religions have a different concept of the afterlife that includes reincarnation with the ultimate fulfillment of Nirvana. Just the opposite in Abrahamic faiths, the ultimate goal is not to live forever in our same personal identities. Instead, adherents look forward to a time when they will lose their personal identities and become one with the Cosmos, much like a raindrop becomes one with the sea. A person reaches a state of Nirvana through right living and enlightenment. Most people in Eastern religions accept the belief that people from other religious traditions can find similar enlightenment. In some Eastern religions, a person can have many different gods and even follow Christ as one of those gods. Many with such a belief would consider themselves very tolerant of other religions, while most Christians would consider such a belief as blasphemous. Compared to Christianity and Islam, Eastern religions tend to place more importance on proper enlightenment rather than absolute truth.

Compared to Abrahamic faiths, Eastern religions are cyclical, not linear. They emphasize birth, life, death, rebirth into another lifecycle, to be followed by another lifecycle, and so on. The Cosmos is not moving forward to some realized kingdom but is constantly changing in its own greater cycle. There is no beginning, and there is no end.

Nature-Based Religions

Nature-based religions have a strong belief system in a spirit world that resides in nature. Though many Christians view these religions as pantheistic and have a low tolerance for such beliefs, some nature-based religions are very monotheistic. In many Native American spiritualties, there is still only one ultimate Creator or Grandfather who created the universe and the world. Yoruba has many *orishas* (divine spirits), but there is still only one Creator. In Nature-based religions, the spirit world serves as an intermediary between humanity and God.

Many Nature-based religions combine elements of the linear and cyclical. Like monotheistic religions, most Nature religions have powerful stories about how God created the world, but like Eastern religions, there is a great sense of appreciation for the circle of life. Nature religions are strongly connected to the seasons of the year, the lunar cycle, the life cycle of plants, and seasonal animal migratory movements. By observing nature, one senses the idea of an ongoing cycle of birth, growth, death, and rebirth. In the afterlife departed souls join the spirit world in this ongoing cycle. In most of these worldviews, there is no exclusive way to the after-life such as the Muslim belief in Muhammad or the Christian belief in Jesus, so many people from Nature-based religions tend to be more tolerant of other belief systems and open to synthesizing their belief system with other religious worldviews.

My worldview is the only way.

People who believe "My worldview (faith or belief system) is the only way" generally view others outside the realm of their faith as in error and lost. We mean the word "lost" here in its evangelical context. A person is on the wrong path and were that person to die, he or she would spend an eternity in Hell.

This faith is typical among fundamentalist and conservative evangelical Christians who place a strong emphasis on God's holiness and judgment. Christians who believe "My religion is the only way" often quote Jesus from John 14:6, "I am the way and the truth and the life. No one comes to the Father except through me." They interpret this passage in its strictest sense of exclusivity, meaning that apart from faith in Jesus Christ, there is absolutely no other means to be reconciled to God and obtain eternal salvation. They believe this is the truth, and any other view or theology that departs from this is wrong. When people accept that Jesus Christ died on the cross for them and place their faith in Christ, they are forgiven of their sins and are able to go to Heaven when they die. There are many passages in the New Testament that point to this type of exclusive faith. Keep in mind, Christians who hold this exclusive belief about salvation still often debate whether such faith is foreordained or left up to a person's free will. Many Christians also argue over whether or not Christians can lose their salvation.

Fundamentalist Muslims have a similar approach to other religions. In Islam, to obtain eternal salvation, a person's good deeds must outweigh his or her bad deeds. Like Christianity, Muslims believe that Jesus was a great prophet. However, they do not believe Jesus was or is God. The idea that Jesus is God and that God somehow allowed himself to be executed as a common criminal is heresy to them. To them, this Christian belief about Jesus is bad enough to condemn anyone to Hell. A Muslim who holds this view could point to any number of passages in the Quran to support such a view and claim, "My worldview is the only way." Muslims who hold such views will often have an extremely low tolerance of other beliefs that oppose their way to understanding salvation.

Religious people who have the belief that "My worldview is the only way" believe they have discovered the absolute truth and are gravely concerned about other worldviews that may take people down a wrong path, especially if that path leads them away from eternal salvation. Therefore, their toleration for other such worldviews is ordinarily extremely low.

My worldview is closest to the truth.

People who hold the view that "My worldview is closest to the truth" are generally more tolerant of other belief systems than those who hold the belief, "My worldview is the only way." They are willing to concede that people from other worldviews may obtain eternal salvation as well.

Many moderate evangelicals tend to interpret theology through the lens of God's love and mercy. Their view about other religions tends to be, "My religion is closest to the truth." They also emphasize a personal relationship with Christ. However, in their understanding of God's mercy, they cannot accept the assertion that God would condemn a person to Hell, especially a good person who simply never knew or understood the gospel message. They believe there is room for the good Muslim or even the good atheist to make it to Heaven. In their theology of the cross, they too recognize the power of Christ's atoning death for the forgiveness of sins, but they also see the cross experience as the greatest moment of reconciliation for the entire world. They would agree with the assertion in John 14:6 that Jesus is "the only way." However, this only way is not always wrapped up in a person's faith in Christ, rather Christ's faith in the person. Even in this theology, there is still a continuum of beliefs: those who believe in a literal Hell and those who do not and those who believe in an ultimate judgment and those who believe in universalism (the belief that everyone will ultimately be saved). Theologians who have these respective beliefs generally have their favorite scriptures to substantiate their beliefs as well.

Likewise, most Muslims do not presume to know the eternal destiny of anyone, not even other Muslims. Granted, they view the Christian belief of a divine Jesus as heresy, but they recognize the many passages in the Quran that teach Muslims to respect the "people of the book" (a reference to Jews and Christians). In their belief they recognize that a person's good deeds can outweigh the bad deeds, even a heretical belief. These Muslims respect Judaism and Christianity and recognize both religions' contributions to Islam, but they see Islam as God's final revelation. So they might say, "My worldview is closest to the truth."

They are apt to be more tolerant of other views than Muslims who make exclusive claims.

Religious people who have the belief that "My worldview is closest to the truth" are concerned about truth, but they concede that people from other worldviews may know enough truth or experience enough of God's grace to make it to Heaven. People with this worldview tend to be more tolerant of other worldviews than those who have the belief that "My worldview is the only way."

My worldview is more enlightened.

Religious people who hold the view that "My worldview is more enlightened" are not as concerned about absolute truth as those in our last two groups. They place more emphasis on having an open mind and a willingness to accept ideas from other worldviews.

People who hold to this thinking are generally not zealous about converting others to their faith or way of life. Since most Hindus and Buddhists believe most everyone will be reincarnated and eventually make it to Nirvana anyway, they are not worried about saving someone from the pits of Hell or getting them to the pearly gates. Liberal monotheists either don't believe in a Hell or don't believe a loving God would ever condemn people to such a place. So they don't agonize about "saving" people either.

However, people who think this way may have a strong desire to bring others to what they believe is a more enlightened and less judgmental worldview. From their perspectives they are not as naïve as people of other faiths who retain silly superstitions and burdensome dogmas.

People who believe that "My worldview is more enlightened" do not generally make claims on absolute truth. So their tolerance for other worldviews is typically higher than our former two groups.

All worldviews are relative.

There is still another approach on our continuum. I have met people who take this approach in all faiths, including Christianity and Islam. Their approach? What difference does it make? All roads lead to the same place. Any religious path/any worldview, as long as people are not hurting others, is as good as any other. They don't believe in exclusive claims to eternal salvation. Therefore, those who believe that "All worldviews are relative" are generally the most tolerant on our continuum of other belief systems.

Nuances in these different approaches

Keep in mind, not every card-carrying member of a particular belief system approves of everything in that system. Hopefully, there is a young Taliban man somewhere in Afghanistan right now who is questioning a command to kill the infidels. This Sunday, someone in the Unitarian Universalist Church will probably question the belief that all religions are relative and will think, "Certainly, somebody has to be right and somebody has to be wrong." This Friday, a father in Turkey, taking his family to a mosque for the Friday prayer service, passing by an Orthodox Church, may wonder, "Maybe those Christians are right about Jesus. "

While Protestants and Catholics agree that salvation comes through Christ and Christ alone, in Catholic theology this grace is administered through the sacraments of the Church. Depending on the Protestant tradition, some see salvation as purely a matter of God's grace while others place responsibility on the believer's faith. Many see a combination of God's grace and the believer's faith.

Fundamentalist and many evangelical Christians proclaim the belief that one can be saved only through faith in Jesus Christ. However, even the staunchest fundamentalist normally makes exception for infants and children who died too young to have comprehended the gospel. In this belief, even though children are tainted by "original sin," they are only responsible for their eternal life when they reach what evangelicals call "the age of accountability." This means that children are protected from Hell because of their naivety. While hardly ever preached this way, this kind of theology implies that children are "born saved," but when they reach the age of accountability, they somehow lose their salvation. To gain or regain salvation (depending on how you look at it), children or young adults must place their faith in Christ, either by freewill or election (depending on your theology). Since there is no definitive chronological age when one reaches the age of accountability, one child may reach the age of accountability by age seven while another may not reach it until age twelve. It doesn't exactly seem fair that the latter child gets an additional five years to hedge his bet against Hell.

Or for that matter, why would a good adult living far away from Christian culture and never hearing the gospel be condemned to eternal punishment? Or a step further, why would a mature adult who has heard the gospel but never comprehended it, be condemned to eternal damnation? Does a God of love visit finite sin with eternal punishment? One explanation is that God is also a God of judgment, and if you believe in freewill theology over predestination, then people make their ultimate choices, not God. They are responsible for their decisions. If you believe in extreme predestination, then God has already chosen those who are saved and those who are not, and there is absolutely nothing anyone can do to change God's mind. Some Christians take an even more exclusive belief; that God holds infants, children, and persons with severe mental retardation accountable for "original sin." In other Christian theologies, even strongly committed Christians, according to Catholic theology, would go to Hell if they were to die in a state of un-repented mortal sin. In most Holiness theologies, any un-confessed sin, no matter how trivial, would send a person to Hell if they died in an unrepentant state.

Volumes have been written on these various theologies, and I apologize if I seem to be trivializing these deeply held beliefs. I am not being cynical; merely pointing out that even those who hold such exclusive theologies have varying degrees of tolerance for nuanced beliefs that are different from theirs.

Most Christian denominations have their own faith statements regarding how one obtains eternal salvation. While a denomination may have a particular stance, that does not mean everyone in that denomination agrees to it. My denomination takes the position that apart from Jesus Christ there is no salvation. Yet individual Southern Baptists still debate and wonder about the exclusivity of salvation. For those who are absolutely convinced of the truth of the gospel, they would probably say, "My religion is the only way." Still, there are some who are not as easily convinced and may wonder about the validity of other faiths and the testimony of other religious believers. They make allowances in their mind for people of other faiths who have never heard the gospel. They may think, "My religion is closest to the truth," or "My religion is more enlightened." A few Baptists find such exclusivity impossible to accept, so they re-interpret the dogma to fit their own spirituality and may actually believe, "All religions are relative."

Various controversies throughout the history of the Southern Baptist Convention have actually centered on these lively debates; however, the denomination as a whole took a much more certain stance after conservative evangelicals gained control of the denomination in the 1980s. With liberal theology out of the way, conservatives then argued over predestination versus freewill (Calvinism versus Arminianism), basically arguing about how certain a person can be about salvation. These arguments may seem rather silly for Christians who are not so certain in matters of faith, but these are serious debates for those who are certain.

Humanists and atheists would see such arguments as ridiculous. Yet atheists have their own debates. Some are just as convinced about their perception of absolute truth as the radical Islamist or staunch fundamentalist Christian. Such atheists believe, "My worldview is the only way." In their belief, they are absolutely convinced there is no god and believe that anyone who believes otherwise is in grave error. In their belief, once people eradicate superstitious religious beliefs, they are free from the chains of religion to find real meaning and purpose in life. To use an evangelical term, this freedom is "salvation" for them, and they have an extremely low tolerance for other beliefs.

Other atheists are likely to be more tolerant of other belief systems. They may think, "My worldview is closest to the truth." While they are convinced of their belief system, they still appreciate the supernatural religious stories, but they "demythologize" the stories to find what they believe is the kernel of truth. Others may be even more tolerant and concede that the existence or non-existence of a god cannot be proven. They generally believe that "My worldview is more enlightened." Since all atheists believe oblivion waits us all, some atheists may conclude, "What difference does it make what people believe, so long as they do their best in this life?" In a group of atheists, they probably have the highest tolerance for other worldviews.

Summary

Let's look at the continuum again.

- My worldview is the only way.
- My worldview is closest to the truth.
- My worldview is more enlightened.
- All worldviews are relative.

If you did not decide earlier, which statement best reflects your worldview?

These statements are not given in any particular order of priority. We are not saying a person will begin at one end and finish at the other. Based on heredity and a constant changing environment, we may change or tweak our worldviews over a lifetime. This chapter is about our belief system and the way we tend to focus more on absolute truth or proper enlightenment and the way these approaches impact our toleration level of other belief systems.

However, there can be an enormous difference in the way we tolerate other worldviews versus the way we tolerate or respect other people who hold those views. This will be the subject of the next chapter.

Chapter 8

Approaches to People

How good and pleasant it is when
God's people live together in unity!
Psalm 133:1

An atheist by the name of Mr. Bowen taught me to play chess. He worked for my father and invited our family to his home for supper one evening. Before we arrived my father warned me about Mr. Bowen's beliefs. I was 13 years old and to my knowledge had never met an atheist, at least one who freely admitted it. It wasn't the kind of thing a person from the Deep South would brag about, but in hindsight I don't think Mr. Bowen was a Southerner. I kind of halfway expected him to be a mean-spirited, mad-at-life person, but we had an enjoyable experience with Mr. Bowen and his wife around the dinner table. After supper when grown folks talk about what they do and teenagers drift off, I wandered over to a chessboard on a coffee table in Mr. Bowen's living room. I didn't know how to play. I picked up a few of the classic Staunton chess pieces and examined them.

Mr. Bowen noticed my curiosity, left the grown folks' conversation, came over to where I was sitting and asked, "Would you like to learn how to play?" He patiently spent the rest of the evening teaching me how to play chess. He showed me how each piece moved and after my newfound knowledge, he challenged me to my first game of chess. He took it easy on me, encouraging me to consider the second and third order effects of each move. He was graceful and allowed me to take back my bad moves, pointing out the consequences of such moves. At some point, he knew my family had to go home, so he went ahead and checkmated me, but he encouraged me and told me that he believed I would be a great chess player one day.

Mr. Bowen began my chess journey. My parents soon bought me a cheap, cardboard chessboard with varnished black and white wooden Staunton pieces. I taught my sister. We played every night for weeks. A few months later when we opened gifts on Christmas morning, I opened a package from my parents containing an elegant, black case that contained a vinyl chessboard and plastic gold and silver, life-like, medieval chess pieces, each resting in its own red velvet shell. That chess set became the local chess set in my neighborhood where I honed my chess skills and beat nearly every buddy that came over to play.

About a year after meeting Mr. Bowen, I tuned in every night on our television to catch the world news about the "match of the century," the World Chess Championship of 1972 in Reyjavik, Iceland. Bobby Fischer, the American challenger, another chess-playing atheist, captured the imagination of many Americans when he challenged Russian Borris Spassky to unseat 24 years of Russian domination of the game.

I taught my son how to play on that same vinyl board with the medieval replica pieces. The first few years I let him win from time to time to keep his spirits up. As he grew older and got better, my winnings did not come so easily. I hardly ever beat him now. The son surpassed the father.

The best chess player I ever played against was a Muslim inmate who worked for me as my Chapel clerk in prison. He did not brag about his ability because he knew as many Muslims do that the Prophet Muhammad forbade the playing of chess. In Muhammad's day, chess was blamed for drawing young people into long periods of idle chess gaming when they should have been studying or getting their chores done. In current Muslim schools of thought, playing chess is still not generally permitted.

I am grateful to Mr. Bowen for fostering in me a love for the game. About two years after my first chess encounter, Mr. Bowen died. In spite of what I had been taught on atheists not making it to Heaven, I couldn't help but wonder if Mr. Bowen made it. My father reminded me of Mr. Bowen's honesty and his hard work and devotion to his family and nation. He was not at all what I had expected an atheist to be like. Mr. Bowen loved life and lived well.

Before I met Mr. Bowen, I had pre-judged him based on my own views of his beliefs, but once I got to know him, I had great respect for the man. In the last chapter, we discussed the way we view the belief systems of others, based on our worldviews. In this chapter, we look at the way we respect people with different worldviews and suggest **the way we respect others is often more connected to our individual spiritual and emotional maturity than our worldviews.**

The popular, politically correct culture would have us believe that in order to respect others, we must respect their beliefs as well. This is a ridiculous assumption. Even if we generally associate conservative traditions with being less tolerant of other views and liberal traditions as being more tolerant of other views, this does not mean conservatives are less tolerant of people who differ from them, or that liberals are more tolerant of people who differ from them. This is an erroneous conclusion because a person can have a low tolerance for a certain belief or practice, yet still respect the person who believes or acts a certain way. A person's conservative worldview may even strengthen his or her resolve to respect others. Likewise, it is presumptuous to conclude that people with more tolerant belief systems are more tolerant of those who believe differently than they do. A person might have a high tolerance for different beliefs and practices but still have a low tolerance for the person who has such beliefs.

Billy Graham, revered by Protestants and Catholics alike and even by people of other religions, proclaims that Jesus is the only way. Graham makes no apology about it. He admits that the message of the cross is often offensive to people who don't understand it. He wants people to turn away from beliefs and practices that lead them away from Christian conversion. We can logically conclude that Billy Graham has a low tolerance for competing views about the path to eternal salvation.

But does this mean Billy Graham does not tolerate or respect the people who have these views? Of course not. Billy Graham proclaims the gospel because he loves the world and wants all people to know that God loves them. Billy Graham does not proclaim an exclusive message because he is an intolerant person. He may have an exclusive faith, but he is an inclusive person.

The same can be said about many Muslim inmates in prison or Jehovah's Witnesses canvassing the neighborhood. Many people spread their message because they want others to know the "truth" or have "enlightenment."

True, not every evangelical is a "Billy Graham" nor is every Muslim concerned about spreading an altruistic message. Many Christians, Muslims, and people of other worldviews proclaim exclusive messages out of fear, guilt, or anger. Such insecurities affect the way they wield their faith on others. We will examine this immaturity in the next chapter.

The same things can be said for atheists. Sure, some are led by hedonistic lifestyles and hate religion. Some are driven by unreconciled issues from their past. They are angry at the world and channel their anger through mean-spirited lawsuits against religious people. If they could have it their way, religious people would not be allowed to express any religious view in a public forum and would be subject to fines or imprisonment for doing so.

Yet there are atheists who love and live well and find joy and peace in life. They may privately roll their eyes at religious beliefs and practices, but they respect those who have such beliefs and would never think to insult them. They share their message of atheism because they believe they have found meaning in life without the trappings of religion, and they want other people to find this same meaning.

Summary

There is a difference between respecting a belief and respecting a person. We do not have to respect beliefs that we do not agree with in order to respect the person who has such beliefs. It's possible to hate the belief, but love the person who has the belief. While worldview plays a significant part in the way we respect others, our level of emotional and spiritual maturity is highly connected to the way we approach and respect people who believe differently than we do.

However, it is quite another matter to hate the belief and the person. This will be one of the subjects in the next chapter along with other volatile religious cocktails.

Chapter 9

Volatile Religious Cocktails

When the missionaries came to Africa they had the Bible and
we had the land. They said, "Let us pray." We closed our eyes.
When we opened them we had the Bible and they had the land.
Bishop Desmond Tutu

W hile writing this book, one of my colleagues, a married Army
chaplain was stripped of his rank, dishonorably discharged, and
sentenced to prison for committing adultery and allegedly threatening to
kill his mistress when she tried to stop the affair. I do not know this
chaplain, but I am certain he did not begin his ministerial career planning
to hurt people and end up in prison. What happened?

With nearly three decades of ministry in prison and military
environments, I have observed three behaviors that, when mixed with
religion, make for very volatile religious cocktails. They are escapist faith,
exploitive faith, and enraged faith.

- Escapist faith twists religion to affirm emotional insecurities.
- Exploitive faith manipulates theology to exploit others.
- Enraged faith hijacks religion to justify malicious acts.

When there is no vetting process, slick religious leaders with these volatile mixes often slip through the cracks into pastorates and other positions of religious leadership. We are familiar with the sex and money scandals of fallen priests and pastors and the violence of radical imams.

It is often said that religion is a major cause of most wars. Indeed, it would be naïve to discuss the wars in Afghanistan or Iraq without addressing the differences between Sunni and Shia or the differences in Wahhabi faith and moderate Islam. We cannot contribute to peace in the Middle East without addressing the differences in Muslim and Jewish perspectives on the Holy Land.

However, while religion is often the cause of war, religion is also often the reason for peace and begs the question. Does a bad person shape a bad theology, or does a bad theology shape a bad person? Or could it be a combination of both? We will look at the possibility of all three answers. Over years of observing the behaviors and religious beliefs of my parishioners in prison and the military, I believe that theology certainly shapes a person, but individual emotional and spiritual maturity also impact the way a person interprets theology, for good or for bad.

One way some psychologists assess emotional maturity is by using a measurement called Emotional Quotient (EQ).[41] There are several variations of EQ, but basically, EQ addresses four questions.[42]

1. How well do you handle anger?
2. How well do you delay gratification?
3. How well do you understand your own emotions?
4. How well do you understand the emotions of others?

---

[41] John Mayer, University of New Hampshire, and Peter Salovey, Yale University, offered the first formulation of a concept called *emotional intelligence*, later known as *emotional quotient*. See Daniel Goleman, *Emotional Intelligence* website, http://danielgoleman.info/topics/emotional-intelligence (accessed 27 Nov 2011).

[42] There are several constructs for emotional intelligence (EI) or emotional quotient (EQ): the Mayer-Salovey Four Branch Model, the Trait Meta-Mood Scale, the Bar-On Model of Emotional-Social Intelligence, and the Trait Emotional Intelligence Measure. Each indicator measures slightly different variants of emotional quotient, but they generally cover the four questions I have listed here. The reader should also note that psychologists do not universally accept EI and EQ as valid scientific measurements.

Generally, escapist, exploitive, and enraged faiths are the results of emotional immaturity. Before we blame religion on the outcome of these volatile faiths, we ought to first consider the emotional maturity level of the people who have such faiths. The more we study our sacred texts and the more we relate with our faith community, the more emotionally mature we ought to become. Unfortunately, some people, whether conscious of it or not, twist the teachings of their faith tradition to suit their own emotional immaturity.

Escapist Faith

Escapist faith is often found in people who have co-dependent relationships. The classic example is the wife with poor self-esteem who stays married to an abusive, alcoholic husband. She could make demands from her husband or perhaps leave him. However, because of her poor self-esteem, she tiptoes around his drunken fits of rage and always nurses him back to sobriety, neglecting her own needs and safety, awaiting the moment he will get drunk again and fly off the handle. If she is a religious person, she is likely to quote scripture to justify staying with the abusive husband.

Does the Lord really want her to live in such abuse? She does not make a stand or leave her husband because it actually makes her feel good to be needed by her alcoholic husband. So she dutifully waits on him and never finds her own emotional independence. Her faith is escapist faith. It is delusional faith. She follows the parts of the Bible she likes that justify her emotional and spiritual insecurities, but ignores or denies the parts of the Bible that would free her from a disastrous marriage. Or in some cases, the wife of an abusive husband may actually want to leave a disastrous marriage, but members of her church tell her to hang on and make her feel guilty for wanting to leave. People with escapist faith twist religion to escape their challenges rather than face them. Sometimes avoidance is the only option, but generally speaking, avoidance is the worst way to handle conflict.

Some use religion to avoid challenges with authority. Every time they run into a difficult situation at work, they do not examine what they could do differently. Instead, they believe God would not want them to be unhappy, so they "blame the man" and go from one dead-end job to another, following the Lord's so-called "will" and never learn how to deal with authority issues.

Some who live in poverty accept their poor condition as their lot in life. They focus on the mansion in Heaven for their future as a way to escape thinking about their economic condition in the present.

Some who are rich justify their stinginess with the belief they are somehow special in God's eyes and avoid helping the poor because of a perception that the poor are lazy and undeserving of God's blessings.

Sometimes people use religious services like a drug. A young woman may be clinically depressed and find the worship service at her church her only solace. Her temperament may relish the quiet, contemplative worship of the church, the classical music, the smell of incense, the candlelight, and the gentle encouragement from her priest. These experiences take her away from her unhappy life, if only for one hour.

Or an angry man with a completely different temperament may attend a charismatic church service to find relief from his bitterness. He enjoys the contemporary praise band, dancing in the aisles, and a fiery sermon from the preacher.

The problem is not their church attendance but what they do with the worship experience after the service. People who are growing spiritually take the worship experience and apply it to the rest of their lives. People who are not growing spiritually will not move beyond their present emotional and spiritual state and will return week after week, not necessarily to worship God but to get a quick fix of feel-good religion.

The main reason we should do religious work is because of our love for God and others and to grow spiritually, but our motivations are not always altruistic. I admit in my own life, it makes me feel good to be needed. There is nothing wrong with this unless it becomes my only reason to do religious work or if I am actually doing harm in the work.

It is not always easy to spot the selfish motivation in our own lives or the lives of others, and it can be very difficult to point this truth out to others, particularly if they are not willing to hear the truth, but delaying the truth can be hazardous. I have seen it time and time again when well-meaning church folks praise a choir member for singing a solo in church and go on and on about his "magnificent" performance. Everybody knows the performance was at best, mediocre, but they exaggerate (lie) to encourage him, to help him feel good about himself. Such affirmation is generally fine until the person convinces himself he is a virtuoso and cannot believe it when the choir director does not want to use him every Sunday to perform a solo.

We do this in other areas of the church too. Many churches are in such desperate need of help that people are often placed in positions of leadership before they are ready. We may task a person to teach Sunday school, but their teaching style is boring or they have little, if any, biblical training and background. We may praise a person for giving a testimony and convince him he ought to be a preacher when his gifts and talents belong in other areas. We have coaxed many people along the way to spend years of preparation to enter professional ministry when in reality occupational ministry was never their God-given calling. They would have been great successes in other careers had the church led them in the right direction. Some ministers realize their poor choice of occupation too late in life and then stay in occupational ministry because they do not know what else to do. They continue to bore their parishioners or worse, drive them away. These ministers may be good people, but their churches did them a great disservice early in their lives by not helping them to find their rightful calling.

Escapist faith is not faith in God. It is faith in what a person wants God to do for him or her. Some people view God, the Almighty Creator of the Universe, as a little fairy godmother or a genie in a bottle. If they just pray hard enough, all their wishes will come true. This kind of faith often falls to pieces when a significant crisis comes along and God does not grant their requests.

Escapist faith engenders laziness and leads to such thoughts as: "God is going to take me when it's my time, so I don't need to worry about what I should eat and how I should exercise. If God wants to save my marriage, God will change my spouse, so I don't have to work hard at this relationship. The Lord is coming back soon, so I don't need to make financial investments in my children's future. God is going to get me out of prison five years before my sentence is over, so I don't need to work on gaining a GED or college degree while I'm in prison."

Escapist faith infects more than the individual. It can infect an entire culture. After the Civil War, many Southern whites felt their way of life was gone. They felt oppressed by the Federal government. In reaction, many white Christians, by the thousands, joined the Ku Klux Klan and twisted the Bible to justify their beliefs in a superior white race. They fought their perceived oppressors by oppressing African Americans. A few generations later, Nation of Islam leaders twisted both the Bible and the Quran to create their own myth of black racial superiority. When a culture feels oppressed by another culture, the oppressed culture often rewrites history to justify its predicament. Since there is often no hard scientific evidence to support a lot of religious beliefs, religion is an easy target for such re-writes.

In summary, people use escapist faith to justify emotional immaturity and avoid their real challenges.

Exploitive Faith

When I was in the Federal Bureau of Prisons New Chaplains Training Course, I met another Bureau chaplain who was also a chaplain in the Air Force Reserve. He was charismatic, gregarious, and appeared to a born leader. I thought he might one day become the Chief of Chaplains of the Federal Bureau of Prisons or the U.S. Air Force.

About three years later I learned he was fired and sentenced to serve six months in one of our Federal prisons for having had sex with female inmates. The female inmates may have considered their sexual encounters with him as consensual, but the Federal government does not. Inmates are considered wards of the state, and as such, staff members are responsible to take care of them, not exploit them.

Exploitive faith is another form of escapist faith, but there is a difference. Escapist faith may or may not harm someone else, but exploitive faith manipulates others. People with exploitive faith use religion or their position of religious authority to exploit the vulnerabilities of others.

Here is a typical scenario. A godly Christian woman has a troubled marriage. Her husband has stopped doing the little things he used to do for her and is not romantic anymore. The flame in the marriage has gone out. She feels unloved by her husband.

So she goes to see her highly respected pastor for counsel about her marriage. The pastor is a good man, known for his integrity. But unknown to her, the pastor and his wife have not felt close lately. He has been extremely busy in the ministries of the church and has partly neglected his home life, a dangerous pitfall for any minister. When the pastor finally gets around to paying attention to his wife, he is usually in the mood for sex, but she is not. His wife needs to be wooed and not treated like a sex object. He is too tired to expend the energy to woo her, so they go to bed each night with unmet intimacy needs.

During the course of several counseling sessions behind closed doors, the young lady in the troubled marriage is amazed at how well her pastor understands her. She wishes her husband understood her the same way. The pastor compliments her on traits her husband used to notice. In deep gratitude she tells the pastor how much she appreciates him and hugs him. He has not felt such an embrace in months. His passion is aroused.

The pastor and the lady arrange several counseling sessions over the next few weeks. They become intoxicated in their feelings for one another, and the counseling sessions turn into rendezvous. To justify their new relationship, both of them ignore everything they were ever taught about boundaries.

He continues preaching and leading the ministries of the church, and she continues in her drab marriage. They live a lie in front of the church and in front of their families, but eventually one of them makes a mistake, and a vindictive deacon exposes the affair.

They go into survival mode, and within a matter of days, their attraction for each other vanishes, but it's too late. The woman has enormous guilt. Her husband threatens to divorce her and to kill the pastor. The church fires the pastor. His career is over. His family and church feel betrayed. His indiscretions taint the way some young people in the church will view religion for the rest of their lives. Some, disgusted by the hypocrisy, leave the church. Both the pastor and his one-time mistress leave behind them a wake of hurt people in their church and families.

I suppose we could blame the deacon or the lady's husband. We could blame the woman with marriage challenges, but the pastor, the authority figure, bears the ultimate responsibility. He was trained or should have been trained in what psychologists call "transference." Both the pastor and the young lady transferred their unmet needs onto one another. As the pastor, he bore the responsibility to protect her vulnerability and to give her wise counsel. Instead, he exploited her, crossed an intimacy line, and justified his actions to fulfill his own selfish needs.

In this scenario the minister's judgment was clouded by his own emotional neediness. This is the reason strong taboos exist in various cultures to prevent men and women from crossing the line. In most Muslim, Orthodox Jewish, and in some Christian cultures, even a public handshake between a man and a woman is forbidden. Others outside these religions may see such taboos as primitive and suppressive, but the taboos exist for a reason. When a man and woman of the same approximate age develop a spiritual kinship, the desire to consummate the relationship can become irresistible.[43] Taboos exist in these cultures to prevent a man and woman from getting close to that line. It is easy to confuse sexual intimacy with altruism. In healthy marriages sexuality is a

---

[43] The best description I have read on this phenomenon comes from Chester P. Michael, *Arise: A Christian Psychology of Love* (Charlottesville, VA: The Open Door, Inc., 1981), 126-127.

great physical, mental, emotional, and spiritual expression of love. Outside the realm of a healthy marriage, sexuality can be used like a drug to meet unhealthy emotional needs. Religious people are not immune from this challenge.

In the scenario of the unfaithful pastor, the minister may have actually convinced himself he was doing the right thing. That does not make it right, but it helps us to understand him. Worse are sexual predators who know what they are doing is wrong and exploit vulnerable people to simply satisfy their sexual desire or to have a feeling of power and control over their victims.

There are other forms of exploitive faith. Some religious people take advantage of others by stealing money, time, or loyalty. Some ministers manipulate their parishioners to give financially beyond their means. Quoting scriptures about the tithe and "giving above and beyond," they take advantage of poor people with escapist faith. The tithe and other financial offerings are great spiritual disciplines for people who have the wherewithal to give. However, when a preacher convinces a poor single mom who barely has enough money to feed her children, let alone pay her bills, to give to his special fund, then something is wrong. Jesus saw through such ruses and cited a similar story about self-righteous leaders who gave their money to temple ministries at the expense of neglecting their own parents.[44] In the same way, ministers can use guilt as a powerful tool to steal precious family time. As important as religious institutions are, no institution should take precedence over the family institution. Decent religious programs balance the needs of the religious community and the families involved in the community. Unhealthy religious communities compete with family time and resources and manipulate members to prioritize the community above family. This is often how religious cults are born. Perhaps the worst is the religious person who exploits the poor or the disenfranchised to join him in a reign of terror. But this volatile religious cocktail belongs in a group all to itself.

---

[44] Mark 7:9-13

Enraged Faith

Anger is a natural emotional response that informs us something is not right and compels us to action. Jesus expressed anger against the moneychangers in the temple who used sacred space for personal gain. The Book of Psalms contains numerous songs that declare anger against enemies and even against God. See Psalm 88 for an example of a blatantly angry Psalm. Anger is a normal phase of grief. When we lose an important relationship, status, freedom, or important possession, we may become angry and blame something or somebody, often ourselves. When someone dies, it is not uncommon for close family members of the deceased to blame God. They may not express their anger in spoken word because they feel guilty for being angry with God. Nevertheless, this kind of anger is often a natural response to death, especially when it concerns the death of people taken before their time or in some horrific way.

We are not wired to forget painful memories. Those who have been victimized by rape, other forms of violence, and betrayal may suffer from Post-Traumatic Stress Disorder (PTSD) for a lifetime. Painful memories are remembered with exactness, but sometimes they are suppressed into the subconscious. Suppressed feelings may explode, and anger only becomes wrong when we allow it to enrage us and we respond in a disproportional way, or we allow it to destroy us and other relationships around us.

Some use religion, not as a way to confront anger but as a way to justify hate and their prejudices. Throughout history people have used religion to commit slander, murder, and genocide. This is the reason many humanists despise religion. They know about atrocities committed in the name of religion, and such knowledge negates anything good religious people tell them about faith.

Most of the Muslims I have known do not believe the Quran condones terrorism any more than Christians and Jews believe the Bible condones it, yet the 9-11 terrorists found passages in the Quran to justify their slaughter of nearly 3,000 people. Most Christians do not believe the Bible condones terrorism, yet Crusaders slaughtered Cathars, Muslims,

Jews, and other Orthodox Christians, allegedly all in the name of Christ. Even in the history of our nation, many deeply committed Christians justified slavery and the killing of entire communities of Native Americans. How did people of religious faith come to such positions? How did the Ulma (Muslim community) and the Church (Christian community) allow these atrocities to happen? It is important to struggle with these questions in order to prevent such catastrophic events from happening again.

Back to our questions – Does a bad person shape theology, or does a bad theology shape a bad person? Or how is an innocent person misguided into terror? In reviewing a number of books about religious terrorism (written a few years prior to 9-11 and in the years immediately following),[45] I synthesized the authors' findings into a general list of characteristics often found in the religious terrorists.

From a sociological perspective, the religious terrorists ordinarily:
- Were male, in their late teens to middle-age
- Felt their specific culture was marginalized and victimized
- Bonded with other men in the same struggle
- Viewed modern Western Civilization as immoral
- Were unwilling to co-exist with certain people groups
- Did not see their culture as part of the existing political regime
- Developed a political radicalization
- Viewed violence as a symbolic act to demoralize their enemy

From a psychological perspective, they generally:
- Were driven by a male psyche to fight
- Had no empathy for their victims
- Were altruistic for their own people
- Had an inflated view of their personal sacrifice

From a theological perspective, they typically:
- Saw their struggle as a cosmological struggle
- Had legalistic interpretations of their sacred texts

---

[45] For a listing of these books, see Sources Consulted, page 295.

- Wanted to impose their application of the texts on others
- Regarded those with alternative interpretations as heretics
- Trusted only a select group of religious authorities
- Wanted a trusted authority to bless them for their acts of violence
- Hated the West and apostate regimes
- Believed their cause was a just war
- Demonized the enemy
- Saw their acts of violence as sacramental
- Believed they would be rewarded for their actions in the afterlife
- Believed they were fighting for God, family, their group, and honor[46]

I made this review in 2011. The prevailing notion then was that most religious terrorists came from poor economic and educational conditions and were lured into their causes with the promise of 72 virgins in the afterlife and the confidence someone would provide for their disenfranchised families once they had paid the ultimate sacrifice.

Just when we thought terror could not get any worse, the Islamic State seemed to come out of nowhere. We have witnessed a significant rise in the recruiting of women and even children to commit horrific acts of violence in the name of religion. And their recruits are not all poor and disenfranchised people living in squalor. Lest we forget, Osama bin Laden and Aymin Al-Zawahiri were wealthy and highly educated. A number of the 9-11 terrorists were well educated as well. The current leader of the Islamic State, Abu Bakr al-Baghdadi, is a highly educated person with resources that bin Laden could only dream about. He proclaims himself as the new caliph of Islam and is recruiting college-educated, young people.

The theology here does play a significant role in their decisions and behaviors. They believe the Caliphate should be restored, as do many other moral and upright Muslims. However, Islamist radicalized terrorists ignore a modern-day application of Islam to coexist with people of other faiths and the Quran's various passages to protect defenseless people.

---

[46] Carlton Fisher, *The Commonalities of Modern Religious Terrorists*, a research report submitted to the faculty of Air War College, Maxwell AFB, 26 September 2012.

Instead they focus on the Quran's passages to kill the infidel and apostates, wanting to return to what they consider the authentic Islam of the 7th century.

True, the Bible contains stories about God directing his followers to annihilate entire communities because those communities worshipped other gods, and the Bible includes commandments to stone people for adultery and blasphemy, but believers in the Bible have not carried out such practices in centuries. Rather they have interpreted such texts in light of all the other commandments in the Bible about love and in light of a modern day application. No decent religious person, whether Jew, Christian, or Muslim, wants to return to 7th century violence or to a Nazi-type violence of the 20th century. The Islamic State and the Nazi Party are prime examples of a theology or ideology "gone bad."

Soon after 9-11, President Bush referred to "evildoers" in a speech to motivate Americans to combat terrorism, but many Americans took evildoers to a new level. Some believed every Taliban warrior should be hunted down and killed. From my stint in Afghanistan, I discovered most of the people in remote areas of Afghanistan could not read or write and lived in what most Americans would call abject poverty. Massacring the Taliban would only give rise to thousands of other enraged terrorists. Some are now calling for the total annihilation of all Islamic State jihadists. Granted, they have to be stopped, but are we not stooping to their level if we have a let's-kill-them-all attitude? Killing one terrorist often gives rise to ten more and hundreds more if we happen to kill innocent people by mistake. The terrorists will simply use these mistakes for their social propaganda. As we meet them with appropriate violence, it is important for the West to remember principles of Just War Theory and for the many Muslims who are fighting radicalized Islamists to remember the righteous applications of jihad.

There are hundreds of young men, right now, sitting behind computer screens and looking at extreme jihadi websites. They are stuck between competing ideologies and have yet to make up their minds. Will they join a group of perceived holy warriors? Will they kill infidels and alleged apostate Muslims? Or will they be attracted to a practical Islam for the 21st century, an Islam that honors and respects people of different faiths and beliefs?

If we intend to stop the tidal wave of the Islamic State and other religious terror groups, we must do more than meet brute force with brute force. We have to examine what makes young people attracted to such groups in the first place, especially the social media that influences them. Malicious social media must be countered with savvy social media that attracts young people in a different direction – a direction that shows love over fear and makes religious terror groups look foolish.

When people are passionate about their worldviews, they naturally want to spread their worldviews. Most Muslims really do want to see Islam become the global religion, just as Christians want every person around the globe to accept the gospel message. Most humanists want people around the world to accept their message. As Americans who believe in freedom of speech and freedom of religion, we ought to champion these liberties around the globe, but there is bound to be conflict with competing messages.

How we spread our message is a major factor in what makes an ideology bad or good. We will save a greater discussion for this on a subsequent chapter on Christianity and Other Religions. Suffice it to say here, all decent religions have in common the love ethic. They encourage their adherents to love God (or their concept of a higher power) and to love and respect others (and in some religions, this includes loving your enemy). The theological opposite of love is fear. A bad religious ideology uses violent fear as a weapon to spread its message.

This brings us back to a major point of this book. Is a person or a group motivated by love or by fear? Granted, we all fall prey to our fears from time to time, but we don't have to be defined by them and live a life of enraged faith.

Using Chaplains at the Strategic Level to Influence Peace

In the introduction to this book, I quoted Secretary of State Madeleine Albright. "As Secretary of State you have all kinds of advisers – economic advisers and arms control advisers and climate change advisers – and the point I want to make is that it would be good to have some religious advisers too."

Our national leaders need the help of mature, seasoned religious leaders. There are numerous places to find such expertise, but one pool of advisors is already available at the national level.

While military chaplains mainly provide religious leadership, freedom of religion, and pastoral counseling, they also provide advisement to their commanders on the impact of religion in military operations. Chaplains provide information regarding various religious cultures in the commander's area of operation. They interface with clerics and faith-based organizations of other traditions, often working as liaisons for the commander or synchronizing humanitarian missions. Chaplains have a long history of providing leadership in peace making and peace building operations. In recent years, many chaplains met with local imams in Afghanistan and Iraq to engender relationship building and to help prioritize the type of humanitarian assistance best needed for their commander's area of operation.

Likewise, many chaplains in the Federal Bureau of Prisons (BOP) and the Veterans Administration (VA) also have much to offer in the area of religious advisement. Whether from the Army, Navy, Air Force, BOP, or VA, these chaplains are commissioned to serve God and country in their own faiths, yet champion the religious freedom for people of all faiths. They represent Judaism, Christianity, Islam, Buddhism, Hinduism, and other religions, and the vast majority of them work well together. Many of them are well versed in world religions, conflict resolution, and spiritual formation.

Granted, not every chaplain is cut out for religious area advisement or religious leader engagement, and chaplains have no business providing advice on how to win wars. This violates their non-combative status. However, many have capabilities to provide advisement on how to prevent wars and shape peace and stability operations around the globe. Most seasoned chaplains know how to work well with clerics from other nations who know the nuances of their own cultures. Likewise, they know how to work with intelligence personnel who understand demographics and can work well with social-media experts who understand media influence. The right team of chaplains could provide courses of action to inevitably influence young, budding terrorists, sitting behind their computer screens, to make the right decision and turn toward a religion that prioritizes love rather than fear. Many seasoned chaplains from Jewish, Christian, and Muslim faiths work well together and understand the dynamics of religious tension in violent conflicts that impact the world today. Whether politicians like it or not, the major violent religious conflicts in the world today cannot be solved with merely secular solutions. These challenges demand the capabilities of skilled religious leaders who understand such conflict.

We will look at other ways to turn the tide of enraged faith in a chapter entitled "Steps to Reconciliation" and in another, "Christianity and Islam."

Summary

Escapist faith twists religion to affirm emotional insecurities. Exploitive faith manipulates theology to exploit others. Enraged faith hijacks religion to justify malicious acts.

If you have become disenchanted with religion, I encourage you to go back and look at the difference between mainstream religious teaching and the religion that was twisted, manipulated, or hijacked by emotionally immature people or infected with a bad dose of fearful ideology. You may be blaming the wrong thing or the wrong people.

Religious institutions attract people who are emotionally wounded, and rightfully so. Decent religious institutions exist to help hurting people. However, wounded people ordinarily need to be healed first before they can treat other wounded people, and hardly ever should an emotionally insecure person be put in any leadership position in a religious institution. It is a recipe for disaster.

Chapter 10

Making Sense of the Journey

Breathe Deep, Seek Peace
James Gurney from *Dinotopia*

S o what do all these continuums, stages, approaches, and volatile mixes have to do with anything? For starters, I have not forgotten the hot question. Are Allah and God the same? Your answer depends partly on your worldview. Which one of these statements best reflects your worldview?

- o My worldview is the only way.
- o My worldview is closest to the truth.
- o My worldview is more enlightened.
- o All worldviews are relative.

How certain are you of your worldview?

- o No certainty, all mystery
- o Some certainty, mostly mystery
- o Mostly certainty, some mystery
- o All certainty, no mystery

If you are a Muslim or Christian and have a belief system that has little room for tolerance of other worldviews, your answer is likely that Allah and God are not the same. You point to differences in what it takes to achieve eternal salvation, beliefs about Jesus, and to alleged textual and historical errors in each other's holy book. And if you are certain in your worldview, you have definitely made up your mind on this question. If you are a Muslim or Christian and have a belief system that is more tolerant of other worldviews, then you probably believe that God and Allah are the same. You note that *Allah* is the Arabic word for God and that Arab-speaking Christians refer to God as "Allah." You point to the many cultural, historical, and theological commonalities. And especially if you are not certain in your own worldview and are more comfortable with mystery, then you are even more likely to see God and Allah as the same.

Yet there are other factors to consider. Where do you see yourself in your spiritual journey?

o   Disorder
o   Duty
o   Doubting
o   Discovery

If you are in a stage of spiritual disorder, the question about whether God and Allah are the same is probably of little concern to you. I would be surprised if you made it this far in this book. I mean no offense by this, other than to suggest this subject probably seems ridiculous to you. If you are in a stage of duty, you probably accept whatever your belief system teaches you, and you have already made up your mind. If you are in the stage of doubting, this discussion has prompted more questions. If you are in the stage of discovery, you may have ceased to dwell on this question. Rather, you simply enjoy the mystery of your faith.

Regardless of your answer to the question about God and Allah, your answer to this question does not necessarily predetermine your tolerance level of those who believe differently than you. There can be a vast difference in the way one tolerates another worldview versus the way a person tolerates others who hold the view. Akin to your spiritual growth is your level of spiritual and emotional maturity and love for others.

How well do you generally:
- o   Love instead of fear?
- o   Trust instead of despair?
- o   Forgive instead of resent?
- o   Choose right instead of wrong?

How well do you generally:
- o   Handle your anger?
- o   Delay your gratification?
- o   Understand your own emotions?
- o   Understand the emotions of others?

Which statement best describes the way you love?
- o   I love myself for self's sake.
- o   I love God for self's sake.
- o   I love God for God's sake.
- o   I love myself for God's sake.

Nor are we immune to volatile religious cocktails. I have had my own failures. Are you currently struggling with any of these issues?

- o   Escapist Faith
- o   Exploitive Faith
- o   Enraged Faith

These issues definitely impact the way a person views God and tolerates others.

Yes, theology shapes a person, but theology does not tell the whole story of a person's faith. Other environmental and genetic factors shape faith as well, and the more we understand these factors, the better we can understand our own faith and the worldviews of others who believe very differently.

This has tremendous impact in a politically correct world that demands neutrality in public and often disparages those who have exclusive views in their religion or way of life. The new religion of tolerance can often be very intolerant. At the same time, religious people should exercise their spiritual and emotional maturity in determining the right times to express religious faith to others and in public settings.

When U.S. military chaplains met with Muslim clerics in Afghanistan and Iraq, there was always the possibility that conversations could explode. However, the chaplains and the imams did not use religious belief as a litmus test to gauge the success or failure of their talks or projects. They worked together to facilitate humanitarian efforts.

To get along with the other, we have to see beyond the dogma on both sides. Even to get along with ourselves, we have to see beyond our own dogma and see what makes us who we are.

Think back over your life. Look at your education, work, physical and mental abilities and limitations, blessings and challenges, and failures and successes. Examine your unique personality temperament, your family and cultural dynamics, and the quantity and quality of love you received as a child. All of these factors have shaped your worldview.

If you haven't answered already, what are your answers to the following questions?

1. How well do you generally:
    o   Love instead of fear?
    o   Trust instead of despair?
    o   Forgive instead of resent?
    o   Choose right instead of wrong?

2. What kind of faith do you have in your worldview?
    o   No certainty, all mystery
    o   Some certainty, mostly mystery
    o   Mostly certainty, some mystery
    o   All certainty, no mystery

3. How do you approach worldviews different than yours?
    o   My worldview is the only way.
    o   My worldview is closest to the truth.
    o   My worldview is more enlightened.
    o   All worldviews are relative.

4. Which word best describes your current stage of spiritual development?
   o Disorder
   o Duty
   o Doubting
   o Discovery

5. Which statement best describes the way you love?
   o I love myself for self's sake.
   o I love God for self's sake.
   o I love God for God's sake.
   o I love myself for God's sake.

6. Are you currently struggling with any of these issues?
   o Escapist Faith
   o Exploitive Faith
   o Enraged Faith

7. How well do you generally:
   o Handle your anger?
   o Delay your gratification?
   o Understand your own emotions?
   o Understand the emotions of others?

These questions are not posed in any particular order of importance, and I have purposely posed these questions in different orders along the way in this book to show their interrelatedness.

The way we understand others and ourselves is far more complex than a set of beliefs. When statesmen and military leaders make strategic decisions about people from other cultures based on generalized ideas about a belief system and ignore other factors, they miss opportunities for shaping peace and stability and often make decisions that lead to disastrous consequences. At the individual level, when we judge others solely on ideology, we risk being offensive to those who hold such beliefs and miss opportunities to build relationships with them. When we assess ourselves solely on a set of beliefs, we miss opportunities for deeper self-development and stymie our potential personal growth.

Of course, we cannot forget about dangerous ideology, but it helps to understand why a person might be attracted to such ideology in the first place. Or if a person is raised in a bad ideology, what might cause him to turn away from it.

Over the years I have watched prisoners of different faiths interacting with one another. Prisoners in the duty stage, regardless of their religion, formed cliques in their own religious communities. They built imaginary walls around their cliques to inoculate themselves from outside influence. They harshly judged others outside their cliques and suspected those in their own religion who differed from them as being heretics. Suppressing their doubts and mistrusting any guidance outside their group, they hindered their own emotional and spiritual growth. When they mixed in a little rage, emotional neediness, or sexual repression, they created a volatile religious concoction.

Those in the discovery stage were far different. I observed the behaviors of prisoners who were emotionally mature and seasoned in their worldviews. They came from Jewish, Christian, Muslim, Native American, Rastafarian, humanist and other worldviews. They were not afraid to talk with one another and were willing to be open about their own respective vulnerabilities in life and faith. They did not form cliques. They often had more in common with people of other worldviews than those stuck in the duty stage within their own worldviews or faith traditions. I often spotted them sitting and laughing together over lunch in the chow hall. These inmates were doing their best to prepare other prisoners to go home to be good fathers and husbands and contributors to their communities.

Summary
If you want to understand the faith or worldview of the other or to understand what makes you tick, then consider all the environmental and heredity factors that include ideology and theology, but also understand:

- Level of spiritual maturity
- Degree of certainty or mystery in a belief system
- Approach to other belief systems

- Stage of spiritual growth
- Capacity to love
- Unresolved emotional issues that impact faith
- Level of emotional maturity

The knowledge of these seven factors, regardless of how they are racked and stacked, helps us to understand our brother's faith without compromising our own. If our agenda for peace is to make others into our likeness, then the pursuit of peace will fail. It is not necessary to have the same worldview to get along, but it is necessary to want to understand. In the next chapter, we will take it to the next level and look at basic steps toward resolving conflict and finding reconciliation.

Chapter 11

Steps to Reconciliation

If anyone is in Christ, the new creation has come:
The old has gone, the new is here!
All this is from God who reconciled us to himself
through Christ and gave us the ministry of reconciliation.
II Corinthians 5:17-18

S ome say the opposite of love is hate. Others say fear. M. Scott Peck, author of *The Road Less Traveled*, said the opposite of love is laziness. He was right. It's easy to love when everything is running smoothly in a relationship, but when relationships get off track, it requires hard work to get them back on track. No wonder so many people give up on their marriages and prefer divorce or cultures give up on each other and prefer war. In his book, *A Different Drum: Community Making and Peace*, Peck outlined four stages to reach a healthy relationship, or what he calls "community."

1. Pseudo Community
2. Chaos
3. Emptiness
4. Community

"Pseudo community" is the initial stage of any new relationship. When we first meet a person, we typically avoid deep and intimate subjects. Initially, the relationship may appear friendly, but it does not mean we are friends. We customarily keep our conversations safe and pleasant. We have not learned to trust one another.

As relationships develop, we become aware of habits, behaviors, and views of others that annoy us. Likewise, they discover things about us they do not like. Thus enters "chaos." When we reach this stage, we have three choices. Stay in chaos. Go back to pseudo community. Or work hard to take the relationship to the next level. Few people want to remain in chaos. The only people I have ever known to enjoy chaos were those with antisocial personality disorders in a maximum-security penitentiary. Unless a relationship is dear to us, we ordinarily just take the relationship back to pseudo community.

If we want a meaningful relationship, we must work hard to develop trust, which means revealing our truer selves, including our vulnerabilities. This is the stage of "emptiness." In this stage we do not necessarily give up our opposing views, but we do give up our need to be right. In this sense we empty ourselves to each other, making the relationship a higher priority than our own unique individualities.

This is risky. When we expose our vulnerabilities and weaknesses in a relationship, we are not certain what the other person will do with this information. For trust to take place in a relationship, all parties must empty themselves at some level to one another. We must use discernment and common sense in this phase. We simply can't trust everyone. Some people exploit the vulnerabilities of others while hiding their own. Peck called such people the "people of the lie." We discussed such personalities in the section on exploitive faith.

However, when we are honest about our vulnerabilities in a healthy way, we develop deeper trust with others and enter into a stage of "community." In this stage people feel safe in the relationship and trust is a common denominator. Obviously, levels of vulnerability and intimacy in community vary according to the type of relationships but the principles are the same in any relationship, whether with friends, dating couples, spouses, believers in a cause, nations, cultures or between parents and children, supervisors and subordinates, or believers and God.

The four stages are fluid. We do not arrive at community and just stay there. On any given day, we might revert back to pseudo community or chaos, then have to empty ourselves again to put our relationship back on track. In a marriage, a couple might drift apart. Two married people who once enjoyed deep intimacy might gradually fade back to a relationship of pseudo community. They talk, but they avoid their serious conflicts. When they discuss their conflicts, they erupt into chaos. Healthy couples empty themselves to one another on a regular basis. They work through their conflicts, accepting responsibility and encouraging one another. Unhealthy marriage relationships stay in a flux of chaos and pseudo community and rarely or never find the relief of emptiness. They continue in a cycle of avoidance and confrontation until the only thing left is divorce. Nations and cultures that once flourished in a common alliance can become bitter enemies.

I have missed cues in inter-faith dialogue, thinking I was getting close to people only to realize I had been in a phase of pseudo community. A few Muslim Iraqis and Afghans told me we would be friends forever, but when I returned to the United States, in spite of traded e-mail addresses, I never heard from them again. Perhaps our exchanges of friendship had been nothing more than their efforts at good Middle Eastern hospitality. There were plenty of times when I tried to reach out to inmates of other faiths, and our relationships were going fine until theological differences were exposed. Then we simply returned to a stage of pseudo community.

Fortunately, I have also broken through ideological barriers with others, but it is hard work. Even when relationships deepen, we have to continually re-visit the emptiness phase, and all parties in the relationships have to do their part.

Forgiveness and Reconciliation

Reconciliation is the centerpiece to any healthy relationship, whether between friends, neighbors, family members, neighborhoods, or nation-states. Genuine reconciliation involves vulnerability, accountability, and responsibility. It also involves seeking and extending forgiveness.

They are not necessarily the same

Sometimes religious people confuse forgiveness and reconciliation. Forgiveness is part of reconciliation, but forgiveness does not always lead to reconciliation. For genuine reconciliation to take place, the offending party has to seek forgiveness and attempt to make amends. If the offending party ignores or refuses responsibility, the offended party must choose between retribution and forgiveness or a combination of the two.

Some religious people say, "If you forgive, then you forget." They get this notion from a poor understanding of a passage from Isaiah, "I, even I, am he who blots out your transgressions, for my own sake, and remembers your sins no more."[47] They think, "If God can forget my sins, I should be able to forget the wrongs others have done to me." They equate forgiveness with forgetfulness and heap guilt upon themselves because they are unable to let go of painful memories.

If we could exorcise painful memories, we would wake up in ecstasy every day, but we would live in naivety and be destined to repeat painful mistakes. Our brains are hardwired to remember painful memories with exactness. It is a survival mechanism to keep us from harm.

The prophet Isaiah was not saying that the omniscient God was forgetful. He was using hyperbole to make a point. From Isaiah's point of view, God is so forgiving; it is as if God has forgotten. When Jesus said of those who crucified him, "Father, forgive them for they know not what they do,"[48] he knew exactly what they were doing, but he chose to forgive. Our memory is what makes forgiveness powerful. In spite of the painful memory, we choose to forgive. Forgiveness is not necessarily an

---

[47] Isaiah 43:25
[48] Luke 23:34, KJV

emotional feeling. It is a choice not to hold the person's offense against them.

How forgiveness works

Suppose someone borrows $500 from me and promises to pay it back in a month. A couple of months roll by and the person has made no effort to repay the loan. In fact, he ignores me and acts like he owes me nothing. Now I find myself in that awkward position of having to ask for what rightfully belongs to me.

If he continues to ignore my demands for him to do the right thing, I have several options. I can pester him or try to take legal action, but at some point I have to decide how much emotional energy I want to spend to get my money back. It's already cost me more than $500 worth of anxiety. At some point, I will probably say to myself, "It's not worth it. Let it go." So basically, I cancel the debt. This is a picture of forgiveness.

How reconciliation works

However, if he comes back a year later and wants to borrow more money, do you think I will loan him the money? While I may have canceled the debt for my own emotional wellbeing, I did not forget. God gives us memories to help us avoid repeating mistakes. I certainly remember, and I won't repeat the mistake again.

For reconciliation to work, both parties must do their part to mend the relationship. I did my part by letting my friend know that his offense bothered me and by cancelling the debt, but we are certainly not reconciled. Reconciliation cannot take place until he does something about his actions. He has to do something about the money he owes me. First of all, he has to apologize for his actions. He needs to show remorse and make some attempt to atone. He may be poor, so $500 may be a lot of money to him. However, if he wants reconciliation, he has to show some sign of contrition and attempt to repay the debt. There are other ways for him to repay the loan. He could offer to wash my car over the course of a few months or mow my lawn for the summer.

Once I know he is genuine about his contrition and his willingness to repay, I may tell him his service is unnecessary. It was never about the money anyway. It was about the principle. I just wanted honesty in our relationship and needed to know he cared. If I am serious about the relationship, I will probably let him mow the lawn anyway, not because I want him to repay me, but because I know responsibility is important to his self-esteem.

But forgiveness seems so hard

Yes, it is difficult, and neither forgiveness nor reconciliation can be rushed. Forgiveness often takes a long time. A betrayal is a loss. Just as we go through various stages of grief when a loved one dies, we go through the same stages when we experience a betrayal or some other form of offense. We ordinarily have to go through shock, denial, anger, and depression to get to the point where we can begin to accept the fact that the damage was done and begin to go on to reconciliation. It is understandable that the offender might want to rush the process, but these feelings cannot be rushed.

If you find it difficult to forgive, try to go easy on yourself and realize there is a difference in cancelling the debt and forgetting a painful memory. Painful memories are the root of post-traumatic stress. We can ordinarily move past the trauma but not the memory of it. Painful memories often arise when we least expect them. A movie scene, a song on the radio, a story, or some faint familiar smell – the seemingly oddest things can resurface a painful memory. The resurrection of this memory does not necessarily mean you carry a grudge. It means your memory still works.

Nor does offering forgiveness negate the consequences of sin or the responsibility of the offender to pay his debt. In some cases the offended person may forgive, but the offender will still be required to pay a debt to society.

Depending on the nature of the offense, there are some offenses such as murder, rape, assault, and adultery (and especially a string of affairs) that require divine intervention to forgive, and I would never tell a person who is bitter from such traumatic experiences that they should forgive the offender. It is naïve to ignore the pain that such traumas leave in a person's memory.

To find healing after such deep wounds, the offended needs the space and time to go through anger and even anger's harsher side – rage, resentment, and perhaps even hate. However, seething emotions can become destructive if they go on too long. Rage and vengeance will suck the life out of a person and can even ruin a person's physical health and damage other relationships. Yet even in such traumatic experiences, forgiveness can become the tool to help the offended person move beyond the pain. Forgiveness in such cases is not used to relieve the offender of the consequences but to help the offended find relief from the suffering.

For lesser offenses or when the offender has certainly paid his dues, there are times when un-forgiveness comes down to just a plain old grudge. We may find it satisfying to bring up the offense to the offender over and over again, but such grudges are destructive in the long run.

Doing our part to be forgiven

How do we get forgiveness from a person who seems to be carrying a grudge? Is it possible the offended person has a right to keep bringing up the subject? Perhaps trust has not been reestablished. How do we reestablish trust?

Sometimes an offended person, trying to do the right thing, offers forgiveness too soon. Wanting to mend the relationship and knowing the offender needs forgiveness, the offended person may ignore his own hurt and extend words of forgiveness when he is still in the shock phase of the offense.

When rash forgiveness is offered to the offender, the offender is often amazed by such perceived grace and mercy and will try all the harder to repent. In some cases though, such easy forgiveness has the opposite effect. The offender, realizing he got off easy one time, is likely to try the offense again. In either case, with an eased conscience, the offender now feels better and can go on his merry way, as if the sin never happened. Yet the offended person is stuck with a painful memory that may permeate with feelings of anger, resentment, sadness, or a need to get even. Funny how the memory of our offenses against others may become foggy over time, but the memory of others' offenses against us remains crystal clear.

No wonder the offended person brings it up again. Unless a person is bitter, normally a person brings up a past offense, not to rub it in the offender's face but to find some new way to find relief from the painful memory. So if you are seeking forgiveness and you think the offended person is still holding a grudge or has truly forgiven but needs help healing a painful memory, then consider the following:

First, you have to give the offended person time to heal, and naturally you have to take responsibility, repent, and do everything within your power to rebuild trust.

Second, try giving an apology in the right love language. Gary Chapman, in his book *The Five Love Languages of Apology,* says there are generally five different ways of expressing love: through words of affirmation, physical touch, quality time, acts of service, and gifts. According to Chapman, each of us tends to favor one of these ways as a primary way to express love, another a secondary, another a tertiary, and so on. He applies these five love languages to forgiveness as well. Normally, we seek forgiveness based on the way would forgive. We may offer words of apology to mend a broken relationship because if we were the offended person, that is what we would want. Yet the offended person may be expecting a gift or some act of contrition to help mend the relationship. Seeking forgiveness is best done in the love language of the offended person. If we do not know a person's primary love language, it is best to seek forgiveness through all five ways, and depending on the severity of the offense, it may be a good idea to express all five ways anyway.

Third, consider offering an unsolicited acknowledgment. If we have moved on past a shameful or embarrassing time, we don't like to dwell on old painful memories, and the last thing we want to do is dredge these memories up to the person we offended. We typically think this would cause the offended person to relive the painful memories and would make the person resentful toward us again. However, the memories are not dead in the offended person's mind. The offended person may be thinking, "It sure is great he or she has moved on… wish I could… I'd like to talk to him about this subject again, but he'll just say I haven't forgiven." So the offended person suppresses his true feelings, thinking, "I don't think he or she cares anymore about how those offenses impacted me."

This is why an unsolicited acknowledgement can be a powerful tool to help both parties. It lets the offended person know the offender is still deeply remorseful. The unsolicited acknowledgement says, "What I did or said to you still bothers me. If I could do anything differently now, I would go back and change the decisions I made and the actions I took that hurt you." Such an unsolicited acknowledgement gives the offended person a new way to frame the memory and a new way to associate the person with the offense.

If you have done everything within your power to confess, repent, atone, offered forgiveness in all five love languages, and attempted unsolicited acknowledgements, but the offended person still will not forgive, then consider one more thing. You may have to repeat these actions during each phase of a person's hurt: during the anger, sadness, and even acceptance phases. Even when a person has long accepted the hurt and moved on, the memory will still surface from time to time and the antidote of an unsolicited acknowledgement may be just what is needed.

However, if you have done all these things and the person will not let it go, you don't need to grovel and continue to live in shame. At some point, you need to accept God's forgiveness, and in spite of the other person's feelings, you must move on – not necessarily from the relationship and certainly not from the consequences but from the situation. It is out of your hands.

Obviously this discussion does not pertain to heinous offenses. If you have committed a heinous offense, it is unrealistic for you to ever expect the person you offended to forgive you, much less to reconcile. It will take a miracle. While the Lord offers grace to all, we are still stuck with the consequences of our sins and cannot escape responsibility. Penance is an often over-looked factor. Just as important as it is for the offended person to have time to go through shock, anger, and sadness to find healing, the offender must have time to go through guilt, shame, remorse, penance, and atonement.

Rash Confessions

If the person you sinned against will find out, and especially if you keep committing the same secret offense; then the offended person has every right to know and should know in order to protect him or herself against the repercussions of irresponsible behavior. Even if the person is not likely to find out, total honesty is almost always the best policy.

However, let's be honest. While I can give examples to my congregation about things I have done wrong, I would never stand up in the pulpit on a Sunday morning and confess my top ten most shameful moments to the congregation. It would be career suicide. While we can explain to our children what we have learned from our mistakes, it would be counter-productive to confess to our children every little seedy thing we have done in the past.

While confession and repentance are necessary, it is not always a good idea for the offender to acknowledge a secret sin to the offended, i.e. gossip about a person or a one-time affair, specifically when the offender has truly repented and will never do it again and the offended does not know about it or will never know about it. Hold on. I am not dismissing the importance of honesty in relationships. Rather, such quick confessions said only to help the offender relieve his or her guilty conscience can be self-serving. The offender in this case must carefully and prayerfully weigh the unsolicited acknowledgement against how much it will help or harm the relationship. Such unsolicited confessions will be painful to the offended, and the offended person is now stuck with a painful image in his or her mind that he or she may never be able to overcome.

If the offended person can adapt and overcome, and the relationship will be stronger in the long run – then yes, such a confession should be made. However, when relationships cannot sustain such brutal honesty, sometimes such confessions are best said only to God and/or to another mature, trusted friend or minister. I cannot begin to tell you how many relationships I have seen ruined because of rash confessions, said at the wrong time or the wrong place. Sins do have their consequences, and sometimes one consequence is being stuck with a memory too painful to share with the person or people you love the most. If you are in this predicament, weigh the importance of brutal honesty with the importance of the relationship. This is an ethical dilemma and requires wise counsel before making such a confession.

Community Responsibility

The process of forgiveness and reconciliation for individuals works the same way for communities. Only the process is more complicated because a community is made up of individuals who process grief differently and some take longer than others to move through it. Look at Germany's general warm relationship with Israel, and compare it to Japan's general chilly relationship with China. While both Germany and Japan have offered reparations and atonement for war crimes in World War II, their approaches have been different, and many Chinese and people from other Asian countries feel Japan's remorse is too little, too late.

Tensions still remain in our country where many whites wonder, "Slavery was over a hundred years ago. Segregation ended two generations ago. Why don't African Americans just get over it?" Statements like these completely ignore the continued consequences of the old systems and the generational grief that has not faded away from the minds and hearts of many African Americans.

Rwanda offers one of the best examples on reconciliation in modern history. In dealing with the mass genocide of 1994, Rwanda is not denying justice, but its people are focusing more on reconciliation than retribution. Today, Hutus and Tutsis are working side by side to maintain a democratic Rwanda.

In the Federal Bureau of Prisons, the majority of my ministry was with African American men. There are a disproportionate number of black males incarcerated in the United States. These factors include poverty, the lingering second and third order effects of slavery and segregation that still impact African American communities, and unfair sentencing guidelines. Blacks caught trafficking cocaine normally receive harsher sentences than whites trafficking methamphetamines.

For years I resonated with other white voices that said, "I don't know why I need to apologize for what others did in the past. I didn't have anything to do with it." Sure, I had a few kinfolk who were bigots, but I fought and continue to fight hard against racism, and I also have people in my family's history that fought against it as well.

Then it dawned on me a few years ago, "No, I did not have anything to do with slavery, segregation, or racism, but my children still benefit from second and third order effects of an old system of injustice while many children of African Americans still suffer from those injustices." One day in prison church, I brought an unsolicited acknowledgement to my congregation. I told my African American parishioners, "I want you to know I apologize on behalf of my kinfolk, and I am sorry for all the injustices against African Americans. I acknowledge this history. If you know of areas where I can personally or professionally do anything differently to make up for these old injustices, please let me know. I want to do my part to make things right."

Many black men came to me after the service and told me there was no need for me to apologize. Instead, they affirmed me for the work I was doing and reminded me of their own responsibility in African American communities.

Yet the attitude in the congregation changed. By owning up to the issue, it took away the racial prejudices some African American men may have had toward me because I was white. The acknowledgement also had a positive impact on inmates beyond the prison church. In most prisons throughout the country, prisoners sit in racially segregated areas in the

146

chow hall. Prison officials do not segregate them. The prisoners segregate themselves. Soon after my talk with the congregation, some of my black, white, and Latino parishioners joined forces and devised a plan to desegregate the chow hall.

In the United States, we place a high value on individual freedom compared with cultures of the Middle East and other parts of the world where community responsibility is prized. If we truly want to be peacemakers in the world, we need to take a serious look at community responsibility. It goes both ways. Minority communities share responsibility as well as majority communities.

If you are a Christian and want to heal old wounds between Christians and Muslims, consider saying something like this as you develop a relationship with a Muslim person, "I realize that Muslims may judge my faith because of the sins of other Christians, perhaps from the days of the Crusades or perhaps because of current mistakes and failures in the Middle East. I am sad for those who have been victimized by such injustices, and I grieve the way others have twisted my faith tradition. Please know this is not the picture of authentic Christianity. Nevertheless, many Christians have caused this perception. If there is anything I can say or do to show you the true face of Christianity, please let me know."

Likewise, Muslims in this country need to consider the naivety most Americans have about Muslim faith. Most of what Americans know about Islam comes from a jaded media. No wonder so many Americans think a terrorist is lurking behind every mosque. If you are Muslim, becoming defensive does not help your cause. If you want to help your cause, may I suggest that you deal with the person's perception before you defend your reality? You may consider approaching a Christian person in this way, "I realize that Christians may judge my faith because of the sins of the 9-11 terrorists and other radicalized Islamist terrorists. I grieve for all the victims of radicalized terrorism, and I grieve the way others have twisted my faith tradition. If there is anything I can say or do to show you the true face of Islam, please let me know."

Statements like these do not imply individual culpability. It would be wrong to confess something we did not do, but statements like these do admit community responsibility and help to destroy ill-conceived perceptions. I do not recall ever facing an inter-faith challenge that had anything to do with reality. All of the challenges I faced were over perceptions, born out of naivety or lies.

If we want to change the way other people think, we have to start with their perception, not ours. If we want to tear down the wall, we have to start by removing a brick from our side of the wall. When people on the other side see us removing a brick or two, perhaps they will begin to remove the bricks from their side. As the wall is lowered, we may be able to look across the divide and see each other as we really are.

Divine Grace

Were it not for my faith that God sacrificed himself for all of humanity, and were it not for what I believe to be a personal intimate relationship with this all powerful God, I would have never had it within me to forgive myself of my own stupid mistakes, let alone forgive others. We can have the greatest head knowledge in the world about forgiveness and reconciliation, but let's face it. Broken hearts can often only be healed by a touch from the Divine. I have never heard anyone sing a song called "Amazing Justice." We prefer to sing "Amazing Grace." Love is a far more powerful force than fear. As we move into the next section of the book and look at some of the controversial issues that divide people today, we will need that Divine touch.

Part 3

The Hard Work of Peace Making

Blessed are the peacemakers;
for they will be called the children of God.
Matthew 5:9, KJV

In this section of the book, we look at some of the controversial issues of our day regarding differences between church and state, Democrats and Republicans, African Americans and European Americans, Catholics and Protestants, Christians and Muslims, and people of other faith traditions. While we may approach these issues with our minds already fixed on what we believe, we also have the opportunity to do our part in healing old wounds and contributing to the hard work of peace making.

Chapter 12

Church and State

Congress shall make no law
respecting an establishment of religion,
or prohibiting the free exercise thereof...
First Amendment, U.S. Constitution

T he American public may not know it, but if you want to find one
of the finest models for religious freedom in the universe, then
visit a prison, particularly a Federal prison. Drop into the prison on any
evening and you are likely to see a Christian worship service in the
Sanctuary, a Jewish service in the library, a Muslim service in an
education room, a Buddhist service in the prayer room, and a Native
American Service outside in the chapel yard. You are likely to hear Jews
welcoming the Shabbat, Christians singing hymns, Muslims saying the
maghrib prayer (evening prayer), Buddhists saying their *oms*, and Native
Americans beating a drum to the rhythm of a heartbeat.

Before and after services, inmates of different faiths often greet one
another in the hallway and wish each other well, often taking prayer
requests from inmates of other faiths to mention in their respective
services. Some, out of curiosity or friendship, attend each other's

respective religious services. There is often lively debate in the chapel hall over the distinctions of the various faiths. It's not unusual for an inmate to have a better education on world religions than a student in the finest university. Prisoners do not water-down their beliefs on the off chance someone might be offended by their beliefs. Instead, they express their diversity of faith traditions.

Now there are some basic ground rules in such an environment. Prison chaplains customarily maintain a "neutral" chapel. During a religious service, inmates are free to array the chapel space with all kinds of religious symbols according to their particular faith tradition. However, when services are over, specific religious symbols like a cross, crucifix, Star of David, or Muslim crescent moon are ordinarily removed from the chapel walls or stage and stored away until the next service. By doing so, the chapel remains a neutral space when religious services are not in progress, thereby affording a person of any faith to come into the chapel during neutral times to make personal prayers without the awkwardness of praying in front of religious symbols that may be contrary to his belief. However, there are times when allowances are made. During Ramadan, Christians might give up some of their time in the Chapel so Muslims can have all the time they need during their days of fasting. During Advent and Christmas, Christians may keep a Christmas tree in the chapel, but Muslims are permitted to cover it with a sheet when they are in the chapel for their service. In other words, under the direction of a chaplain, inmates work together to practice their respective religions. There is a practical give and take.

Many evangelicals who don't know what chaplains do often think Christian chaplains are not allowed to share their faith in these environments. Because of the way many evangelicals see church and state separated in public school systems and on courthouse lawns, they assume Christian chaplains in federal prisons or the military offer a watered-down version of the gospel. This is not true. Christian chaplains are free to share their faith. What makes these systems work is that Jewish, Buddhist, Muslim, and other faith tradition chaplains are allowed to share their faiths as well. However, any seasoned chaplain, regardless of faith tradition, uses common sense and knows when other people are not interested in hearing about his or her particular brand of religion. They don't force their faith on others. Good chaplains enthusiastically lead parishioners within their own faith traditions, but at the same time, they eagerly champion the rights of others to practice their religious beliefs, even when others have opposing theologies.

Ask the average American what the First Amendment of the United States Constitution says, and he or she is likely to say, "That's the one about separation of church and state." Yet the phrase "separation of church and state" is not mentioned in the amendment or anywhere else in the entire Constitution. The amendment states, "Congress shall make no law respecting an establishment of religion, or prohibiting the free exercise thereof." The framers of the Constitution and the Bill of Rights, both deists and evangelicals, never envisioned a separation of religion and politics. They often blended religion and politics to advance their causes. The amendment was placed in the Constitution to ensure the institutions of religion and politics would not mix, but it was never intended to keep the ideas of religion and politics apart.

Of course, that was a different era. Many of our American founding fathers came from Anglican backgrounds. The Enlightenment and the Great Awakening movements impacted all of the founding fathers. Evangelicals, inspired more by the Great Awakening, were passionate about a personal relationship with Jesus Christ and orthodox Christian beliefs. Deists, more influenced by the Enlightenment, were not generally inspired by orthodox Christian beliefs. Deists basically reduced the essentials of religion to these beliefs. One, there is a God. Two, God is to be worshiped. Three, living right is the best way to worship God. Four, people must repent from bad behavior. Five, people earn their rewards or just due based on the kind of moral life they live.

In spite of the differences between deists and evangelicals on the person of Jesus Christ, they were united in yet one more deist belief and evangelical fervor: that God controlled the destiny of nations.[49] Both

[49] Winthrop S. Hudson, *Religion in America,* (New York, NY: Charles Scribner's Sons, 1981), 92.

sides freely integrated religious language and practice into politics. Winthrop Hudson called this new, united, American religious zeal the "Religion of the Republic."[50] I call it "Americanized Christianity."

It should be noted that American Indians and enslaved Africans, many of whom had different ideas about God, were excluded from contributing any plan to the new government. Nevertheless, the framers, all European American males from Western Christian culture, set the stage for religious freedom for people of all worldviews and cultures. After struggles to defend and define the Constitution through Civil War and Civil Rights, the United States became more pluralistic than the framers ever imagined. Nevertheless, what these early framers established was perfect for the present.

Now people from all different faiths have the civil liberty to follow their own conscience. Freedom of religion is an American right. With such unfettered freedom and current trends in the waning of religious influence in America, other issues are arising.

On one end of the continuum are religious people, particularly conservative Christians who are grieving the loss of religious influence in America. When people grieve, they often go through all the stages of grief, including anger. Some Christians are reacting in a fortress mentality and so staunchly defend the idea that the United States is a Christian nation that they often ignore or deny the voices of people from differing worldviews and religions. Those from other worldviews and religions want their voices heard and their histories remembered as well.

On the other end of the continuum are those from other worldviews who often ignore or deny the significant influence that religion, particularly Christianity, had in the forming of the United States and the influence religion still has in this country. Likewise, they often react in a fortress mentality, many even wanting freedom from religion, something not guaranteed in the U.S. Constitution.

Unfortunately, many critics of Christianity do not understand Americanized Christianity. This type of faith is most often seen in patriotic church services, where Christians freely mingle songs of faith

---

[50] Ibid., 111-114.

with patriotic songs, say the Pledge of Allegiance, and honor various founding fathers. In more conservative patriotic church services, Christians are likely to celebrate individual liberty, emphasize evangelical founding fathers, and call on the country to repent from immorality. In more liberal patriotic church services, Christians are more likely to celebrate community responsibility, emphasize deist founding fathers, and call on the country to repent from social injustices. Americanized Christianity can often be seen in public events where Gospel songs and prayer are often included in the programs.

As a chaplain, I personally thrive at such patriotic worship services and public events, often leading them, but I can see how patriotism and piety can be compromised in an unhealthy mix. Christian critics of such church and public events rightly point out that the gospel is no more an American idea than it is a Russian or Nigerian idea. You are not likely to find an American flag in these critics' churches. It's not that they are anti-American. They just focus more on separation of church and state, claiming this as a more laudable American value. They want to keep the church pure from a perception of American ethnocentrism and normally advance messages on tolerance and inclusivism.

However, if the gospel is authentic and transformational, it must be relevant with other cultures. Americanized Christianity has its place in the church and the public just like Russianized or Nigerianized Christianity has its place in Russia or Nigeria. If patriotism is expressed in private and public life, why can't it be expressed in church life? Conversely, if Christian faith is expressed in private and church life, why can't it be expressed in public life? There is a way to synchronize patriotism and piety without jeopardizing the integrity of either.

Christian critics of Americanized Christianity also empathize with non-Christians at public events where Gospel songs and prayers are incorporated into such events. But non-Christians respond in several different ways. Some actually join in on the songs and prayers because they may not be that fervent in their own beliefs. Others, more committed to their own faiths, remain awkwardly silent but still support the practices because they respect the majority's wishes around them.

Others would stop such practices because they believe in freedom from religion at public events and don't want to place themselves or their children in circumstances where they feel a religion is being forced upon them, or that somehow their patriotism is judged inferior because they don't jump up and sing a rousing Gospel song or throw in with a prayer. Some don't mind at all but do wish such events included a venue for their beliefs as well.

The debates continue. Should the majority sacrifice its religious expression in public for the sake of a minority? And if Christians can express their authentic faith in public, then why not people from other faiths as well? Shouldn't the minority have a voice as well? With the current decline of Christian preference in the United States and the rise of no religious preference at all, we need to review our history, how we got to where we are, and look for ways to work together.

Church and State in Western Civilization

Jesus was basically apolitical. He said his kingdom was not of this world.[51] He avoided the affairs of Roman politics, saying, "Give to Caesar what is Caesar's, and to God what is God's."[52]

The Apostle Paul believed all governments were ordained of God and considered civil authorities to be ministers of God's justice.[53] He believed government was necessary to protect citizens and to punish those who broke the law.

Jesus was so otherworldly that when he was accused of treason, he completely trusted God and did not defend himself. Paul was more pragmatic. He used the Roman court system to defend himself and apparently took pride in being a Roman citizen,[54] but like Jesus, he did not see himself as a change agent for civil government. Rather, he saw himself as a change agent for the Church.

In the early years of the Roman government, Rome generally extended religious toleration to its citizens and subjects, with one caveat.

[51] John 18:36
[52] Matthew 22:21
[53] Romans 13
[54] Romans 22:25-28

Various emperors demanded that their subjects give offerings to the Roman gods. For pagans of course this presented no challenge, and even if Roman citizens doubted the validity of other gods and especially that of the emperor as a god, they still saw no conflict in making the offerings, particularly after considering the repercussions for refusal.

However, homage to Roman gods was anathema to the monotheistic Jews and Christians. In Paul's day, cooler heads prevailed. Roman administrators understood the convictions of monotheistic believers and made exceptions for Jews. So long as Jews respected Roman authority, Roman authorities allowed them to practice their religion as they wished. However, as more despotic emperors came to power, they demanded all their subjects to pay homage to the gods. Roman persecution of Christians began under Nero, and persecution of Jews began under Caligula. Roman persecution of Christians continued off and on for nearly 300 years until Emperor Galerius issued an edict of toleration in 311. In 313, Emperor Constantine issued an edict to grant freedoms to Christians. His edict also mandated that state confiscated Christian properties be returned to the rightful Christian owners.

By the time of Constantine, Christians outnumbered pagans in the Roman Empire, and Constantine saw Christianity as a way to unite his divided kingdom. However, Christians were divided along theological lines, and he would have to unite them first in order to unite his kingdom. In 325, Constantine summoned a Council of bishops and church leaders to meet in Nicaea to settle the disputes, out of which later came the Nicene Creed. This creed today is still recognized by the Catholic, Orthodox, Oriental Orthodox, and most Protestant churches as the standard for orthodox Christian faith. Nicaea began the emperor's involvement in directing the affairs of the Church.

In 391, Emperor Theodosius declared Christianity the official religion of the Roman Empire, outlawing the old pagan ways. The tables were turned. The Christian majority began to persecute the pagan minority, even persecuting other Christians who did not fully embrace all the tenets of the Nicene Creed.

In the early fifth century, Augustine combined the Christianity of Jesus and the Christianity of Constantine in his famous work, *The City of God*. Augustine believed there were two great kingdoms on earth. The first was the city of God represented by the Church, and the second was the city of man represented by civil authority.

Augustine's view of these two kingdoms had much in common with Jesus and Paul's view, with one exception. Jesus and Paul viewed Roman authority as a bystander to the spiritual world, to be used of God when and if God needed her, much like the Bible says God used Babylon to carry out God's will on ancient Judah. Augustine took it a step further. He did not see Rome as a mere pawn to be used when and if God needed her. As the ancient prophets saw Israel's relationship with God's covenant people, Augustine saw Rome and the Church in a similar light. Just as the "good" kings of Israel and Judah worked in concert with their priests, so Roman rulers worked with Christian leaders.

Augustine's philosophy influenced church and state relationships in Western civilization from Rome to Constantinople and would later impact mosque and state relationships in the Muslim world. As Islam spread throughout Northern Africa and Europe in the seventh and eighth centuries, caliphs saw themselves as protectors of Islam. To this day, most Muslim countries freely integrate Sharia to varying degrees into the laws of government, and most Muslims cannot imagine a civil government without Islamic law.

The Merovingian and Carolingian kings saw themselves as protectors of the Church. Pope Leo III crowned Charlemagne as Emperor in the Basilica in Rome on Christmas day in the year 800. This coronation moved much of Western world power from Constantinople back to Rome and officially empowered the Roman emperor to become the protector of the entire Church. The emperors of the West enjoyed the title of Holy Roman Emperor for over 1,000 years until Francis II abdicated his throne in 1806 during the Napoleonic Wars. Even when the Western and Eastern churches split in 1054, the Byzantine Empire continued an Augustinian model with the Orthodox Church.

Over the millennium, church and state leaders did not always see eye to eye. Popes and emperors, and at lower echelons, bishops and kings often vied for power. During the early years of the Holy Roman Empire, popes held sway, especially during the Crusades. Few events highlight papal supremacy more than King Henry IV kneeling in the snow for three days outside Canossa castle, begging Pope Gregory VII to admit him back into the graces of the Church. The tables turned a few years later when Henry IV deposed Pope Gregory VII.

Few kings exerted more power over the church than King Phillip of France. When Pope Boniface excommunicated King Phillip in 1302, Phillip simply retaliated and placed Boniface in prison. When Boniface died a year later, Phillip appointed his own pope and moved the Holy See from Rome to Avignon, France. When the monastic knights of the Knights Templar opposed Phillip, he crushed them.

Regardless of whether a king or bishop controlled a kingdom, ordinary citizens and serfs could have never comprehended our modern understanding of separation of church and state. In their worldview, like the Muslim view of mosque and state, church and state were inseparable, even when church leaders and government leaders disagreed. The institutions had a symbiotic relationship, with kings protecting the church and bishops blessing the government. It may have been tumultuous at times, but it was a marriage nevertheless.

When Luther, Calvin, and Zwingli swept their reforms through the Church, they challenged centuries of Roman Catholic tradition, but they did not change the Augustinian model. Lutherans and Calvinists formed their own church states. The followers of Zwingli made church decisions through city councils. Catholics and various Protestants fought each other, killing one another on a mass scale, over claims of new church-state jurisdictions.

In contrast, the early Separatists (Mennonites and Anabaptists) saw hypocrisy in church-state relationships and believed church and state were two separate entities. They believed an apolitical approach was more akin to the Jesus way and refrained from politics and serving in the military and civil service. They prohibited their children from being baptized into a state church. Many were persecuted for their beliefs and fled to America to freely worship apart from government interference.

However, many did not find instant freedom in the new world. The Puritans were attempting to create their own church state in New England. Puritans believed they were led by God to create a new Israel in the new world where they would integrate their understanding of God's law in their new civil government. Roger Williams, a Baptist at the time, did not accept their exclusive views of a church state and was persecuted for his beliefs. He left the colony of Massachusetts where the Puritan church state was being formed, and he subsequently established the colony of Rhode Island for Baptists and people of other faiths to practice religious freedom. William Penn, a Quaker, did the same for Quakers and people from other traditions in the colony named after him.

As distance and especially time separated the colonists from an English way of life, English leaders realized they could not force the Anglican Church on Separatists and free-spirited pioneers who often disdained organized religion. If they expected the colonists to remain loyal to England, they knew they would have to offer religious toleration in exchange for loyalty and revenue.

Through and after the American Revolution, deist and evangelical founding fathers agreed they did not want a church state or a state church. Deists, like Thomas Jefferson, James Madison, John Adams, and Benjamin Franklin, were not orthodox Christians. They believed in natural religion. Ethan Allen and Thomas Paine were outright critical of Christianity. Men like them would see to it there would be no church state. Evangelicals, like Patrick Henry, Samuel Adams, John Jay, Benjamin Rush, and John Witherspoon, did not want state interference with the church, and they would see to it there would be no state church.

John Leland, a prominent Virginia Baptist preacher, abolitionist, and friend of both James Madison and Thomas Jefferson, shared his concerns about religious freedom with Madison. Leland pledged to support Madison as a delegate from Virginia to ratify the Constitution if Madison agreed to amend the Constitution to support individual religious freedom. This was Leland's view:

"No national church can in its organization, be the Gospel Church. A National church takes in the whole nation, and no more; whereas, the Gospel Church, takes in no Nation, but those who fear God, and work righteousness in every Nation. The notion of a Christian commonwealth should be exploded forever... If all the souls in government were saints of God, should they be formed into a society by law, that society could not be a Gospel Church, but a creature of the state."[55]

Leland was equally concerned about religion meddling in the affairs of state. He supported Jefferson's opposition of assessing taxes to support Christian missions. After the Constitution was adopted, Leland exclaimed that it would now be possible for the "pagan, Turk, Jew, or Christian" to be eligible for any post in the government.[56] He envisioned a nation where American Indians could practice their native faiths and African descendants could practice their respective homeland religions.

This First Amendment changed over a thousand years of church and state relationships. In the new American republic, the amendment created a healthy way for church and state to coexist. Baptists no longer had to "separate" from government in order to practice their faith. They could participate in government, knowing the government would not attempt to change their faith. Deists, like Jefferson, could administer the government, knowing that some state church would not interfere with government. Spain had her Roman Church, England her Anglican Church, Scotland her Presbyterian Church, and the Ottoman Empire had the Caliphate, but there would be no Church of the United States, and both sides saw to that.

The phrase "separation of church and state" does not exist in the Constitution. In 1802, President Thomas Jefferson wrote a thank-you letter to the Connecticut Danbury Baptist Association where he referred to the First Amendment as a "wall of separation between Church and

---

[55] L.F. Greene. *The Writings of John Leland* (New York, NY: Arno Press, 1969), 107.
[56] Ibid., 191.

State."[57] It was not a legal document. It was a thank-you letter meant to endear Baptists to his cause of religious freedom.

Nearly 150 years later in 1947, Supreme Court Justice Hugo Black borrowed Jefferson's phrase when he declared the "wall of separation between church and state must be kept high and impregnable."[58] In this case, a taxpayer in New Jersey challenged a state law that authorized local school boards to pay transportation costs for children to attend private Catholic schools. The justices ruled in a five-to-four decision in favor of the state law. However, the case is remembered for Justice Black's rhetoric about the First Amendment.

Since then, the phrase "separation of church and state" has been used so many times that many Americans actually believe it is part of the Constitution. Opponents of religious influence in government cite it as their source of authority, and many religious people who fight to maintain a religious presence cite it as their source of authority.

The founding fathers found a common sense way for religion and government to coexist. Even the deist founding fathers would have never considered the notion of outlawing prayer in public school. They ensured that chaplains opened Congressional sessions with prayer. Chaplains still do this. George Washington, claimed by both deists and evangelicals, inaugurated a Chaplain Corps in the First Continental Army. We still have a Chaplain Corps. A relief of Moses and the Ten Commandments is sculpted on the front of the Supreme Court Building. By the way, a relief of Muhammad is also included, something that disturbs many Muslims because they see it as a graven image. The Ten Commandments are engraved on the oak doors that open to the Supreme Courtroom. The Ten Commandments are displayed on the wall behind the justices where they preside over American justice. Benjamin Franklin envisioned a great hall in Philadelphia where deists, evangelicals, and Muslims could interact with lively discourse.[59]

---

[57] Thomas Jefferson, *Writings*, Vol. XVI, 281-262, to the Danbury Baptist Association on January 1, 1802.

[58] *Everson v Board of Education*, 330 U.S. 1 (1947)

[59] H.W. Brands, *The First American: The Life and Times on Benjamin Franklin* (New York, NY: Anchor Books, 200), 149.

Granted, when most of the founding fathers thought about what we now call religious diversity, their idea of diversity was normally limited to Judaism, Catholicism, Anglicanism, Congregationalism, and the growing Baptist, Methodist, Quaker, and Unitarian Protestant traditions. They would be shocked to see the religious diversity we have now. Yet a few deists like Franklin and evangelicals like Leland knew the First Amendment was broad enough to cover people of all faiths.

The Way Ahead

The common ground for people of all worldviews is the acceptance of the United States as a republic for all people. The Pilgrims may have wanted a Christian nation, but the founding fathers ensured no particular church or religion would force its doctrine on its citizenry. Conversely, people from non-Christian worldviews should take a look at the significant impact Christianity and Judeo-Christian values had in the forming of this country and the impact those values still have on this nation.

A few years ago in my home state, the Alabama Supreme Court ordered the removal of a monument of the Ten Commandments from the Alabama Judicial Building rotunda. Those who filed the lawsuit claimed the monument's placement in a public building was a violation of their First Amendment rights; that a particular brand of religion was forced on them in a public setting. When the defendants for the monument pointed to the portrayals of the Ten Commandments in the Supreme Court building as a precedent, the plaintiffs claimed the Supreme Court replicas were reminders of the Ten Commandments' historical contributions to our justice system, not religious contributions. They claimed the Ten Commandments monument displayed in the Alabama state judicial building was placed there solely for religious reasons.

In a public outcry, approximately 4,000 Christians marched on the Alabama state capitol and claimed their First Amendment rights were violated when the monument was removed. They argued the monument in the U.S. Supreme Court Building honored both historical and religious contributions and were angry over the disparity. I wonder how many of the protestors could have actually recited the Ten Commandments. I suspect many of them were more worried about their American religious rights than they were the Ten Commandments. But I also doubt the founding fathers would have been worried over the display in the state building and may have found the whole argument trivial. If we can honor the traditions of Judaism, Confucianism, Christianity, and Islam in the Supreme Court Building, from a historical or religious perspective, why not other public places?

Why should a few people, so mortified by the words on a block of granite, get their way at the expense of the majority? But fair play is fair play. Why not allow people from other traditions to erect their own monuments next to that one? I concede, in some cases this would not be practical as some groups don't have the resources to fund such projects, and in other cases, there simply isn't enough room for everyone to have it his or her way.

But there is also a practical limit to fairness. Sometimes prisoners grumbled to me that other faith groups had it better than their particular faith group in the prison, and that it wasn't fair. So I would ask them, "What do you want me to take away from the other faith groups to make it fair for you?" If they didn't get my message, I showed them the religious services schedule, pointing out one particular group, the Moorish Science Temple of America (MSTA) that met very infrequently. There were just a few MSTA men in the prison and their wants for the group were few. Then I took the complainers to the chapel library and showed them the only two books we had for the MSTA and then told them about the one official visitor that came to see the MSTA once every other year. Then I politely challenged them, "If you want me to be fair, then I need to reduce all the religious groups, including the General Christian Community that I lead, down to what the MSTA inmates have"

Before they countered my argument, next I gave them an unsolicited and unwarranted apology, "If I have done or said anything in my leadership to give you the impression I do not care about you or your faith group, please let me know so I can accept responsibility, ask for forgiveness, and do something about it." In an environment where they were not used to hearing staff members or inmates accept responsibility for anything, they were shocked, and they normally began to back down from their accusations of unfairness.

Then I asked them what they really needed. I usually discovered all their religious needs were basically met. So I followed with another question, "What do you want?" There is a difference in a need and a want. The Federal government is ordinarily required to accommodate basic religious needs but not necessarily all wants. I told them I would take care of their wants if I could.

They often responded by wanting to know how much of the chaplaincy budget was allocated for their specific group. I managed a modest budget to buy liturgical and educational resources, maintain the chapel, and pay for the services of our contract rabbi, priest, and imam. They were normally shocked when I told them I didn't have an exact apportionment for the different groups. I said the Christian group was the largest group on the compound, but proportionately, I spent the least on the Christian inmates since the Federal government already paid me to be their pastor, and I could find plenty of Christian volunteers in and around Montgomery, Alabama. I used more than half the money to pay for the contractors, and that after spending money on maintaining the chapel, there was relatively little left over to purchase liturgical and educational resources. However, since the Christian, Jewish, and Muslim groups had support from the outside community, I typically spent the remaining money to purchase items for the Rastafarian, Hindu, MSTA, and other such groups that had little or no representation from the outside community.

Once the inmates knew I really did care, their whole notion of needing to be fair went away. They left my office, generally confident that if they were patient enough with the system and with me, they would not only get what they needed but what they wanted as well.

If we are looking for a way to be fair across the board with people of so many different worldviews in this country, there is only one way to do it. We have to strip all groups down to the lowest common denominator and become like old communist Russia. Russia had a system in place that prohibited religious expression in a public format and ensured everyone was equal. We see where that ended.

On the opposite end of the continuum, if we are looking for a model where one dominant worldview runs a nation, then look to Saudi Arabia. If you are not a Muslim, try getting a visa to go to Mecca and see where that gets you. Or if you are fortunate enough to go to Saudi Arabia, try proclaiming a faith in public that is different from Islam and see where you end up.

Do American Christians really want a Christian nation that prohibits others from practicing their different faiths? Or for that matter, do American Muslims, Jews, Hindus, or Humanists just want the United States their way?

Even in chaplaincy, there is no one cookie-cutter model. At the prison camp, we had to build an outdoor chapel for the Native American, Wiccan, and other faith groups that traditionally practice religion outdoors. But if they could worship outside, why not other groups as well? Some of our most memorable Christian services were outdoors.

While many military and most Federal Bureau of Prisons chapels have one chapel to accommodate all faiths, this is not always the case. On some military bases, there is a separate Catholic chapel and Protestant chapel. On U.S. military installations in Middle Eastern countries, bases often have separate Muslim prayer rooms, apart from chapels, to accommodate Muslim personnel working on those bases. Many Muslims in these countries don't have the same ideas about religious toleration as we have in the United States. They would never consider saying their prayers in the same building used for other religions. Such an idea is blasphemous to them, so no sane chaplain would ever try teaching them the benefits of using a so-called neutral chapel.

The point of these anecdotes: There is no way to be fair in all circumstances, but respect and common sense go a long way. Watering down religious expression in the public arena does not resolve our national debate over religion. Why can't people from all faiths and worldviews fully express their opinions in public in keeping with a few common sense guidelines? Yes, this freedom creates edgy conversation and lively discourse, but our founding fathers intended this lively freedom.

When I was around Christian soldiers in Iraq, Afghanistan, Qatar, and Kuwait, they did not get angry when they heard the daily Muslim public calls to prayer. Instead, the Muslim calls to prayer were a reminder for them and me of our corporate and private need to revere God. For soldiers who did not care for religion, the calls to prayer helped them at least to understand the culture of these nations. The Muslim public expressions of faith did not detract from our Christian faith or offend us. It helped us.

At the same time, Iraq and many other nations are not even close to where the United States is on religious freedom. During the war, many Iraqi Christians and most all Iraqi Jews fled the country for fear of losing their lives. Shia and Sunni Muslims were in bitter conflict. We may have edgy debate in the United States over religion, but we do not kill each other over our views. Instead, we offer safe haven for people of all faiths.

Summary

Men with Judeo-Christian values, and under the influence of varying degrees of orthodox Christianity and the Enlightenment, implanted their values into the Constitution of the United States. Christianity had and still has an impact on shaping this nation. Americanized Christianity has its place in the national fabric. Yet this nation also contains people of other faiths and worldviews who want their voices heard and their histories remembered as well. They too are part of the national fabric. There is a way to coexist. The First Amendment is still the answer, and we can learn from prisoners, soldiers, and chaplains that know how to uncompromisingly proclaim their own faiths, yet champion freedom of religion for people of all faiths and worldviews.

People from all over the world come to the United States to find freedom they cannot find in their own countries. They dream about what we as Americans often take for granted. The coexistence of religion and government is not always easy, but this edgy mixture is one of the great hallmarks of our republic. We need to protect this mixture, not water it down. Christians, Muslims, Jews, Humanists, and people of other faiths and worldviews can use the First Amendment to find common ground and use common sense. The United States does not belong exclusively to any particular worldview or religion. As such, the United States is not a Christian nation, an atheist nation, or any other type of religious nation. It is a republic for people of all worldviews and faiths.

Chapter 13

Blue and Red

Let us not seek
the Republican answer or the Democratic answer,
but the right answer.
John F. Kennedy

Americans who have never traveled through the Deep South are surprised to discover there really are churches on nearly every street corner. Many typical, county seat Southern towns were built in the 1800s around a railroad line, cotton gin, and textile mill. As these towns sprang up, churches were built on prominent street corners not far from the courthouse. The prominent street corners normally include a Southern Baptist Church (typically called the First Baptist Church), a United Methodist Church (typically called the First United Methodist Church), a Presbyterian Church, and either an Episcopal or Lutheran Church. These churches saw their heyday in the 1950s and 60s but are aging now and likely waning.

Prior to the Civil War, whites and blacks often worshipped together, albeit in separate parts of the church, but after the war, African American denominations experienced exponential growth. These historical black churches in county-seat towns are often quite literally located on the other side of the railroad tracks where we are likely to find a National Baptist Church, an African American Episcopal (AME) Church, or an AME Zion Church.

After the Azuza Street Revival in the early 1900s,[60] Pentecostal churches, affiliated with the Assembly of God (mostly all white) or Church of God in Christ (mostly all black), sprang up on the outskirts of towns. In some towns we might discover an independent, storefront Pentecostal Church (generally all black) in a depressed business area of town. It was likely started by a small group of members who left their mother churches because they believed the traditional churches were not "sanctified" enough.

Where the white mill workers once lived, we are likely to find another Southern Baptist Church, founded as a mission church by the First Baptist Church to meet the spiritual needs of the white, working poor. In this same area of town, we might spot an Independent Fundamentalist Baptist Church, chartered by members who left the First Baptist Church in the 1960s or 70s because they considered the mother church too liberal. In towns large enough to sustain a Catholic community, we are likely to find a Catholic Church, nestled in a pastoral setting just outside of town, and just a little farther down the road, we are likely to find a windowless Jehovah's Witnesses Kingdom Hall.

In the modern suburban area, we will probably discover a non-denominational Community Church, founded in the 1980s. This church synchronizes Baptist and charismatic styles of worship. The Community Church and the Jehovah's Witnesses Kingdom Hall are likely to be the only houses of worship where blacks and whites collectively meet to worship.

In this part of town, we might also find a Presbyterian Church of America and an Anglican Church, formed by members who respectively left their mother denominations, the Presbyterian Church (USA) and the Episcopal Church because these churches had become too liberal. On the other hand, we might find a Cooperative Baptist Fellowship Church,

---

[60] Birthplace of a major Pentecostal movement in the United States.

formed by members who left the Southern Baptist Convention (SBC) because they considered the SBC too conservative.

If we use our imagination, we can see a blue or red flag over the steeples and roofs of most of these churches. The blue flag, representing the Democratic Party, flies over the black churches of the National Baptist, Church of God in Christ, African American Episcopal, and AME Zion churches. It is likely flying over certain white churches like the Presbyterian (USA), Evangelical Lutheran, Episcopalian, Disciples of Christ, and liberal Methodist churches. Not all members of these churches identify with the blue flag. These congregations likely include a few members who are more conservative than their pastors, especially the pastors educated in liberal seminaries.

The red flag, representing the Republican Party, flies over the Presbyterian Church of America, Assembly of God, Southern Baptist, Missouri Synod Lutheran, conservative Methodist, and independent fundamentalist churches. There are exceptions in the red churches as well. These churches likely have a few blue members who are more liberal than their young pastors who were educated in conservative seminaries.

The color of the flag is harder to discern over the local Catholic Church. It depends on the culture where that church is located and whether or not church members and the priest are more inclined to social ministry issues or moral issues. The color is also difficult to discern over the Community Church. There is no flag over the Kingdom Hall and independent holiness churches. Members of the Jehovah's Witnesses community or the Holiness Church are likely to recoil from the affairs of state.

I have obviously painted broad-brush strokes. If I omitted your particular denominational or non-denominational church or over generalized your church as white or black, blue or red, please accept my apology. I am simply trying to make a point. Generally speaking, Christians in the South and many other areas of the country segregate themselves according to race and politics.

For several years in my hometown church in early November of every election year, someone placed "Christian" voter guides on a table in the church vestibule. For a few years the voter guides were inserted into the worship bulletins. Although our pastor clearly informed us God was not a Republican or Democrat, the guide was obviously slanted toward Republican candidates. The guide showed how candidates voted on issues like abortion, traditional marriage, public prayer, and support for the military.

Not mentioned in the voter's guide were issues like the environment, social justice, helping the poor, defending the oppressed in third-world countries, battling racial injustices, and striving toward peaceful resolutions in armed conflicts. Aren't these issues important for the Christian as well? The Bible speaks more about helping the poor than any other cause in the entire Bible. However, this and other such issues were not even mentioned in the "Christian" voter guide.

Blue Lines and Red Lines

Christians in the South typically have to choose a side. Again, these are wide sweeping generalizations, but generally, this is how the sides line up.

Democrat Church	**Republican Church**
For national health insurance	For individual health insurance
Champion same-sex marriage	Champion traditional marriage
For gun control legislation	For rights to keep and bear arms
Maximize public school support	Maximize private school support
Neutralize prayer in schools	Support public prayer in schools
Maximize social programs	Minimize social programs
Protect illegal immigrants	Deport illegal immigrants
Increase environmental regulation	Decrease environment rules
Minimize military defense budget	Maximize military support
Against social media restrictions	For social media restrictions
Pro-choice on abortion	Pro-life on the abortion issue
Against capital punishment	For capital punishment
Pro-affirmative action	Against affirmative action

There are plenty of exceptions, and the issues change over the years. When I was a boy, most Southern Christians supported the Democratic Party. The Democratic Party once favored rehabilitation programs over get-tough-on-crime laws, but when both parties realized district attorneys could get elected on their 98% conviction rates, whether the convicted were innocent or not, both parties got tough on crime. So I acknowledge that Christians and even the political parties often change sides or switch positions.

However, most of our churches are divided along the left and right. I have heard people say, "I don't see how anyone can be a Democrat and claim to be a Christian." On the other hand, I was sitting one day next to a highly educated Presbyterian minister in the Columbia Theological Seminary dining facility. He knew I was a prison chaplain but did not know anything about my connection to the Army. He automatically considered me a liberal kindred spirit because of my connection to Jesus' emphasis on helping prisoners.[61] In our conversation he wanted me and everyone else at the table to know, "I don't see how anyone can ever consider himself a Christian and favor a pre-emptive strike diplomacy (referring to our military's attack on Iraq)." When he learned I was a chaplain for soldiers as well, he offered an insincere apology and avoided me for the remainder of my time at the seminary, never knowing where I actually stood on the issue. While I understand the remarks from both sides, they reflect a condemning attitude that those on the extreme left and extreme right have of one another. Because of these extremes, many people choose to avoid the church scene altogether, opting for other worldviews or for alternative church subcultures.

Christians have squabbled over issues since the Church began. In the New Testament we find Christians arguing over biblical interpretation, the role of the Holy Spirit, religious rituals, speaking in tongues, dress codes, abstinence of alcohol, end times, politics, sexuality, and women's roles in the church and home. Two thousand years later, we still fight over the same issues.

---

[61] Matthew 25:31-40

The trump card we Christians often play is to claim that "God is on our side," as if we are the enlightened group of Christians and other Christians just don't get it. During the first Great Awakening, Christians used the terminology of "Old Lights" and "New Lights." New Lights considered themselves empowered by a new sense of spiritual freedom and considered the Old Lights a bunch of old fuddy-duddies, too legalistic to experience God's enlightenment. Conversely, the Old Lights considered the New Lights out of touch with reality.

In the 1800s, American Christians divided over state's rights, slavery, and the Civil War. My own denomination was formed in Georgia in 1845 when Baptists in the South split from northern Baptists, partly because of issues related to slavery. It took 150 years, but in 1995 when Southern Baptists met for the annual Convention, the Convention passed a resolution that confessed complicity in the old racial injustice system and sought atonement. In 2012, the Southern Baptist Convention elected its first African American as President of the denomination.

In spite of periods of political turmoil, there were also periods of great unity among the various churches. The Great Awakening brought more unity than it did division. Churches of various denominations exchanged preachers and formed missionary societies to collectively fund missionaries. Quite a number of churches merged and formed new denominations. In the late 19th and early 20th centuries, conservative and liberal churches joined hands to promote literacy, especially through Sunday School programs. Churches worked together to champion child labor reform and declared war on poverty and alcoholism.

Biblical Interpretation and
Individual Freedom versus Community Responsibility

Our current divisions today are rooted in two main controversies. One is over how we interpret the Bible. The other is which is more important: individual freedom or community responsibility?

For about 1,700 years, the Western Church, influenced by Origen, a Second century Church Father, focused on an allegorical method to understand the Bible. Origen was a student of Philo, a First century

Jewish philosopher who merged Greek philosophy into Judaism. Basically, when Philo and later Origen approached a biblical text, they looked for three specific meanings of the text. First, they wanted to understand the literal meaning of the passage. Second, they looked for a practical application, and third, they looked for the hidden meaning of the text. They believed the Bible was filled with hidden revelations, and if one had the spiritual eyes to see such revelation, a person could understand the Bible at a much deeper level. In time, some of these "deeper" revelations became traditions of the Church. When the Protestant Reformation came along, Protestants rejected many traditions of the Catholic Church, but many of the new Protestant churches did not jettison the allegorical approach to understanding the Scripture.

It was not until the Enlightenment and the introduction of scientific methodology that many Protestants began to question many of the traditional interpretations of the biblical stories. Thomas Jefferson is a classic example. He basically cut and pasted various parts of the Bible to form his version, *The Life and Morals of Jesus of Nazareth*, now commonly known as the *Jefferson Bible*. There is some disagreement over why he did this, but most scholars agree this was Jefferson's attempt to sift through what he considered the fables of the Bible to get to the nuggets of Jesus' ethical teaching.

The new emphasis on scientific methodology gave birth to the behavioral sciences, and if scientists could apply scientific methodology to the new fields of anthropology, psychology, and sociology, then why not theology? The Bible was no longer immune from critical analysis. Many theologians began to use various forms of historical and literary criticism to attempt to discover the oral traditions that led to the written biblical accounts. Applying scientific methodology, many discarded literal interpretations of the supernatural stories, some even discounting a core Christian belief, the bodily resurrection of Jesus. Embarrassed by "old superstitious stories," they believed they were stripping away the husk to find the kernel of truth, the lost meaning behind the stories.

The new field of historical criticism made it easier for "enlightened" thinkers to accept the Bible. They could now find other meaningful applications of the supernatural stories without having to take the stories literally. Many of these thinkers had already discarded the doctrine of Jesus' substitutionary atonement. They could not accept the belief that a loving God would condemn his own son to death because God could not stand to look at the sins of humanity; let alone believe that God would condemn a vast majority of the world's population to a literal Hell just because people could not believe or were never told the gospel story. So using their perception of scientific methodology, the new liberal theologians stripped away nearly 2,000 years of traditional understanding of the gospel to apply a newer meaning, or in their way of thinking, the original meaning of the gospel. Walter Rauschenbusch, a leading theologian around the turn of the last century, explains his evolution of thinking.

> The social gospel is the old message of salvation, but enlarged and intensified. The individualistic gospel has taught us to see the sinfulness of every human heart and has inspired us with faith in the willingness and power of God to save every soul that comes to him. But it has not given us an adequate understanding of the sinfulness of the social order and its share in the sins of all individuals within it... The social gospel seeks to bring men under repentance for their collective sins and to create a more sensitive and modern conscience.[62]

Rauschenbusch no longer believed in substitutionary atonement theology. Instead, he saw Christ's selfless sacrifice as a call for society to repent and atone and address social injustices. He became known as a leading figure in the Social Gospel movement in the early 20th century.

In time, the critical method of interpreting the Bible and the Social Gospel merged into a collective stream of thought. Many of the new liberals in mainline Protestant churches no longer prioritized personal relationships with Christ and salvation. Some outright rejected this theology. Rather, they saw the gospel as a means to cure the social ills of

---

[62] Bruce Shelly, *Church History in Plain Language* (Nashville, TN: Thomas Nelson, 2008), 414.

their day and promote a better society. Many prominent universities and seminaries, once founded on orthodox Christian beliefs, became proponents for this new "enlightened" version of Christianity.

Naturally, many Christians from evangelical and charismatic traditions, especially from the Bible Belt, reacted with a fortress mentality. Few events highlight the debate more than the 1925 "Monkey Trial." John T. Scopes, a high school teacher in Dayton, Tennessee, was brought to trial for violating a new state law that prohibited public school teachers from teaching evolution. The trial became a media circus when the famous defense attorney Clarence Darrow, representing Scopes, was pitted against the state's major witness, Christian populist William Jennings Bryan, also a former Secretary of State and three-time U.S. presidential candidate. The liberal press, and later the movie *Inherit the Wind*, made the populist hero (known for both his progressive social agenda and evangelical fervor) look like a fool for believing the supernatural stories of the Bible. Yet even Bryan did not accept the 24-hour, six-day creation story as literal. Even the Scofield Reference Bible, still a favorite Bible commentary for dispensationalists, left room for interpretations beyond a literal 24-hour day interpretation.

But the trial became the last straw for many conservative Christians and stoked the flames of the fundamentalist movement. The growing dispensational theology (that began with John Darby and popularized in America by John Inglis and Cyrus Scofield in the late 1800s) became a staple in conservative Christianity. Compared to the new liberal theology that allowed one to question faith, dispensational theology provided answers. To counter new liberal interpretations of Scripture, fundamentalist Christians amplified literal interpretations of the Bible. Through their new understanding of the Bible, they explained the allegorical stories in Daniel, Ezekiel, and Revelation. They presented a timeline of the history of Israel, the Church, and events leading up to the return of Christ and his millennial reign into a neatly packaged theology that fit with all the Biblical prophecies. Since they could no longer trust the liberal seminaries, they formed their own Bible colleges. In time, they produced their own version of scientific methodology to prove the

Genesis creation stories took place as literally explained in the texts. They also typically enforced strict disciplines on their young people such as abstinence from alcohol and dancing and forbade them from going to the movies, bowling alleys, clubs, and other places they believed the devil might get a foothold. Most importantly, fundamental churches clung to the gospel and its relevance for individual relationships with Christ and salvation, often eschewing the new liberal emphasis for community responsibility.

As the liberal churches continued to mock fundamentalist theology, fundamentalist churches dug their heels and fought back. In time, the two sides ripped the ministry of the Church into two separate camps: social ministry espoused by liberal churches and soul winning espoused by fundamentalist churches.

Generally speaking, until that time, the two ministries were basically one in the same. For example, the abolitionist movement was a social ministry movement ignited in England by evangelicals like William Wilberforce and John Newton. In the United States, evangelicals like Benjamin Rush and John Quincy Adams continued to carry the abolitionist torch. Church leaders during this time period sent missionaries to share the gospel and feed the poor. They would have never thought about separating the gospel and social ministry. Populist William Jennings Bryan, both a social progressive and fundamentalist evangelical, would have never separated the gospel and social ministry. How could one give a cup of cold water to a person and not care for his soul? Conversely, how could one care about a person's soul and not care about his physical wellbeing?

In a wide speaking generalization, the divisions we have among Christians in the United States today boil down to two questions. Where do you stand on the Bible, and where do you stand on individual freedoms versus community responsibility?

Regarding the Bible, many of the left say the Bible has more to do with humanity's understanding of God than it does with God's direction to humanity, that the Bible contains numerous errors and its stories ought to be interpreted in light of modern scientific revelation. As societies change, some biblical teaching ought to be ignored or re-interpreted to fit modern circumstances. Some propose omitting certain books from the Bible deemed as no longer relevant and adding new books to the Bible in light of recent discoveries of ancient religious texts.

On the far right end of the continuum is the fundamentalist belief that the Bible is without error in regard to any historical or scientific fact and that every single word of the Bible was written by the biblical writers as dictated by God. Less fundamentalist is the belief that the Bible is infallible, that the biblical writers were subject to what they knew about science and history at the time, but that they were inspired by God to write what they did. Regardless of how far to the right, most conservative and evangelical Christians would say the word of God cannot change, does not change, and will not change, and the teachings of the biblical writers are applicable to all times and cultures. Evangelicals range in belief from fundamentalist to moderate, but nearly all would say the Bible is God's guide for humanity.

The way one interprets the Bible does impact the way one looks at the gospel story and its relevance toward individual and community responsibility. If a person does not accept Christ's sacrifice as a substitutionary atonement for individuals, then what did Christ die for? From this perspective, it must have been to redeem society. Hence, the more liberal churches focus their theology and ministries on changing society – community responsibility. Anxious about the left's loose interpretation of scripture and flippant approach to Christ's substitutionary atonement, evangelicals from conservative and fundamentalist camps tend to prioritize saving individual souls over community responsibility.

No other country has given more freedom to exercise religious liberties than the United States. The United States is the culmination of Western influence on Christianity. In the feudal days of Europe and state churches, very few people grew up thinking like modern-day heroes and heroines, "One of these days I am going to get out of here. I've got to be me and follow my dreams." To the contrary, old-world heroes lived, not to be independent, but to fit in and be a part of their existing community. They sacrificed themselves for the community's survival.

However, the Protestant Reformation, particularly the Separatist movement, lit a fire and many people who felt suppressed by their state churches found a new sense of freedom in their new individual religious experiences. Some, like the Puritans in Massachusetts, had hopes of establishing their own new state church, but men like Roger Williams, a Baptist at the time; William Penn, a Quaker; and later John Leland, a Baptist saw to it that the emerging new nation would protect individual religious liberties.

While religious freedom increased in the United States, it was not like the kind of pluralism we see today. In the early 1800s, most any American claiming to be a Christian or part of Christian heritage belonged to one of these churches: Catholic, Episcopal, Congregational, Presbyterian, Baptist, Methodist, Lutheran, Quaker, or Unitarian. Those were the basic choices. It was not uncommon for mainline Protestant churches to work together on common mission projects. Blacks and whites often joined in revival meetings and worshipped in the same houses of worship, albeit normally apart, with whites having the best seats.

However, the dominance of these few churches did not last long. With the influence of men like Richard Allen, John Jamison Moore, and E. C. Morris, African Americans formed their own respective churches: the African American Episcopal, African American Episcopal Zion, and the National Baptist Convention churches. Many whites, like Joseph Smith, Alexander Campbell, William Miller, Charles Russell, and Mary Baker Eddy, concerned that mainline churches no longer represented authentic Christianity, formed their respective churches: the Mormon, Church of Christ, Seventh Day Adventist, Jehovah's Witnesses, and Christian Scientist churches. In time, some of these churches split, like those from the Alexander Campbell movement, forming the more conservative Church of Christ and later the more liberal United Church of Christ and the Disciples of Christ. Churches continued to split over social issues like slavery, poverty, and prohibition and over theological issues like the liberal-conservative controversy and the Pentecostal movement. In the more independent churches, if a person did not like the preacher, got mad at the church over a personal or theological issue, did not like the color of the carpet or playing the piano in church, he or she could just up and leave and form his or her own church. The religious liberty afforded in the United States is a uniquely American phenomenon. Where else can a person go in the world to find such religious diversity?

But to the thinking of emerging liberal theologians and even many evangelicals, too much emphasis on individual freedom led to the neglect of community responsibility.

A number of denominations did try to find a balance. My own denomination, particularly during the 1960s and 1970s, was very diverse and included those who prioritized soul winning, the "conservative agenda" and those who prioritized social ministry, the "liberal agenda." The various Southern Baptist seminaries became known for their respective conservative, liberal, or middle-of-the-road theological agendas. Southern Seminary was known for its more centric agenda and had a school of evangelism in the tradition of Billy Graham and a school of social work and emphasis on pastoral care in the tradition of Wayne Oates. Many Baptist associations employed directors of church and community ministries to champion both evangelism and social ministry. The Southern Baptist Convention established a first-class World Hunger Fund and Baptist Disaster Relief, empowered women in ministry, and sent missionaries with specialized skills to third-world countries to combat poverty, disease, and hunger, all while spreading the gospel.

The Two-Party System in American Christianity

The liberal-moderate-conservative diversity in my denomination drew to a close in the 1980s with the groundswell of a conservative resurgence. The conservatives believed the denomination had moved too far to the left, particularly on biblical interpretation. In time, many moderate and liberal leaders were either run off from the Southern Baptist Convention or left it and formed the Cooperative Baptist Fellowship or went to other denominations. Southern Baptists were not alone in their theological in-house fighting. Several other mainline denominations were hemorrhaging as well over biblical interpretation and priorities about community responsibility versus individual freedom. The conservative resurgence in Christian denominations paralleled political movements in the country.

In 1976, the South helped elect Jimmy Carter, a self-proclaimed born-again Christian Democratic candidate to the White House. At the time, most white Southerners still voted predominantly for Democratic candidates and were eager to support an evangelical, but when Carter came to the White House, he did not focus on the agenda of conservative resurgents. Inspired by his own understanding of Christ's teachings on social concerns, Carter championed community responsibility issues like the environment, world peace, poverty, racial equality, and the rights of women. In the minds of many Southern conservatives, Carter was a huge disappointment. They wanted to see him champion individual freedom and conservative moral issues such as prayer in public school, anti-abortion laws, promoting a strong military, and taking care of the home front before helping developing nations. With a run-away inflation economy, many conservative Christians found no issue with switching sides. The Moral Majority was born and joined forces with the Republican Party to support Ronald Reagan who at that time did not even claim a born-again Christian faith.[63] However, Reagan championed the Moral Majority's individual liberty and morality causes. For perhaps the first time in American history, many evangelicals were willing to give up a person who shared their most fundamental belief rather than support a president who supported community responsibility over specific individual American rights.

Many Christians in the Deep South, particularly white conservative evangelical Christians, jettisoned the Democratic Party because the party went too far to the left for them, particularly on the abortion issue and

---

[63] See http://www.reagan.utexas.edu/archives/speeches/1984/100784a.htm, "Debate Between the President and Former Vice President Walter F. Mondale in Louisville, Kentucky, October 7, 1984" for President Reagan's response to the question, "Would you describe your religious beliefs, noting particularly whether you consider yourself a born-again Christian...?"

later on the Lesbian, Gay, Bisexual, Transgender (LGBT) issues. They see the Republican Party as the best political party to represent their Christian values, particularly the values that pertain to moral issues, family values, and individual freedoms. However, most African American churches, while often far more conservative than white churches on abortion issues, LGBT issues, and the Bible, remain loyal to the Democratic Party. This is largely due to the party's identity with Civil Rights, Jack and Bobby Kennedy, Rev. Martin Luther King Jr., and because they see the Democratic Party as the best political party to represent community responsibility, particularly on caring for minority groups and the poor. Latino and Hispanic voters are often divided into two camps. One camp contains refugees who fled from Cuba in the 1950s and their children or grandchildren who favor the Republican Party for its stance on individual rights. They remember what Castro was like. The other camp contains thousands from Mexico and other Central American nations. They favor the Democratic Party for its stance on community responsibility. They know what poverty is like.

Of course, there are plenty of churches that do not fit neatly into these categories on the far left and right, and we will address them in our conclusion of this chapter. However, for the sake of understanding the right and left divide, let us look at the issues.

Churches on the far left generally champion the greater good of the community over the rights of the individual and select their favorite biblical passages or interpretations of the passages to support their agendas. They favor a national health insurance in order to safeguard the larger community. They support lesbian, gay, bisexual and transgender (LGBT) rights because they believe that humanity has evolved to a higher level of understanding love. The biblical references against homosexuality are ignored or re-interpreted in light of the Bible's greater theme on love. They are willing to forgo any personal need to own a weapon in order to safeguard the community. They support public schools in order to educate the larger community. Regarding public prayer in schools, their concern is to create a harmonious community where no one is offended. They are not against home-school education, but they are not willing to support it at the expense of taking money from the greater community's education. They want to protect illegal immigrants, increase environmental regulation, and minimize defense spending because their sense of community extends beyond the borders of the United States. They also want to protect the environment because their understanding of community extends beyond the human realm to include animals, plants, earth, and sky. Regarding communications restrictions, they are concerned about protecting individual free speech, but their main objective is to have an open and free web for the entire global community. They are against capital punishment because the community should not stoop to the level of the individual. Regarding the abortion issue, this issue is not just about the rights of one woman. It is about the emancipation of women in general. They support affirmative action because it enables minority groups to have greater power in the greater community. They support increasing government programs because they generally trust the Federal government more than individuals, corporations, and religious organizations to take care of the country, and they are willing to increase their individual taxes in order to help the greater good.

Churches on the far right generally support the rights of the individual above the community and pick their favorite biblical passages or interpretations of them to support their agenda. They are against national health insurance because it forces an individual to purchase insurance and takes away the individual's right to personalize his own health-care plan. They point to biblical passages that clearly state that homosexual acts are wrong. The Bible says it. That settles it. Individuals should be able to keep weapons in their homes to protect their personal safety and their family's safety. Conservatives support public schools, but they believe individuals should have the right to express their religious beliefs in a public setting and government should support a parent's choice to educate their children in their own homes. Conservatives are not against helping illegal immigrants in crises, but they generally want to deport them if they compete for American jobs. Conservatives want a clean environment too but not at the expense of hassling individuals and companies with overburdened regulations and expenditures. They want a strong military in order to protect the individual freedoms of Americans. They want to increase communications restrictions to protect their individual families from pornography and child predators on the Internet, and they also want the government to have easy access to find predators and terrorists on the net to protect the security of the nation. They favor capital punishment because murder is the ultimate crime against the individual. They are against abortion because they want to protect the individual rights of unborn children. They are against affirmative action because they see it as a discriminating program that often ignores the most qualified individuals. They want to sharply reduce government programming because they believe individuals, states, corporations, and religious organizations can do a far better job of taking care of people than the Federal government.

Political debates over biblical interpretation have simmered down because several denominations have already splintered over this issue and have settled comfortably into their own views; however, political debates remain hot over individual-versus-community responsibility. The good news is most of the issues do not necessarily fall into someone's category of absolute right or wrong. Most people who care about community responsibility still care about individual rights, and those who care deeply about individual rights don't normally forgo community responsibility. They just prioritize them differently. Yet there are two issues that belong in the right-or-wrong category, and few are able to find a neutral position.

The No-Compromise Issues

No other issues arouse more heated emotion than the abortion and Lesbian, Gay, Bisexual, Transgender (LGBT) issues. This is because there really is no solid middle ground to take. On these two issues, we are bound to stay divided, but we can do so with greater respect.

Christian supporters of LGBT rights and same-sex marriage are not lobbying for unrestrained sexuality. They support boundaries that respect and protect families and children, albeit their definition of family is broader. They are simply asking, "Why shouldn't LGBT people have the same rights as heterosexuals?"

Christians on the left do not necessarily disclaim various verses in the Bible about homosexuality, but they correctly point to far more passages in the Bible about heterosexual sins than homosexual sins. Taking a more liberal approach to biblical understanding, they either ignore specific passages condemning homosexuality as outdated for modern times or interpret those texts in light of the Bible's larger theme on love. Many cite the love between David and Jonathan as an example of gay love in the Bible. They also point to examples in nature of homosexual behavior. They advocate LGBT rights in the same way Christians from earlier generations promoted freedom for slaves and equality for African Americans and women, and they often see those who disagree with them as unenlightened or homophobic. They want society to see LGBT lifestyles as normal. They want to be treated equitably by church and state. Many are seeking justice and affirmative action to right the wrongs of the past and are pleased to see the government celebrating an LGBT month that honors their intimate relationships and the contributions of notable citizens with LGBT orientation. They are rejoicing in a new era of acceptance and see themselves as progressive and enlightened. Even many straight people now take pride in having gay friends and view any ardent adherent to traditional marriage as ancient and old school.

When sexual preference is placed on a continuum, some people by nature or environment have straight preferences and others by nature or environment have gay or lesbian preferences. Away from the ends of the continuum and toward the middle, some heterosexual people occasionally have homosexual desires, and some homosexual people occasionally have heterosexual desires. Right in the middle of the continuum are those with a bi-sexual preference. By far the majority of people lean toward heterosexual orientation, but sexual orientation cannot be easily changed, particularly if a person is far to one side of the continuum. It would be just as difficult for a totally gay man to change his sexual preference as it would be for a totally straight man to change his. Even many conservative pastoral counselors do not necessarily attempt to change sexual preferences of their gay clients. Rather, they attempt to redirect behavior associated with the preference.

This leads precisely to the point of Christians who advocate for LGBT rights. They are saying, "Just because a custom has been treated as a tradition for hundreds of years doesn't make it right. Slavery was once an accepted practice. We now know how wrong slavery was. Society for too long has disparaged us. The new tradition must include consenting adults of heterosexual, homosexual or bi-sexual preferences. We should have our rightful place along our heterosexual brothers and sisters, whether in marriage, Church or State."

Most Christians on the right do not discriminate against sexual orientation. They realize heredity and environment shape a person's sexual orientation. They understand that people with LGBT thoughts struggle with sexual temptation in the same way straight people struggle with theirs, but they seek to defend sexual intimacy within the boundaries of marriage between a man and a woman as culture's norm.

When they approach the biblical passages on homosexuality, they interpret the passages literally and accept the teachings with universal and timeless application. To ignore such passages would be ignoring the word of God. They view the claim that David and Jonathan were gay lovers as a non-scholarly interpretation of the biblical text.

Christians on the right point to homosexual behavior in nature as an exception to nature's norm, not the norm. The first commandment of the Bible is "Be fruitful and multiply."[64] If homosexuality were the norm, our species would die out within a few generations. Only heterosexual behavior is pro-creative. Taboos exist in all cultures to ensure a culture's survival. Christians on the right wonder where the breaking of such taboos will end. And while many Christians empathize with the LGBT community, they feel awkward at government sponsored or sanctioned LGBT celebrations and ceremonies. For them, sexuality is something celebrated behind closed doors, not something to be flaunted in public. Even if public heterosexual celebration events were to become the new rage, they would not want to attend such events. However, many feel

---

[64] Genesis 1:28

they have to attend for fear of not being seen as politically correct and then risk losing status at work or opportunities for promotion. They now feel they are being discriminated against.

Most Christians on the right define marriage as exclusively between one man and one woman. They say to LGTB people, "We respect your sexual orientation; however, we do not advocate normalizing sexual behavior outside the realm of traditional marriage, whether homosexual or heterosexual. Just because a movement is popular doesn't make it progressive or enlightened or superior to traditional marriage. We are procreative people, supporting nature's way and the institution of the family as ordained in the Bible."

Abortion is equally as tough an issue. Christians on the left do not see abortion as a normal means of birth control, and it is not their mindset to kill babies as their critics claim. They acknowledge abortion as a difficult decision and recognize the emotional pain and suffering a woman is likely to experience before, during, and after the abortion. They promote other means of birth control and view abortion as a last resort, but they staunchly defend a woman's right to choose abortion when she has been raped, exploited, or when continuing the pregnancy would impede her from reaching her goals in life. They believe she has the right to govern her own body, including her choice to terminate or continue her pregnancy.

Christians on the right are often criticized as being insensitive to the rights of women on this issue. This is hardly ever the case and is used as a smokescreen to cover the real issue. Many Christians on the right champion women's rights, but they are also concerned about innocent, defenseless children. The argument boils down to this critical question. Is the life growing within the womb a mere fetus or a human being? Christians on the right recognize this life as a human being with a soul, deserving of human rights and dignity. They also point to nature. In some circumstances the mother in some species may kill her sick or deformed offspring. In dire circumstances she may kill weaker offspring to ensure her strongest offspring will survive. However, no other species except humans wields abortion as a wholesale means to control the number of its species. In this sense abortion is not natural. Christians on the right are sympathetic to a woman's plight, but given the tough dilemma of choosing between a woman's right to control her own body and the life of an innocent child, they default to protecting the life most innocent and vulnerable. It should be noted that even pro-life Christians argue about when abortion may be acceptable as in cases of rape, incest, or when a woman's life is at stake.

Some Christians have been cruel on both sides, and each side has used the other's cruelty to cover up the real issues. The LGBT issue and the abortion issue are at a deadlock. However, we can extend better understanding and join forces on other issues that contribute to solving common social challenges. On the abortion issue, what are we doing to address economic and social issues that lead to unwanted pregnancies? What are we doing to liberate women? What kind of role models do we provide for families? What are we doing to address poverty? How do we help young people when they are tempted in inappropriate relationships? What are we doing to fight pornography? If other animal species have their exceptions, what might be ours? What do we do about pregnancies involving rape and incest, or when we know that the unborn child will be born severely deformed? Do we have too many laws? Granted, the Republic must have laws to protect children, but when a woman or family is faced with an ethical dilemma regarding an exception to the norm, what gives the Republic the right to interfere? Who should be involved in these decisions? Certainly the pregnant mother, but what about a loving father, other family members, and the doctor sworn to the Hippocratic Oath?

On sexual issues in general, the Church has historically made a bigger fuss over sexual sins than the crueler sins of greed, vengeance, and exploitation. At various times in history, the Church mixed platonic philosophy and guilt to make people feel guilty for enjoying sex even in the context of marriage. No wonder so many people have left the Church. Thankfully, in recent years many churches have championed healthy sexuality by advancing marriage retreats and helping sexually frustrated marriages to reawaken passion.[65] Perhaps churches on the right and left can find common ground in helping those wounded by sexual exploitation, pornography, repressed sexuality, or sexual assaults. Young people who maintain their virginity and celibacy in a sexually expressive Western society are to be applauded because the temptations are fierce. Whether they have homosexual, bisexual, or heterosexual thoughts, how can the church best support and affirm them in their commitments to the Lord?

These two hot issues boil down to these two questions: Is the life within a womb a fetus or a child? Is sexual expression outside the realm of marriage between a man and woman right or wrong? There is no middle ground for these answers. However, we can find common ground on many of the societal issues that lead to these challenges, and we can do a better job trying to understand the other side.

The Other Issues and Reconciliation

As we mentioned earlier, other issues can be boiled down to a difference of opinion on how to solve a common issue. The right and left are both concerned about poverty. They just have different ideas on the best means to help people get out of poverty. Both are concerned about the effects of crime. One side believes individuals need guns to protect themselves and another side believes if there were fewer guns, there would be less crime. The right and left simply prioritize community responsibility and individual rights differently.

Sometimes when the state goes too far to the left or right, churches on the left and right occasionally link arms to champion a common cause. When the state of Alabama passed one of the toughest laws on illegal immigration in the country, conservative churches joined with liberal churches to help exploited Mexican workers and families and worked together to attempt to repeal the law. A few years earlier, conservative and liberal churches in Alabama linked arms to campaign against a state lottery in order to combat the social ills associated with

---

[65] For examples, see Catholic Marriage Encounters, Gary Chapman or Mark Unger's Marriage Seminars.

gambling. Currently, churches from both sides are trying to influence Alabama state legislators to pass laws to prevent payday lenders from exploiting the poor with exorbitant, ungodly interest rates.

The churches on the left and right make a bigger impact in the world when they work as one Church, rather than as a divided Church. Even when we cannot agree on the issues, let us seek first to understand the other side. The Apostle Paul said,

> If anyone is in Christ, the new creation has come: The old has gone, the new is here! All this is from God, who reconciled us to himself through Christ and gave us the ministry of reconciliation: that God was reconciling the world to himself in Christ, not counting people's sins against them. And he has committed to us the message of reconciliation. We are therefore Christ's ambassadors, as though God were making his appeal through us. We implore you on Christ's behalf: Be reconciled to God.[66]

The gospel message is not an either/or message regarding individual freedom and community responsibility. The gospel does not separate evangelism and social ministry. They are connected. The gospel calls individuals to be reconciled to God, to one another, and to be reconciled within a community. There were times in American history and politics when Christians did not so easily separate evangelism and social ministry.

There are many paradoxes in arguments given by both the left and the right. How can a person be so against capital punishment and for the protection of animal rights, yet not stand up for life within the human womb? Or on the other side, how can one so staunchly defend the rights of the unborn child and not care about the plight of poor children from Central America who made it across the Mexico-US border? Does God draw a line between countries to separate people? The Bible is loaded with admonitions to help the poor and the stranger.

Who can do a better job of tackling these issues: big government, local churches, businesses, states, or individuals? Well, it depends. I have worked in the local church and for the Federal government, and I have

---

[66] II Corinthians 5:17-20

experienced occasions where churches and small groups solved community challenges much more efficiently than big government. Likewise, I have experienced challenges where big government was the best or only solution. I have seen waste on both sides as well as creative and efficient productivity on both sides in private public partnerships. During national emergencies and natural catastrophes, I have witnessed government and non-governmental organizations, religious institutions, and private citizens work collectively at their best.

Summary

Many of the debates among Christians in the United States boil down to two questions: Where do you stand on biblical authority, and where do you stand on community responsibility versus individual freedom? Many would say if you believe in more literal interpretations of the Bible and favor individual freedom and the associated conservative moral issues over community responsibility, then you must be a Republican. If you believe in more liberal interpretations of the Bible and favor community responsibility and the associated liberal social issues over individual freedom, then you must be a Democrat.

Perhaps there is a middle road, a stronger road. Many of our left and right differences today over the Bible could be settled if we only tried to understand the original intent of the biblical authors and used common sense in applying their teachings in a modern world. Jesus never intended to separate evangelism and social ministry. I envision churches where Christians can freely debate political issues without condemning one another; where neither the blue or red flag is hoisted but where the gospel transforms the national divide.

If you are a Christian, remember the words of the Apostle Paul, "There is neither Jew nor Greek, slave nor free, male nor female, for you are all one in Christ Jesus."[67] Is there not room here for "Democrat and Republican" as well? What actions can you take to remain

---

[67] Galatians 3:28

uncompromising in your own faith; yet begin to heal the left and right divisiveness in the Church?

If you are an American, remember the Preamble from our Constitution, "We the people." This "We" includes the far right and the far left, and interestingly, the Preamble contains the same hot issues we squabble over today. "In Order to form a more perfect Union," how do we "establish Justice, insure domestic Tranquility, provide for the common defense, promote the general Welfare, and secure the Blessings of Liberty to ourselves and our Posterity?"[68] What actions can you take to remain uncompromising in your own convictions, yet respect those from the far left or right as citizens of our great Republic?

Some on the extreme sides claim those who will not take a stand with them are straddling the fence. However, is it possible it may take more courage to work together than to take a side? This book is basically an invitation for that discussion and a challenge for Christians of all colors and cultures and Americans of all worldviews to at least try to understand respective countering viewpoints on race, religion, politics, and power.

---

[68] The Constitution of the United States of America, "Preamble"

Chapter 14

Black and White

We must learn to live together as brothers
Or perish together as fools.
Martin Luther King Jr.

T his is a chapter I mulled over for years, re-writing and editing more times than I can remember. I was beginning to think there was no longer a need for this chapter as I was sensing that racial conflict was becoming a thing of the past in the United States. After all, I was working in the Deep South with black and white soldiers and black and white minimum-security inmates who were getting along fairly well. Surely if black and white prisoners were getting along, then blacks and whites were getting along in American towns and cities. I was clearly naïve and proved wrong by the racially charged protests in 2012, sparked after George Zimmerman, a young white Hispanic man, shot and killed Trayvon Martin, a black teenager in Florida. One side saw it as a case of self-defense. The other side saw it as a racially motivated murder. Then came the riots in Ferguson, Missouri in 2014 sparked after a white police officer shot and killed Michael Brown, a young, black man. Once again, one side saw it as a case of self-defense. The other side saw it as racially charged brutality. Then came the protests and vandalism in Baltimore, Maryland in 2015. These protests were ignited after Freddie Gray, a young, black man, died while in police custody. The outcry from blacks and the defensiveness of whites clearly show that racial conflict in the United States is still alive in the early 21st century. So I decided to keep this chapter in the book. In this chapter I attempt to weave my own calling of reconciliation in with my failures and successes at attempting to bring blacks and whites together in a prison in Montgomery, Alabama. I close this chapter by offering a few thoughts on racial reconciliation.

If there is one word that describes my passion in life, it is "reconciliation." I have always been drawn to it – mostly for noble reasons but some perhaps not so noble. This passion is connected with my natural personality temperament. Admittedly I'm a touchy-feely guy who likes to see the big picture and wants everybody to get along. Now I am not stupid. I could have never survived a career in the Federal Bureau of Prisons and the U.S. Army if I always catered to this side of my temperament. So I learned to develop my analytical and thinking side to balance my temperament. However, if given my preference, I naturally want to see everybody get along. Reconcilers crave this.

Children with these types of personalities generally need a lot of affirmation. I was born in the late 1950s, and parents of that era in the South, especially fathers, did not typically dote on their children and remind them every day they loved them. Their way of showing love was to provide for their children and to give them strong discipline, but I craved words of affirmation as well. Consequently, I quickly learned to get affirmation from others, especially my grandmothers. Now I never recall my grandmothers telling me, "I love you," but they would often tell me what a good boy I was and tell my parents and other kinfolk, "Carl is my favorite," sometimes even in the presence of my sister and cousins. This did not exactly endear me to them. So I admit it. I have always had a need to be liked.

I was the firstborn. My father was the firstborn of four children. He grew up in a relatively poor home where he was embarrassed by his mother's fits of rage and his father's alcoholism, so he left home when he was 15 years old and moved in with his maternal grandparents. Daddy felt like he had to work hard in his early life to earn a good family name. My mother, the youngest of four children, grew up a few miles down the dirt road from my father's home. Her father died when she was four years old, so she was raised in a strong matriarchal household with a stepfather who came in and out of her mother's life. Hardly any family had considerable money during the Depression, but my mom's family owned a sizeable farm and lived in the big house on the hill. Her family had issues too, but her mother was a respected member of the Daughters of the American Revolution (DAR) and the United Daughters of the Confederacy (UDC). She was considered "high society." Consequently, my mother's family protected its secrets, and Mama learned early how to protect her good family name. Subsequently, I grew up in a home where my parents worked hard to earn and/or keep a good name.

My parents made sure they taught me right from wrong, took me to church, and my mother was quick to point out the faults of my father's family and her own family so I would not repeat extended family mistakes, especially alcohol abuse, promiscuity, trashy talking, and racism. As a child I absorbed everything they taught me, but sometimes I thought my mother was overly critical of others, and I felt empathy for the recipients of her criticism, though I dared not question her. While I did not comprehend the reasons at the time, early in life I yearned for family members to get along.

While my mother may have been critical of her own family members, she taught me to be respectful of different cultures and ethnic groups. My parents' teaching were in contrast to the pejorative views that many whites had of blacks in their day. This further flamed my passion for reconciliation. As a teenager I used to fantasize about becoming a civil rights leader, following in the steps of Martin Luther King Jr.

All of these factors – firstborn son, a need for everybody to get along, a strong sense of right and wrong, a passion for social justice, and an inner calling that began when I was twelve years old – destined me to become a preacher with a passion for reconciliation.

My first full-time ministry job filled this passion. I served as a director of Christian social ministries for a Baptist association, working with 55 churches in a five-county area. We supported ministries that addressed various social concerns such as poverty, homelessness, spouse and child abuse, and prisoner rehabilitation.

When I became a chaplain, I fancied myself as a reconciler. In the Army Reserve, I saw myself as a symbol of God's peace, albeit a very imperfect symbol, among warriors who carried weapons. In the Federal Bureau of Prisons, I saw myself as a symbol of God's freedom, albeit a very imperfect symbol, among prisoners behind bars.

I had plenty of passion, but my leadership skills did not match my passion. With the exception of a six-month stint serving as the pastor of an Army chapel community at Fort Bragg during Desert Shield and Desert Storm days, I had never served as a supervisory chaplain. I had worked as a staff chaplain in a maximum-security penitentiary and a medium-security prison, but I did not chart my own course as a supervisory chaplain until I came to the Federal Prison Camp in Montgomery, Alabama.

The Mess at the Joint

When I arrived in Montgomery, I was stoked. Montgomery is the Cradle of the Confederacy and the Birthplace of the Civil Rights Movement. Jefferson Davis was sworn in as President of the Confederacy at the state capitol. Less than 100 years later and right across the street at Dexter Avenue Baptist Church, Rev. Martin Luther King Jr. led the fight for civil rights. Just a few miles away in the prison camp, I would bring my righteous fight to the prison.

When I first got there, I may have thought I was ready, but I soon found out I did not know how to bring strong-willed prisoners to come together in any form of reconciliation. I still had a need to be a people pleaser.

My predecessor was a charismatic African American Baptist preacher. He had certainly set the stage for religious freedom in the prison and was a tough act for me to follow. It would have been better had I followed his predecessor. His predecessor was a white Methodist minister who went by the book, kept inmates in check, and was known among many staff members and inmates as being more of a cop than a chaplain. He maintained a tight schedule in strict accordance with Bureau of Prisons policy, and if an inmate didn't like it – well, that was just tough. He led the main Protestant service, the only weekly Protestant worship service, in a structured liturgical tradition. He taught inmates how to toe the line and the importance of respecting authority. Much to his credit, he was personally responsible for designing and supervising the construction of the current chapel at the Federal prison camp.

The black Baptist minister who replaced him, my predecessor, was exactly the opposite. According to policy, inmates were not permitted to lead religious services unless a chaplain or community volunteer could not be found to do so. Also according to policy, only one religious worship service was required per week per major faith group. My predecessor greatly relaxed the policy and basically turned inmates loose regarding religious freedom. If there was room for it on the chapel schedule, he scheduled almost anything the inmates wanted. There were several different varieties of Protestant services: one catering to blacks, one to whites, one to a mixed Pentecostal audience, and several to Latinos. There was not a vacant spot anywhere on the chapel schedule for anything new. While it was a full schedule with plenty of unique worship opportunities, there was relatively little offered in the way of practical Christian discipleship or practical life-skills training to prepare the men to return to their communities on the outside.

While I appreciated what he had done for religious freedom, I was overwhelmed by how I would ever be able to bring these men together in a united effort to worship and prepare them for returning to their communities. I would have been much better off had I followed the other chaplain. I knew if I wanted to accomplish what I had in mind, I would have to go through a time of being perceived as the bad guy, and I did not relish that, nor did I know how to do it.

As chaplains, we wear two hats. Under one hat we champion religious freedom and serve people of all faiths, and under another hat we lead religious services and lead those within our own faith tradition.

So I was working at reconciliation on two fronts: one from an inter-faith perspective and another from an ecumenical (Church) perspective. While the government expects chaplains to lead religious freedom, there is a practical limit to it. To use Judaism as an example, there are many different forms of Judaism such as Orthodox, Conservative, Reformed, and Reconstructionist. While Jewish prisoners are allowed and encouraged to practice their own individual faith as they desire, it is not possible to have enough time on a chapel schedule to have services to accommodate every single nuance of Jewish faith. And if you do it for one faith group, well – you have to do it for everybody else – the Muslims, the Rastafarians, the Buddhists, the Christians, and so on. So the services offered to Jewish prisoners were not officially "Orthodox Jewish," "Reformed Jewish," etcetera. They were simply "Jewish."

It is even more complicated in Christian traditions. In a prison and military environment, the chapel schedule includes at least one Catholic service and one Protestant service. An Orthodox service is scheduled when there are enough Orthodox parishioners and an Orthodox priest is available. The reason for the separation and lumping Protestants together is because Catholic and Orthodox churches do not generally offer the Eucharist to Christians outside of their respective traditions. Mainline Protestant churches generally do offer Communion to Christians of all traditions. "Protestant" is generally a catchall group that encompasses liturgical, charismatic, and evangelical traditions that follow the tenets of the Nicene Creed. In addition, the chapel schedule typically includes other Protestant groups that don't fit neatly into mainline Protestantism or "orthodox" Christianity.

So the only Christians in a prison setting that generally don't get to have a service in their specific Christian tradition are those within the general Protestant category. Since there is no way to accommodate all the different Protestant groups, most Federal prison institutions just lump them all together: Episcopalians, Presbyterians, Baptists, Independents,

Non-Denominationals, Pentecostals, and so on, regardless of differences in culture, theology, and styles of worship. A Protestant chaplain is assigned to lead them and just figure it out. Even as a Baptist minister, by policy I was not generally permitted to lead a regular Baptist service. If I did, then what kind: Southern Baptist, American Baptist, Conservative Baptist, National Baptist, Baptist Alliance, Missionary Baptist, or Cooperative Baptist Fellowship? No, the government expected me to be a good "Protestant" chaplain.

But I did not mind. I wanted to figure it out. After all, like many other chaplains, I became a chaplain answering a call to ecumenical ministry and reconciliation. While we Protestant chaplains ascribe to the tenets of our individual Protestant traditions, I have found that most of us thrive on balancing and blending a rich diversity of Protestant traditions. Many of us are also searching for ways to reconcile with Catholic and Orthodox Christians as well.

And that is what I felt called to do in Montgomery – to reconcile. So under the multi-faith hat, I often served as a mediator or leader in helping Jews to get along with other Jews, Muslims to get along with other Muslims, Rastafarians to get along with other Rastafarians, and those in other inmate religious groups to get along with others in their respective groups. I often had to play referee and help these various groups get along with each other. I led inter-faith classes to address our common concerns and interfaith services such as Thanksgiving and Memorial services. Peacekeeping was hard work, peacemaking even tougher, but the payoff was always worth it. As the men learned to get along within their groups and the groups learned to get along with each other, reconciliation spilled over onto the compound and impacted other staff and inmates who witnessed it.

As difficult as that was, the other hat was heavier, trying to bring Christians together to collectively worship and work with one another. I certainly give my predecessor his due. He broke the sterile mold of a Protestant service and empowered religious freedom. However, unfettered freedom with little regard to whom was leading what created cliques and divisiveness in the Christian community on the compound.

There were basically several different informal churches on the compound, a Southern Black Church, a Southern White Church, a Latino Church, a Pentecostal Church, and a Catholic Church.

I naturally took over the main Protestant service my predecessor had led, the Southern Black Church. By policy I had every right to end all the other inmate-led Protestant services like my predecessor's predecessor would have done, but I knew such a move would not have endeared me to the other factions.

So I spent my first year trying to build friendly relationships with the inmate Christian leaders and the volunteers from the outside community, figuring if they just liked me, we would make it all work out. The inmate leaders had powerful, charismatic personalities. It was easy to see why they had a following. I shared my pulpit with a few of these inmates and the community volunteers and explained to them how great it would be if we all worked together, but basically, all I got was lip service in return. In fact, by sharing my pulpit and affirming them, I actually handed them greater power to keep doing what they were doing. The Sunday white service continued to hold its own. Only a few of the white men who attended the service ventured to the main service that I led. Since I was not as skilled as my predecessor in leading a black service and since I was trying to make it a more balanced service anyway, many African American men started to drift away from that service to find more common ground in the weekly Pentecostal service, which offered a more passionate style of worship.

At this point you may be thinking, "What's wrong with that? Everybody should get to worship the way they want. Was your ego not able to handle the rejection?"

Even today on most major military installations, there are generally three different styles of worship services offered to Protestants in order to accommodate different cultures. The typical base chapel on a major military installation offers a "Traditional Protestant Service" with traditional liturgy and hymns to cater to those who want a more traditional service, a "Gospel Service" with lively preaching and Black Gospel singing tailored toward "traditional" African American worship, and a "Chapel Next Service" with contemporary praise music for young adults. So I could have continued the culturally unique Protestant services in the prison.

And if you are thinking my ego couldn't handle the rejection, you are partially right. I have freely admitted part of my passion for reconciliation comes from my own ego needs. But I can honestly say I wrestled with this dilemma and was able to divorce my needs from the needs of my parishioners and what I believed God was calling me to do. As a reconciler it was my job to do everything possible to reconcile these men to God, to their families, to their communities, and even one to another. And the prison environment is different from the military environment. I knew that if Christian prisoners could learn to get along together in a community of faith in a prison, then they could learn how to get along in the families and communities to which they would return. If I was giving them what the government wanted me to give them, then I had succeeded. But if I were giving them what I believed God wanted me to give them, then I was failing.

The cliques had created a mess on the compound. Men from the various cliques fussed over who deserved more time for services and argued over who was right or wrong regarding various nuanced Christian theologies. Their divisiveness contributed to racial segregation on the compound. Prisoners typically sit in segregated areas in the chow hall. There are customarily black, white, and Latino sections. Staff members do not create these segregated areas. Prisoners do so themselves. The divisiveness in the Christian community only contributed to the segregation in the chow hall and on the prison yard. It got so bad that Muslim prisoners actually pointed to the divisiveness of the Christian community as a recruiting tool, "Look at them. They can't even get along with each other. Why would you ever consider Christianity?" The Muslim inmates had a great point.

So I began to prayerfully consider what I needed to do to bring this motley group of Christian prisoners together. First of all, our church needed a name. How can you bring people together to something if you don't even know what to call it? Working with a few inmates I knew I could count on, we decided to name the church, "Peace Community Church," partly in honor of my wife whose maiden name is Peace but mainly because the name defined our mission. We wanted the church to be an authentic community of people who followed Jesus, and we wanted to be known as peacemakers, reconciling people to God, family, one another, and the communities to which they would return.

Telling It Like It Is

Next, I appointed two inmates, both African Americans who were raised in a church culture, Steve Shaw and Larry McNeil, to help lead our music in Peace Community Church.

The musical talent available in a prison rivals Hollywood. I knew some talented inmates were not exactly walking the talk, but knowing they could draw a crowd, I encouraged Steve and Larry to invite talented artists to sing or play in our main Protestant service. Some of these talented men strutted to the rostrum and showboated their musical talents, and we actually began to grow a sizeable, raucous congregation, but the spirituality in the chapel was about as shallow as a saucepan.

One night when I had taken as much flimflam religion as I could stand, I did what a preacher should hardly ever do. I told my parishioners exactly what I thought of them.

On this particular night I had invited one of our volunteers from the community, a Church of Christ minister, to lead our congregation in Communion at the beginning of the service. I had also invited a preacher from the local Church of God in Christ to deliver the sermon that night and for his choir to lead the praise and worship component. Well, I was already mixing two denominational styles of worship and theology that don't ordinarily mix well. Although I have to say, the two ministers were very open to working together.

Only a handful of my parishioners showed up for the Communion service, but as word got out on the compound that women were in the visiting choir, the inmates began to pour in and pack the chapel. The Church of God in Christ is a Pentecostal tradition. So when it was the choir's turn, along with the singing, they danced in unison, and in an environment where women were rarely seen, let alone dancing in the Spirit, the inmates' eyes were glued on the "gyrating women," and I knew it wasn't because the inmates wanted something from the Lord.

I was sitting beside Larry. Right before the guest preacher got up to preach, I stood up and told the congregation what I thought, "I can't believe it. We just had a sacred Communion service and hardly any of you showed up. I don't guess it was good enough for you. But we bring a few women in here, and you can't wait to get in here and gawk. I don't care if you ever come back."

I sat down next to Larry, feeling good to have gotten that off my chest. Larry looked at me with a smile and wide eyes. I thought he was showing approval. I was to later learn it was a forced smile and he was really thinking, "Have you lost your mind?" The guest preacher skillfully encouraged the congregation through this awkward situation to support their chaplain and then transitioned to his sermon.

Larry and Steve were already having a tough time following my direction to bring this motley crowd together. I did not know it at the time, but after my brief statement to the congregation, they were ready to quit on me. However, before throwing in the towel, Steve came to my office and addressed me in a way that few inmates would dare. He called me by my first name and said, "Carl, what's wrong?"

I leveled with him and told him I was failing miserably in bringing our church together into a ministry of reconciliation. He decided then and there to commit to a vision of reconciliation and to see it through to the end of his sentence, even if we were the only two guys left in the Sunday service.

His prediction came close. As a consequence of my "honesty" that Sunday night, only 13 men showed up the following Sunday, and that number included Steve, Larry, and me. Larry had decided to stick it out too. He was soon released from prison, but Steve had another two years left.

With true grit Steve appealed to the white guys, and I appealed to the black guys. Most of the black inmates thought Steve had turned his back on them, and most of the white guys thought I had turned my back on them. I have to give Steve credit. I could go home every night, but Steve was stuck in prison and had to endure a 24-hour struggle every day. He took great risk in a prison environment to join an unpopular chaplain, but he did not give up.

At first, we thought a blended service included equal parts of loud Rap Gospel and twangy Hillbilly Gospel with a smidgeon of Latino Gospel thrown in to appease the minority group of Latinos. Well, the blacks endured the so-called white music, and the whites tolerated the so-called black music. Both blacks and whites, not understanding a single word of Spanish, tolerated the Latino Gospel music.

The Epiphany

It seemed like we were fighting a losing battle. So I was relieved when I had a chance to get away from the battle for a few weeks. My Army Reserve unit was taking part in a mission called *Nuevos Horizontes* (New Horizons) in El Salvador. Our engineer unit worked with El Salvadoran soldiers, military engineers, local government officials, clergy, and educators along with United States Army Special Forces and Joint Forces. The mission was to drill wells, build schools, and repair bridges and roads; offer medical, dental, and veterinarian services; and deliver clothing and school supplies – all to the populace in a rural, jungle-type environment. I had worked with my community church and several people to send clothes and school supplies. I will never forget the opening ceremony for one of the schools. El Salvadoran and U.S. Army soldiers stood at attention around the American and El Salvadoran flags. The local poet laureate read his poem and then the El Salvadoran school children, all dressed in their school uniforms, sung their national anthem.

In my euphoria during this reconciling mission, I had temporarily forgot about the mess in Montgomery, but somewhere during my time in El Salvador, I heard a "still small voice" speak to me. I am not the kind of person that says, "God told me this or God told me that," but this experience came as close as I ever recall to perhaps hearing the literal voice of God. Here is what the voice said, "Carl, you came down here to get away from what I need you to do in that prison. You know what I have called you to do. Now go back and kick some ass."

I knew this voice was not some directive to go back and be mean to my congregation, but it was a voice that confirmed me to stay the course. So while in El Salvador, I prayerfully reworked the prison religious services schedule and planned courses of action.

When I got back I announced to our inmates and the volunteers that beginning in one month, we would only have one main General Christian service per week. We would call it a General Christian service, not a Protestant service, because we were not "protesting." We wanted the service and our church to be accommodating to all orthodox Protestant traditions and to be Catholic friendly. Anyone interested in a leadership position, whether inmate or community volunteer, would have to be gospel focused, committed to orthodox Christianity, and above all, committed to loving God, loving others, and a spirit of reconciliation. The gospel was our message and music would be a major medium.

We would not entirely get rid of other types of Protestant services, but instead of a weekly white service, Pentecostal service, and other flavors, we would have one General Christian worship service per week. In addition, we would have one other weekly Christian worship service that alternated worship styles: Pentecostal one week, Liturgical another, and so on. Any inmate or volunteer helping to lead one of these services had to join me in the mission on reconciliation and be a supporter and participant in the General Christian service as well.

This plan also freed the chapel schedule to offer programs relevant for their emotional and spiritual development. We would concentrate on basic Christian discipleship, parenting skills, marriage skills, coping with anger, dealing with authority issues, servant leadership, resolving conflict, handling grief, dealing with pent-up sexual desires, and the like. I would recruit new community volunteers to lead these courses and also empower inmates I could trust to lead discipleship groups as well.

Some of the volunteers balked. I told them they were welcome to teach one of the new weekly covenant groups or lead a worship service in their tradition once a month. If they didn't like that, they could leave.

Some inmates, urged by disgruntled volunteers, complained to the warden, but I had already briefed the warden. While he did not always agree with my methodologies, he supported me.

At first, I held on to inmates who I thought represented the old cliques. I thought I needed them to influence their followers. Several of these clique leaders were rigid in their dogma, had an unforgiving spirit, and were hard to work with. After a while I realized I had made a mistake by holding on to these guys, so as their time came to leave prison, I did not replace them with other members of their cliques and in some cases just got fed up and fired them. This was difficult for me. I did not want to hurt their feelings. They went running back to their cliques to rally a move against my leadership.

However, it only took a few days for me to get over firing them. I did not know it at the time, but other inmates on the compound had been waiting for this to happen. The only reason they had not been attending church was because they couldn't stand these guys. With the annoyances out of the way, church attendance picked up immediately.

Shortly after Steve left prison, I recruited Chuck Latham, a local African American minister in the community, to become my associate pastor. Chuck was active in both a local Southern Baptist Church and a Holiness Church. Later, he became active in a National Baptist Church and an Anglican Church. Like me, he loved working in a multi-denomination and multi-cultural environment. Chuck was also a retired Air Force officer.

As a military man, he wanted to know the mission. So I told him, "Reconciliation." He joined me to lead our inmates and a small group of community volunteers to intentionally reflect the demographics of the prison population in our prison church. About 40% of our prisoners were African American, approximately 40% European American, and roughly 20% came from Latino cultures with a few guys from other ethnicities and cultures.

I continued to recruit Christian community volunteers to lead covenant groups and empowered the right inmates to do so as well. Chuck also had a gift for helping our Latino brothers. We intentionally included our Latino men in the weekly Christian service, had an additional weekly worship service in Spanish, and attempted to offer the same covenant groups in Spanish that we offered in English. We eventually recruited an associate pastor from the outside community to better represent the Latino needs of the church.

Lisa also increased her volunteerism and became known as the First Lady of Peace Community Church. She and I began to lead marriage classes for prisoners and marriage retreats at the prison for inmates and their spouses (This was a minimum-security prison where inmate spouses were able to visit for extended visiting hours over the retreat period). Whenever I was away on extended military deployments, Lisa and Chuck made sure the church kept on with our vision while I was gone.

We created a group called the Seven Shepherds, basically a kind of deaconate made up of seven selected inmates that rotated on and off. Of the seven, four represented the functions of the church: worship, ministry (evangelism and ministry), education, and fellowship. We also included a Latino to represent our Latino population on the compound, another shepherd to help us with the administration of our programs, and lastly, a shepherd to help us keep reconciliation as a major emphasis in our church. We ordinarily chose a Catholic person as our reconciliation shepherd to ensure we kept our services and programs Catholic friendly.

We also ensured that appointees on the Seven Shepherds reflected the ethnic demographics on the compound, and we tried to keep a balance of shepherds to represent liturgical, charismatic, evangelical, conservative, and liberal traditions.

If we were to err in any way at our attempt at racial balance, we would err toward having more African Americans. I did not want my parishioners to ever get the idea the white chaplain was trying to stack the deck with whites. This was disconcerting to some whites. They argued, "But shouldn't you select the best man for the job, regardless of color?" At some level, I agreed with them, but I reminded them we were not fighting a battle against reality. We were fighting a battle against perception, and until we could change perception, we could not change the reality. In hindsight I believe the men we selected were the best men for the jobs anyway.

The Controversies

From time to time various theological controversies surfaced in our little prison church. These controversies usually started from inmates who held strong beliefs far to the left or right of the Nicene Creed or believed their church tradition was the only way to eternal salvation. However, theological controversies typically did not last long.

Chuck and I quickly discovered that when we challenged these controversies from the pulpit, we just stirred the pot and empowered the naysayers to strike back. We learned to minimize the influence of these controversies by talking one-on-one to gullible inmates and empowering the church inmate leaders to address the issues off-line with the troublemakers.

You, my reader, may be wondering, "Were you actually trying to stop these so-called 'troublemakers' from expressing their own religious beliefs?" The answer is "No." In addition to the weekly Catholic and General Christian worship services, we made chapel space available to a number of different nontraditional Christian groups, and I often served as a referee helping them to get along with one another. Even prisoners who create their own religions are allowed the freedom to practice their faith in prison so long as their practices do not interfere with the safety or security of the institution, but we did not schedule chapel time for every nuanced belief because it was impossible to give space to every single belief system in a limited chapel schedule. Therefore, if these guys did not have their "own" church to go to, some of them ended up in our motley prison church, and quite a few of them gave Chuck and me a few headaches over the years.

Yet theological controversies paled in comparison to controversies over styles of worship, and particularly regarding the differences in the way blacks and whites generally prefer to worship. Blacks typically clap on the upbeat and whites on the downbeat. No one took this seriously, and we often laughed at ourselves, especially when whites were trying to catch the right beat. However, many of my parishioners argued endlessly over the style and length of sermons and songs and the volume of the sound coming from the amplifiers.

Many whites complained to me about how they felt the services were out of control. These issues were not new. Prior to the Civil War, when blacks and whites often joined together for revival services, whites often complained about the unrestrained passion and spontaneity of the services.[69] African Americans had a reason for singing long and passionate choruses. When slaves worked in the fields, they often sang such choruses to help them adapt to and overcome the hard work. They naturally brought their style to the revival services. In those dark days for African Americans, the corporate worship experience gave them the opportunity to celebrate their momentary freedom and the everlasting freedom that would be theirs one day. Why restrict such a celebration to an hour? Such services were the weekly highlights of their hard lives.

A few whites complained to me about "whooping," a style of preaching that uses cadence, rhythm, and shouting, often in synch with accompaniment from a piano. Whooping is used to emotionally connect the congregation with the preacher. With the exception of some Pentecostal and Appalachian mountain cultures, whooping has nearly disappeared from most white Christian cultures. While both black and white styles of whooping include shouting, the styles are very different in cadence, rhythm, and accent.

I am not a whooper. I did not grow up with it, and I would not feel natural doing it, but I do admire preachers who do it well. Still popular in many African American churches, whooping is typically inserted near the end of the sermon to bring the congregation to a state of passionate response or outright euphoria. I consider it both a spiritual gift and an art. Done right, it endears the congregation to the preacher and enriches congregational involvement in worship – similar to singing a hymn together. This is one reason charismatic churches have better success in attracting blacks and whites to worship together. This success in unity is

---

[69] Nathan O. Hatch, *The Democratization of American Christianity* (London: Yale University Press), 155.

often attributed to the work of the Holy Spirit, and I don't doubt that, but the success also has a lot to do with personality temperaments that are attracted to emotional styles of worship. I think most of our white parishioners actually enjoyed good whooping.

However, when poorly done, it can be an embarrassing experience for both the preacher and the congregation, and our white guys did not mind letting me know. Those who grew up with a whooping tradition typically do not like to admit when they hear a bad dose of it. They feel uncomfortable pointing out a bad performance in a ritual that is considered holy. However, when whites heard a bad dose of it, some had a tendency to stereotype African American preachers as uneducated.

I freely shared my pulpit with other ministers: black, white, and Latino. Most of the African American preachers were phenomenal from the pulpit, but every now and then, one of them would lose my congregation with a boring sermon, and to regain the congregation's attention, the visiting preacher would use whooping and the microphone to wake up the congregation. With the volume turned up as loud as it would go on the audio system, the preacher would place his mouth a hair's breadth away from the microphone and scream, "Yeaaa" at the top of his lungs. Those in the congregation who enjoy loud public events would yell back at the top of their lungs, "**Yeaaa,**" creating a cacophony between the preacher and the congregation, "Yeaaa, **Yeaaa**, Yeaaa **Yeaaa**, Yeaaa," and so forth. And if the cacophony was accompanied by an electric guitar and electric key board connected to amplifiers with the volume cranked up as high as it would go, and if the bass from the speakers was booming and vibrating the entire building – all the better. At such moments, a few white guys always snuck out the back door and would later complain to me that their eardrums nearly busted, while the charismatic blacks and whites worked themselves up into worship frenzies and would later tell me, "I don't remember what the message was about, but it sure was good."

Conversely, I often shared my pulpit with white ministers who bored both blacks and whites. My black parishioners would complain to me about the "lack of the Spirit" from such sermons, and when they knew such a preacher was coming back, some of them avoided the church service that day. When I first started preaching, I wrote what I thought were well-written sermons and rarely pulled away from my manuscript when preaching. I quickly learned that if I were to have any success in prison preaching, I had better provide greater spontaneity and passionate preaching.

The Plan

Chuck, Lisa, several other volunteers, the Seven Shepherds, and I prayerfully implemented eight courses of action. We did not come up with the following courses of action as listed below in one fell swoop. I have them listed as they sort of grew with us.

One, we kept with our Seven Shepherd format to ensure the demographics of the prison were represented and integrated liturgical, charismatic, and evangelical traditions.

Two, we did not limit the General Christian worship service to one hour. Instead, we infused it with a philosophy of ending the service with our parishioners wanting more. We found that an hour and 20 minutes was typically just the right amount of time. We saw the worship event as the celebration event of the week and used it to encourage our parishioners to get more from other meetings and covenant groups scheduled throughout the week.

Three, we tried to control the volume on the amplifiers to suit the person in the middle. We were not always successful, but most of the parishioners seemed to appreciate us for trying.

Four, we were honest with preachers who preached too long or bored our parishioners, or we simply did not invite them back. We found that the most successful sermons at the prison church combined some elements of academia but largely centered on great storytelling, passionate energy, and practical application.

Five, we conducted what the Army calls "after action reports." We brought our worship leaders, song leaders, and Seven Shepherds together after each service for a brief meeting to give the service three thumbs up and three thumbs down. Chuck and I made sure our guys knew that we were not immune to their critiques. At first, the guys were slow to catch on. They felt it wasn't right to be critical of a worship service. So Chuck and I had to teach them we were not being accountable to the Lord and the church if we could not afford to be honest with one another. They learned not to hold back, and Chuck and I learned there were quite a few of our own sermons we should have mercy killed. We began to use this kind of honest assessment about every program in the church. Nearly all the leaders caught on, and we began to develop win-win worship services and educational opportunities.

Six, we made sure our inmate leaders in the church were known on the compound for their Christian integrity. In a flimflam prison environment, most prisoners know how to spot a con. The number one excuse I heard for not attending church over the years was, "I don't want to go and worship with a bunch of hypocrites." When our leaders were walking the talk, we debunked the old excuse for not attending church and created an attraction for men who were looking for honesty.

Seven, we focused on music and songs that brought people together. Sure, we always had at least one person who sat stone cold in his chair while the rest of the congregation stood and sang at the tops of their lungs, but such people were not going to be happy anywhere or anyhow, so we basically ignored their complaints. Instead, we found scores of musical pieces, particularly in black and white contemporary genre, that everyone enjoyed. The guys loved many of the old traditional hymns as well. Since many of our parishioners did not grow up in the church, even the old hymns were new to them. I loved it when our singing came to a crescendo and the music accompaniment dropped off, leaving the rhythm of a beating heart, accompanied only by clapping hands and stomping feet and a congregation singing in perfect harmony.

Eight, we were intentional. If we had a string of Sundays where Black Gospel was the dominant form of music or a string of Sundays where Southern Gospel was the dominant genre, we were intentional to steer the ship back toward center. We were intentional in reflecting the demographics of the compound and various denominational flavors. We worked on finding common ground between those who came from liturgical, evangelical, and charismatic traditions. We were intentional in our partnership with the Catholic community, letting our Catholic brothers know they would not hear any anti-Catholic rhetoric from the General Christian pulpit. We often invited the Catholic priest to speak at certain events.

And most of all, I had to be intentional in leadership. When I left for military deployments, I had to do my best to ensure the church would drive on with a ministry of reconciliation in my absence. Nearly every time I spoke from the pulpit, I reminded our congregation of our mission – Reconciliation – to bring people closer to God, to their families, and to their communities, preparing them to be better Christians, fathers, husbands, children, and servant leaders in the communities to which they would return. Like my predecessor before me, I wanted to empower inmates, but anything they wanted to lead had to fall within our greater vision of reconciliation. When I discovered inmates with hidden agendas taking us away from our vision, I removed them from any leadership position in the church. I had to tell people where I wanted them to go and show them how to get there. It was not easy. I had to give myself the grace to fail because we often attempted to blend styles together that did not blend well. However, the freedom I had to lead church in a prison environment gave me the freedom to experiment until we found what worked, and often what worked for a while, did not work anymore, and we had to adapt and overcome again. I had to be willing to change and lead a church that was willing to change.

Those who are unfamiliar with prison environments often think a prison is full of people who have challenges with authority. That assessment is partially true; however, many prisoners crave leadership, and they respect authority once it is earned.

I learned early on to count on many of my African American parishioners for support. It did not matter to them that I was white. What mattered to them was that I was their pastor. This was particularly true among the middle-aged and older black men.

I think there were several reasons for this respect. Historically, black communities have given their pastors enormous respect. In white culture people have always had the opportunity to move up the social ladder in a variety of occupations. This was not so in black communities until recent generations. One of the few occupations available to African Americans for such ladder climbing was that of the pastor. I sense the respect for black pastors is beginning to wane in African American communities, but generally speaking, African Americans still treat their pastors with greater respect than do whites their ministers. Secondly, freedom theology is ingrained in most black churches. It was the place of celebration, the place to celebrate spiritual freedom and the kingdom that would be. For many of my black parishioners, church was not just something they did. It was who they were. So if I preached a bad sermon or we had a string of less-than-passionate services, many of them supported me because it was in their nature to do so.

Lisa too experienced a respect she never expected. In many traditional, conservative white churches, a male pastor's spouse is typically expected to be a gentle, submissive woman expressing her gifts through playing the piano and teaching children in Sunday school. A pastor's wife is actually called the "Pastor's Wife." This is not so in black churches. The pastor's wife is officially known as the "First Lady." When my wife became involved in our ministries at our prison church, the African American men called her their "First Lady" and gave her the kind of respect that soldiers would give a general officer.

This is not to say we did not have strong white support along the way or we never had challenges recruiting African Americans. Many young white men, unfamiliar with church, loved the dynamics of our blended church. They had never heard Southern Gospel, let alone Black Gospel, and they loved it all. I also recall several notable older white men who were deacons or pastors from very conservative evangelical traditions and risked losing status among their prison peers to support our prison church. Unfortunately, I noticed a trend in young un-churched black men who came from gang neighborhoods. Many of them were not easy to bring into church, and as soon as they noticed something they did not like, they quit participating, and it was difficult to bring them back. Yet there were quite a few who broke the mold and faced rejection from their peers to support our motley church.

It took a while to transform the prison church. It happened when I let go of my need to please people at the expense of pleasing God. It happened when I understood the vision of reconciliation for my congregation and led them to it and when we implemented music styles that struck a harmonious chord with all cultures. It also happened when we began to assess our worship experiences with three essential questions. Did the service contain elements of beauty? Did it have integrity? And did it lead to peace?

Over time, we discovered that blending or balance, or whatever you want to call it, was not a matter of having equal portions of black and white music, a smidgeon of Latino music, and playing to the fundamentalists one day and the liberals the next, or doing Low Church one Sunday and High Church the next. In such services factions just tolerated each other to get to the parts they liked. Instead, we discovered our most successful services occurred when we included music everybody liked. Even better, when all the worshippers praised God in song, singing at the top of their lungs – no accompaniment needed, except stomping feet and clapping hands. Services were ordinarily packed for the rest of my career. Oh there were a number of services, including plenty of my own sermons I should have mercy killed, but for the most part, the Sunday service became the highlight of the week for many prisoners. The covenant groups and other discipleship programs became transformative to help prisoners make real changes before going back to their communities in the free world.

Few sights brought me greater joy than watching an old, leathery redneck with slicked-back hair, singing side by side with a young black man, sporting long dreadlocks and a mouth full of gold teeth.

When prisoners were being released from prison, they often asked me, "Chaplain, where can I find a church like this on the outside?" I did not know how to answer them. Since retiring from the prison church, I sometimes miss the beauty, integrity, and harmony I found only in a prison. Lisa and I miss the joyful celebration of the blended cultures and voices. If it worked in prison, it ought to work in the free world.

I think what we attempted will work in most prisons, and I encourage other Christian prison chaplains who may be discouraged in their work. Be who God called you to be. Go kick some ass in a godly way. And for those of you who may be pastors in outside churches, I don't claim what worked for us will work for you in a "regular" church setting. We had an advantage that outside churches do not have. If inmates wanted to go to church, they did not have the option of a hundred churches in town. And I never planned it this way, but it just so happened (perhaps a God-thing), our most influential Christian leaders were typically huge, powerful men with booming voices and charismatic personalities. I often felt physically overwhelmed in their presence, and I can only imagine the influence and the conversations they had with other inmates who may have challenged my authority. They didn't rough anyone up, but they took care of business.

Social Challenges

In my ministry along the way with blacks and whites, I listened to their respective social concerns often about each other, and I use this section to voice their concerns. Whether real or not, these were their perceptions.

"Why don't they just get over it?"

Often I heard well-meaning whites tell me they wished blacks would just get over it. The comments usually went something like this, "I don't get it. I didn't have anything to do with slavery or past racial injustices. And I get tired of being blamed for something I didn't do. Why can't they quit living in the past, take responsibility for themselves, and just get over it?"

I realize other European Americans may not agree with me on what I discovered, but permit me to share what dawned on me. True enough, I did not have anything to do with racial injustices. In fact, I grew up with parents who were raised in a segregated South who taught me to believe differently. As a young person I fancied myself as a modern day civil rights leader, proclaiming racial justice in a nearly all-white high school and was criticized by some of my white acquaintances for taking such a stand. So why should I owe any anything to African Americans?

Nevertheless, I have to admit this. While most of my kinfolk never kowtowed to racial stereotypes, I know some who did. No, I didn't have anything to do with any current inequities, real or perceived, between black and white communities, but I do believe my children are benefactors of the second and third order effects of those old segregated systems, and generally black children are not. And lastly, grief is not something that can be rushed. There is such a thing as cultural and generational grief, and it takes time for a people to collectively get over old wounds.

So I cannot rush a cultural and generational grief anymore than I can rush a person through grief who just lost a spouse, parent, or child. As an American, I take pride in our individual rights, but as a Christian I am also reminded of community responsibility. No, I didn't have anything to do with racial injustices, but I acknowledge these things happened, and if there is anything I can do to help make things right, I want to be involved in that change.

I have made such acknowledgements from the pulpit from time to time, and when appropriate, have made them in one-on-one conversations with African Americans because inevitably in black and white friendships and acquaintances, the subject of racism eventually comes up. And when I did so, I have noticed if there were any prejudices or walls built on their side, I saw the bricks begin to come down.

I have learned as a Christian and as a pastor, if you want to help someone who has been hurt, and particularly if that person blames something or someone else for his or her predicament (whether the blame is appropriate or not), then you have to acknowledge his feelings before he will ever trust you to help. Later on, you can work out who is responsible for what. For any process of reconciliation to work and particularly regarding race relations, it is important to simply acknowledge what happened and the hurt of the other person.

"I invite him, but he doesn't invite me."

On the other hand, whites often complained to me that their invitations to African Americans to come to their homes and churches or to join them for dinner or at public events have not been reciprocated. And in some cases, they hear this response, "Oh, so you can tell your friends you have a black friend." Particularly in prison and military environments, whites have often told me they felt shunned by African Americans at various game events and in an ironic twist, often felt they had to sit in segregated seats on a bus or in a chow hall.

I do not know if this will help you if you are African American, but most whites are not being friendly to African Americans so they can peer into your personal life and claim they have a token black friend. They truly want the friendship.

I can understand the reluctance. If European Americans were the ones who started the mess with slavery and racism in the Western Hemisphere, then I can see why many African Americans carry a generational grudge. However, just because a modern white person's skin is white does not mean he or she believes or lives that old mess. Reconciliation is not a one-way process. It only works when it is reciprocated, and most often, reconciliation begins with the person or party who feels most offended. It may not be fair, but it is the Jesus way. "If someone strikes you on the right cheek, turn to him the other also. And if someone wants to sue you and take your tunic, let him have your cloak as well. If someone forces you to go one mile, go with him two miles."[70] If you are African American and have white friends and acquaintances, celebrate what you are doing to initiate inclusivity. If not, consider what you can do to invite "them" to your home for dinner, out to a game, or to attend your church.

Holding hands

Now, for the touchy subject – interracial marriage. The marriage of a black and white person is still often considered a taboo in the South and

---

[70] Matthew 5:39-41

other parts of the country. I have heard both blacks and whites express their concern about this.

Now I am not encouraging young black and white singles to rush out and marry one another. In fact, I encourage dating couples to have as their number one priority a common worldview. Naturally, common cultures lend to a common worldview. It would be naive to ignore the challenges that some mixed marriages might face. However, it would also be naive to ignore the beautiful blending of cultures created by many mixed marriages that lead to great marriages.

My point here is not to highlight successes or failures in mixed marriages but to say that some black and white Southerners still have a problem with black-and-white interracial marriage. Until we view mixed marriages between blacks and whites as no different than other mixed marriages, we still have a challenge with racial reconciliation in the South.

A few black women have told me, "I wouldn't mind dating a white man, but I feel that I would be letting my sisters down." In a census report noted in an article from a 2011 *New York Times* article, the report suggests that among minority groups in the United States, African American women are the least likely minority group to marry white men.[71] Likewise, some white parents have told me, "I would never let my daughter date a black man."

Generally speaking, when a Southerner, black or white, sees a white man holding hands with an Asian woman, no one raises an eyebrow. Few people would think disparagingly of a European American or African American dating a person of Asian, Indian, or Central American descent, but heads will still turn to see a black man holding hands with a white woman or a black woman holding hands with a white man. However, if someone were to tell the observer, "You know he's from Rwanda... or Jamaica," the person will inevitably respond, "Oh, I didn't know that. That's different." Color is not even the real issue. The real issue is culture. Healthy married couples in a mixed black and white relationship

---

[71] See the statistical chart from Andrew A. Beveridge, Queens College Sociology Department, Census Bureau, in the article from Haeyoun Park, "Who is Marrying Whom," *New York Times*, January 29, 2011.

are to be applauded for their courage for breaking through the cultural barriers.

Summary

Maybe African Americans should not feel guilty every Sunday when they pass by an all-white church to get to their all-black church. Maybe white people should not feel guilty every time they pass by an all-black church to get to their all-white church. Churches, like people, have different cultures, theologies, and personalities and have their own particular niches, most of which are contributing to the greater Church and the communities around them. Perhaps people should not feel guilty when they walk into a cafeteria and want to sit with people with whom they have more in common. And by all means, young people should not rush out and marry people from different cultures just to break old stereotypes.

However, Rev. King once said, "Sunday morning is the most segregated hour of Christian America." Perhaps one of our greatest challenges is that we continue to think in terms of black and white. I have never seen or met a person whose skin color was pure black or pure white. Some came close, but in reality, we are all just different shades of brown. While we don't need to stop churches that have their own particular niche ministries with blacks or whites, maybe it's time we stop creating new ones that do. Let these old church systems fade away. Now is the time to begin new reconciling churches, intentional in bringing black and white cultures together. What can we do to remove the bricks from the wall and tear down the cultural divide?

If you are a Christian, remember the words of the Apostle Paul, "There is neither Jew nor Greek, slave nor free, male nor female, for you are all one in Christ Jesus."[72] I have a feeling had Paul lived to see our day; he would have included "black and white" in this now famous line. If you belong to an all-white church, what can you and your church do to model accountability, responsibility, and racial reconciliation? If you belong to an all-black church, what can you and your church do to model

---

[72] Galatians 3:28

trust, forgiveness, and racial reconciliation? Even more important, what can both sides do to create mixed black and white churches and make this the new order? If prisoners can make it happen in a prison church, certainly we ought to be able to do it in the free world.

Chapter 15

Catholic and Protestant

I believe in the Holy Spirit, the holy Catholic Church,
the communion of Saints, the forgiveness of sins,
the resurrection of the body, and life everlasting.
From the Apostle's Creed

I t has been said the Church was never more united than on the first day of Pentecost as described in Acts. During the annual Jewish celebration of Shavout, Peter proclaimed the gospel to a crowd of Jewish people who came to the celebration. They came from many different countries, cultures, and languages. As Peter preached they all heard the message in their own native tongue. To this day, Christians continue to celebrate the miracle of "tongues of fire" on the annual Day of Pentecost. Yet the greater miracle that day was the unification of such a diverse group of people. Luke says in Acts that 3,000 were added to the Church on that day. These early believers gave away all their possessions to one common community in order to share a common abundance.

The early Church continued to grow exponentially. In the Church's earliest formation, it hardly looked like the institutionalized version we see today. It was more of a movement than an organization, but by the time of Constantine, the Church had become a highly organized institution with bishops maintaining control in Rome, Antioch, Alexandria, and Constantinople.

With such exponential growth church leaders were bound to disagree over theological and cultural differences. The theological differences were normally settled at various ecumenical councils. If other leaders or churches disagreed with the decisions of the councils, they were often denounced as heretical, or at the very least, viewed as outside of communion with the Church at large. Over time, the Church split over theological and cultural differences into three major churches: the Catholic Church (i.e. Chaldean Catholic and Roman Catholic churches), the Eastern Orthodox Church (i.e. Greek Orthodox and Russian Orthodox churches) and the Oriental Orthodox Church (i.e. Armenian and Coptic churches). The three churches were in agreement on the first three ecumenical councils, but churches from the Oriental Orthodox tradition did not agree with decisions made in the Fourth Council and parted ways from the Catholic and Eastern Orthodox traditions. Catholics and Eastern Orthodox remained in agreement through the next three ecumenical councils. However, as theological and cultural tension grew, the churches officially split in 1054 under the leadership of Pope Leo IX and Patriarch Michael Cerularius in what became known as the Great Schism.

By the 1500s, the Roman Catholic Church could no longer hold its authority over nonconforming movements from Anglicans, Reformers, and Separatists. War broke out in Europe where Catholics and Protestants fought over what church would control various state or city governments. About a hundred years later, many Protestants left Europe, particularly England, to establish their own religious colonies in the New World.

As religious toleration grew in the 13 colonies and later when the new republic institutionalized freedom of religion, the United States would become a beacon of religious freedom. At first, the revival movements during the two Great Awakenings in America divided Christians among Old Lights and New Lights, but the revival movements also had a way of bringing various Protestant churches together in a spirit of ecumenical harmony. Pastors from different denominations often shared pulpits. Denominations partnered to form missionary societies to mutually support mission endeavors at home and abroad.

However, by the early 20th century, countless new denominations, independent churches, and Christian sects were formed in the United States as Christians divided into various camps, depending on their views of slavery, the Civil War, the scientific revolution, end times, the Azusa Street Revival, and other issues and movements. With guarantees of religious freedom, the United States became a seedbed to start whatever new church or religion a person or group wanted to plant.

According to the Pew Research Center, 32% of the world's people belong to some Christian tradition. Of those,

Catholics account for	50.1%
Protestants	36.7%
Orthodox	11.9%
Other traditions	1.3%[73]

In the United States, according to Pew, those who claim Christian faith make up 70.6% of the nation's population.[74] This is down nearly 8% since the last survey results in 2008.[75] The second most popular group with 15.8% of the population and perhaps the fastest growing group include those who claim no religious preference at all.[76] The following list from Pew shows approximate percentages of people in the United States who claim Christian faith, including major Christian subgroups, along with the percentages claimed by people of other faiths and worldviews.

---

[73] Pew Research Center Poling and Analysis, "Global Christianity – A Report on the Size and Distribution of the World's Christian Population," December 19, 2011.
[74] Pew Research Center "Religious Landscape Study," 2015 report.
[75] See the Pew Research Center "Religious Landscape Survey," February 2008.
[76] "Religious Landscape Study, 2015.

Pew Research Center U.S. Religious Landscape Survey[77]

Christian	78.4%	
Protestants	46.6%	
Evangelicals		25.4%
Main Line		14.7%
Historical Black		6.5%
Catholic	20.8%	
Orthodox	0.5%	
Mormon	1.6%	
Jehovah's Witnesses	0.8%	
Other Christians	0.4 %	
Jewish	1.9%	
Buddhist	0.7%	
Muslim	0.9%	
Hindu	0.7%	
Other world religions	0.3%	
Other faiths	1.5%	
Unaffiliated	22.8%	
Atheist		3.1%
Agnostic		4.0%
No preference		15.8%

Over the next few pages, I will attempt the impossible of highlighting the major commonalities and distinctions among various churches. Please keep in mind these are wide-sweeping generalizations with many nuanced exceptions.

Commonalities between
Catholics, Eastern Orthodox, Oriental Orthodox, and Protestants

- Dependence on the Bible as authoritative
- Belief in the tenets of the Nicene Creed
- A common understanding of the redemptive nature of Christ's work and a common commitment to the gospel: Christ has died, Christ has risen, and Christ will come again

---

[77] Pew Research Center "Religious Landscape Study," 2015.

Major Differences

Eastern Orthodox	Catholic
The Pope does not have primacy over the Church.	The Pope is the vicar of Christ on earth.
Does not include the *filoque*[78] in the Nicene Creed	Includes the *filoque* in the Nicene Creed
While an intermediate state between an earthly life and heavenly life is recognized, purification occurs in the earthly life.	Purgatory is an intermediate stage between the earthly life and a heavenly life where one is purified or does penance for venial sins.
Does not accept the belief that Mary was born without original sin	Belief in Immaculate Conception (Mary was born untainted by sin)
Emphasis on theology from a mystery perspective	Emphasis on theology from a rational perspective
Priests may be married	Priests commit to celibacy
Use of icons as symbolic imagery	Use of statues as symbolic imagery

Many of the differences in the Catholic and Orthodox Church are more cultural than theological, and attempts have been made in recent years to reconcile the two churches. The churches are similar in their understanding of Catholic sacraments and Orthodox mysteries. The sacraments/mysteries include: baptism, confirmation/chrismation, the Eucharist, reconciliation/confession, marriage, holy orders (the

---

[78] *Filoque* is a Latin phrase that means "and (from) the son." In the Orthodox and Oriental Orthodox versions of the Nicene Creed, there is this statement, "We believe in one Holy Spirit, the Lord, the giver of Life, who proceeds from the Father, who with the Father and Son is adored and glorified." In a later version of the Creed, adapted by the Western Church, the filoque is added. Thus, "We believe in one Holy Spirit, the Lord, the giver of Life, who proceeds from the Father *and the Son* (italics emphasized to show the distinction), who with the Father and Son is adored and glorified." For the Orthodox Church, the inclusion of the filoque undervalues the role of the Father in the Holy Trinity. For the Catholic Church and other churches that include the phrase, the filoque highlights the role of the Son in the Holy Trinity. This is a very simplistic explanation of a complex theology.

ordination of priests, bishops, etc.), and anointing of the sick/holy unction. While most Protestant churches facilitate such rites as well, many Protestant churches do not consider the rites as sacramental; that is the Church actually imparts God's grace through the rituals. Most Protestant churches view such rituals as symbolic, not sacramental. To clarify the difference, some Protestant churches refer to such rites as "ordinances" rather than "sacraments."

Major Differences

Catholic	Protestant
Papal edicts are infallible.	Only the Bible is infallible.
Two sources of final authority: the Bible and Church tradition	Only one source of final authority: the Bible
Sacraments provide God's grace	Sacraments/ordinances are symbolic of God's grace
Belief in Mary's immaculate conception	Belief that Mary was a very holy person but subject to sin as any other person
Belief in Mary's perpetual virginity	Belief that Jesus was virgin born, but Mary later had married sexual relations with her husband and gave birth to other children
Saints are venerated	Saints are respected
Celibacy of Priests	Ministers are ordinarily married.
Belief in Purgatory	No belief in Purgatory
Greater use of statues and symbolic imagery	Prohibition of or minimal use of statues and symbolic imagery

Again, these are wide sweeping generalizations. It should be noted the Anglican, Episcopal, and Lutheran churches are much closer to the Catholic and Orthodox churches on sacramental theology and liturgy (the way people worship).

Major Differences in Protestant Traditions

Reformed (i.e. Presbyterian, Congregational)	**Separatist** (i.e. Baptist, Independent)
Observance of liturgical calendar	Non-reliance on the liturgical calendar
Covenant theology	Conversion theology
Covenantal baptism	Believer's baptism by immersion
History of church and state working together	History of separating church and state
Hierarchical system of governance	Autonomous church structure

Pentecostal	**Main Line Protestant**
A "second" filling of the Holy Spirit is necessary for living a vibrant Christian life[79]	An acceptance of Christ as Savior and an intimate relationship with Christ equates being filled with the Holy Spirit.
The gift of tongues is a result of a Spirit-filled life.	Minimal emphasis or no belief in speaking in tongues

Growing up where I did in the South, there were not a lot of Eastern Orthodox Christians, let alone Oriental Orthodox Christians, but when I was 17 years old I became friends with a Greek American who introduced me to his family and faith, and I went with him several times to his Greek Orthodox Church in Atlanta. Most Protestants, including me, would have been hard pressed to tell you anything about Eastern or Oriental Orthodox churches, but most Protestants could generally tell you what they thought or believed about the Catholic Church.

---

[79] Some Pentecostals believe that unless a person speaks in tongues, the person is not "saved." For them, the sign of tongues is evidence that the Holy Spirit has filled a person, and apart from this filling, there is no salvation.

Protestants and Catholics maintained a chilly theological distance for nearly five hundred years. It's no wonder. After all, during the Reformation, those that were labeled Protestants either turned their backs on the Roman Catholic Church or were kicked out of the Catholic Church. It takes a long time for old wounds to heal. However, in the 1960s, under the leadership of Pope John XXIII in the Second Vatican Council, the Catholic Church shattered the wall of separation. The Council made sweeping reforms in the Catholic Church, changing the liturgy from Latin to the modern language of the people, officially recognizing Protestants as people of Christian faith, and it attempted to bridge the chasm between the Catholic, Eastern Orthodox, and Oriental Orthodox churches.

It took a while for old prejudices to die in the South. Several decades ago the South was still predominantly Baptist territory. There was a Catholic monastery not far from where I lived. My buddies and I used to wonder what the monks did behind those cloistered walls. We thought Catholics worshiped Mary, saints, idols, and relics. With the popularity of Hal Lindsey's *The Late, Great Planet Earth* and the rise of dispensational theology in evangelical churches, we wondered if Pope Paul VI, Henry Kissinger, or Richard Nixon might possibly be the Anti-Christ.

We have come a long way since then. It's nearly impossible to find a Protestant now who doesn't like Pope Francis. We are in a new era of bridge building between Catholics and Protestants, but there is still a lot of work ahead. A few Catholics yearn for the days before the Second Vatican Council and see Baptists and other Protestants as belonging to cults. Some Protestants refuse to see Catholicism as part of General Christianity and even deny the historicity of Protestant churches coming out of the Catholic Church.

Whether from a Catholic or Protestant tradition, it is important to realize we approach our disagreements with different sources of authority. For most Protestant denominations, there is only one final source of authority. It is the Bible. Protestants respect their denominational traditions and authorities but not with equal weight as the Bible. It is one reason we have so many different denominations today. If a particular group of Protestants disagrees with the traditions of its denomination, the group may splinter from the denomination and form another group, based on the new group's interpretation of the Bible. Catholics do not do this because they have two sources of equal authority, the Bible and Church tradition. Thus, Catholics are normally less likely to question their church tradition than Protestants are to question their various traditions.

Therefore, if you are a Protestant and want to quote scripture and argue with Catholics over purgatory, transubstantiation, Mary's Immaculate Conception, different meanings of the sacraments, celibacy of priests, and the like, may I suggest giving your argument a rest? Many Catholics may agree these theological positions cannot be proven outright by any particular scripture, but that does not matter. Most Catholics will tell you these are the traditions taught by the Church, and the Church has rightly interpreted and applied the Bible. Just as staunchly as you hold on to your view of the Bible, the Catholic may hold on to his or her view of tradition. When it comes to issues like these, we are simply at an impasse regarding who has the right belief. If you are a Catholic, may I suggest that you avoid arguments like these with Protestants, and by all means, do not quote Catholic tradition to a staunch Protestant? You should give your argument a rest as well.

However, if you insist on debating the issues and you come from a Protestant tradition, please consider the Catholic, Orthodox, and Oriental Orthodox churches have been around a whole lot longer than any Protestant church. Protestant denominations are relatively the new kids on the block, and most Protestant churches are offshoots in one way or another from the Catholic Church. Before you dismiss what the Catholic Church or other older churches have to say about the Bible, look at the tradition. Is it possible that the older church's tradition is closer to a proper understanding of a Biblical text than the newer Protestant understanding?

On the other hand, if you come from a Catholic or another non-Protestant tradition, please consider that Protestants have only one final source of authority, the Bible. Normally, the thinking Protestant is trying to find and follow the original intent of the biblical authors. Is it possible that leaders in the Catholic Church long ago altered the original meaning of certain texts to fit the philosophical and theological biases of their day? Perhaps Protestants have discovered or gone back to the real intent of the biblical authors in such passages.

Here is the good news. We follow the same gospel, revere the same Bible (almost – there are a few differences in the Catholic, Orthodox, and Protestant versions of the Bible), and follow the same Lord. Most Protestant traditions adhere to the tenets of the Nicene Creed. We have more in common than we are different.

In fact many Protestants do not like being labeled "Protestant" because they do not see themselves as "protesting" against a "catholic" (universal) or "orthodox" (right way) church.

Many Baptists, even some Catholics, do not know the real meaning of the word, "catholic." Baptists who are unfamiliar with the Nicene Creed and visit a Nicene Creed-confessing church for the first time are typically shocked when reading or reciting the Nicene Creed. They recite the creed along with other Catholics, Orthodox, Anglicans, etcetera, surprised to realize they believe the same thing, until they get to the part that says, "We believe in one holy catholic and apostolic Church." At the word "catholic," the Baptist may cringe, unwilling to make any pledge of allegiance to the Catholic Church, headquartered in Rome. He misses the point. The authors of the Nicene Creed did not intend this creed as a commitment to the authority of a church in Rome. The word "catholic" in this context means universal, and it was placed in the creed to refer to the universal Church, meaning all faithful followers of Christ in the Church at large. In the real context of the word "catholic," a Baptist is just as part of the catholic Church as any Roman Catholic.

Some Protestants refer to themselves as "non-denominational" to set themselves apart from any organizational affiliation, as if to suggest they are not tainted by the long traditions of Catholic or Protestant churches and are closer to the one true Church. Yet even many non-denominational churches have characteristics in common and often affiliate with other likeminded churches in their own sort of "non-denomination" denomination. Some Protestants, craving reconciliation with Catholics, Eastern Orthodox, Oriental Orthodox, and other Protestants, use words like "inter-denominational" or "ecumenical" to describe the universal or catholic church. In the Bible, the followers of Christ are simply called, "Christians" or followers of "the Way."[80]

As a chaplain, I rarely led explicit Baptist services in a prison or military setting. I honored my denomination and brought my Baptist distinctions with me to those services, but I attempted to lead "General Christian" worship services. I avoided labeling them as "Protestant services." I wanted the attendees from all Christian traditions to feel welcome, but even in such services; the Communion table remained the issue.

When I first wrote this chapter, I listed Protestant beefs about Catholics and Catholic complaints about Protestants, citing several historical conflicts. I thought I was setting the record straight for both sides to see. Then I realized I was just whining about my own frustration about the universal Church's split over the Eucharistic/Communion table.

This is not just a split between Catholics and Protestants. It is an old rift between Catholics, Eastern Orthodox, and Oriental Orthodox as well. I am not ignoring the theological differences on how we approach the table or serve from it, but it does appear that many of our churches are generally more concerned with "right belief" than "right relationship." Jesus said, "Blessed are the pure in heart for they shall see God."[81] Whether religious institutions will seat them or not, is it possible the Creator holds a seat at his table for all the pure in heart? So I deleted all the petty complaints Catholics and Protestants have about each other and opted instead for a few recommendations on getting along and offering a hope and prayer until that great day when we can all sit together at a common table. To keep it simple, I will just refer to the Communion rift between Catholics and Protestants.

---

[80] Acts 11:26 and Acts 9:2
[81] Matthew 5:8

We are getting closer. Vatican II made it possible for Catholics to attend Protestant services, and when a Catholic Mass is not readily available, Catholics are even encouraged to attend Protestant services.

However, because of theological differences over the table, the Catholic Church prohibits Catholics from participating in any Protestant Communion and prohibits non-Catholics from participating in the Catholic Eucharist. Protestant denominations and churches vary on the issue. Most have an open Communion service and welcome people from all Christian traditions. Still others have closed Communion, welcoming only members of their particular denomination to the table and in some cases, only members from their specific congregation.

As a leader of General Christian services, I feel a sense of communion between Catholics and Protestants in any service until we get to the Communion table. Then Catholics attending the service are placed in that awkward situation of having to decline the General Christian Communion in order to respect their church tradition. Participating Catholics are generally okay with this, but it makes them look odd in the presence of participating Protestants who ordinarily don't understand the Catholic prohibition against Catholics participating in a Protestant Communion. Regardless of the Catholic prohibition, some Catholics participate anyway in the Protestant or General Christian Communion. They usually do for one of three reasons. First, some are naïve of the Catholic prohibition. Second, some compromise their real faith in order to fit in. Three, some are willing to break with their church tradition on this point because they long for unity. They long for "communion" (fellowship) with the lowercase "c" with fellow Christians of all backgrounds, and they long for "Communion" (Eucharist) with the upper-case "C" with fellow Christians of all backgrounds.

I tried to preempt this awkwardness as much as possible by reminding attending Catholics and Protestants of their respective traditions regarding Communion and the Apostle Paul's guidance on Communion,[82] but I led an open Communion service and never forbade

---

[82] See I Corinthians 11:17-35

anyone from receiving Communion. I figured the decision to participate was between God and the person receiving Communion.

Over the years I learned to avoid this awkwardness by ordinarily concluding the weekly General Christian service without Communion and offering a Communion service a few minutes after the main service. This not only gave Catholics an easy way out, but it also excused Protestants who did not feel ready to receive Communion. It also liberated the Communion service, and the people who participated in Communion did so because they truly wanted to be there.

While our General Christian service was jam packed in the prison, we typically only had about 20 men who stayed around for the weekly Communion service that followed, but this turned out to be one of the highlights of the week for them and me. It was a very informal service. We customarily stood in a circle around the Communion table. I offered a prayer of thanksgiving and confession. We made our profession of faith, and I thanked the Lord for the bread and the juice, symbols of God's grace and God's presence in our individual lives and our community. I served the person to my right, saying the words, "the body of Christ, the bread of Heaven... the blood of Christ, the cup of salvation," and that person in turn served the person to his right and so on. Each person in the circle sipped or dipped, and when the cup had made it circuitous trip back to me, I drank the remaining contents of the cup. Then I normally asked the newest person in the group to choose his favorite sacred song. We all joined in, a cappella style, normally in perfect harmony. We had fantastic singers in prison. When the last word of the song was sung, I could feel my lungs take in a deep breath, and I heard my brothers doing the same. In one final sigh of total contentment, we stood there in a holy hush, no one wanting to leave, until finally someone clapped or said, "Praise the Lord." Then we departed, eagerly looking forward to next week's Communion service.

We still held a Baptist-style Communion service every three months or so in our General Christian service. I digressed – back to the divided table.

The divided table highlights the difference in beliefs about the Eucharist/Communion between Catholics and most Protestants. In the Catholic doctrine of transubstantiation, at the moment in the Eucharist when the priest, through apostolic succession, consecrates the bread and the wine, the bread and wine actually become the mystical body and blood of Jesus, and God's grace is imparted to those who receive the blood of salvation and bread of Heaven. For Catholics, sins are forgiven through the ritual itself in this sacramental Eucharist.

Most Protestants view the bread and wine (or grape juice) as symbols of Christ's body and blood. In most Separatist traditions, people participate in a Communion service as a memorial, as a way to remember Christ's sacrifice. In other Protestant traditions believers view the Communion service as a memorial as well but also see the bread and wine as symbolic of Christ's presence in their lives. In their understanding, the Communion service becomes paradoxically a memorial service and a celebration service at the same time. In either case, most Protestants do not believe God literally imparts grace through the priest's words or through the bread and wine (although Anglicans, Episcopalians, and Lutherans come closer to a Catholic view on this subject). For most Protestants, sins are forgiven, not through the ritual itself or the spoken words of a pastor or priest, but by a mixture of God's grace and the believer's faith in what the ritual symbolizes. Depending on the Protestant tradition, some see Communion as more of a symbol of God's grace while others see it more as a symbol of the believer's faith.

There are merits to both Catholic and Protestant positions. Perhaps as Catholicism teaches, Jesus literally meant what he said, "This is my body... this is my blood." Perhaps Protestants who often take such a literal view of the Scripture should re-examine Jesus' teaching from a Catholic perspective. On the other hand, from a traditional Protestant view, this literal interpretation does not fit squarely into the framework of Jesus' ministry, as Jesus constantly challenged the Pharisees to let go of their legalistic ways and follow instead the heart of the Jewish law. Most Protestants doubt that Jesus was introducing a ritual that could only be done in a certain way and only by those in a long line of apostolic succession from one particular church.

If you come from another religious tradition or worldview, these nuances may seem trivial; however, they are not for many Catholics and Protestants and for people from other Christian traditions who believe the sacrament or ordinance must be given in the tradition of that church to be valid. Therefore, while the Catholic Church welcomes people from all faiths to attend Catholic services, non-Catholics are not invited to receive the bread and wine. However, they may go through the Eucharist line to receive a blessing from the priest. Some Protestants are happy to receive the blessing. Others view it as a second-class blessing. Likewise, some Protestant churches have similar prohibitions.

While various churches may impose restrictions on their clergy regarding the Eucharist/Communion, not every Catholic priest or Protestant minister is in agreement with the restrictions.

I recall a retreat I once attended with a small group of seminarians in the very monastery I used to poke fun of as a boy. We stayed there the better part of a week with the Catholic monks, and I finally learned what they were doing behind those cloistered walls. Most of them were several decades older than me, but I could not keep up with them. They got up at 4:00 AM to say communal prayers and met other times throughout the day to say their prayers, read the Scripture, and eat together. They farmed and baked bread and shared their produce and bread with the outside community, and they opened the rooms of their monastery to anyone needing a place to find solace. The monks knew we were Protestants, yet two days into the retreat, the monks wanted to know why our group was not coming forward in the worship services to receive the Eucharist with them. No one in our group had an issue with receiving the Eucharist. We simply did not want to place the monks in an awkward position of having to refuse us in order to enforce Catholic dogma or to accept us and compromise their dogma, but evidently, they were willing to ignore that particular church tradition in order to have communion and Communion with us.

There is a way for Catholics and Protestants to officially have Communion together. This is done in ecumenical services where Protestants line up on one side of the table to receive the elements from the Protestant minister and Catholics line up on the other side to receive the elements from the Catholic priest. It is as close as Catholics and Protestants officially get to a joint Eucharist/Communion, but the fact that there are segregated lines is a testimony to the division.

One time a Catholic priest and I were leading a Kairos Event, an ecumenical program jointly led by Catholics and Protestants in a prison setting. The Catholic priest and I concluded the event with the "official" way to lead a "joint but segregated" Eucharist/Communion service. I was at one end of the table serving Protestants, and the Catholic priest was at the other end serving Catholics. After our parishioners had gone through our respective separate lines, the priest turned to me and offered me the bread from his hand and the wine from his cup. I paused for a moment, shocked. I almost wept and then accepted the gift to have Communion with my brother. I was too emotionally moved at the time to even think about offering him the bread and grape juice from my side of the table.

I know there are Protestants and Catholics who would be offended by this breech of dogma by Catholic priests and Protestant ministers. I know that Catholics and Protestants once killed each other over this very issue. I now understand that some Catholics and Protestants are so convinced of their specific beliefs about the Eucharist or Communion that to deviate even a smidgeon from long standing tradition would compromise their sense of respect for God and their traditions. They see the ritual, rightly so, as an intimate gathering of family, reserved only for those who understand the family and want to be a part of it.

But many Catholics and Protestants see themselves as part of a greater catholic or universal Christian family, regardless of the culture in which they were raised. I was not there in person 2,000 years ago to hear Jesus say, "This is my blood... this is my body." Regardless of centuries of arguments over what he said, I am not certain if Jesus meant it literally or figuratively, but I am comfortable seeing the Eucharist/Communion as a mystery. When I go to the table or serve from the table, I am not doing so because I necessarily have the "right" beliefs and am certain about my church's dogma. I struggle with beliefs regarding various theological issues, but I have placed my faith in the mystery of the gospel that is available to any and all people. I participate in the meal because I see it as Catholics call it, a Eucharist, or a Thanksgiving. I do so because I see it as Protestants often call it, a Communion. The ritual helps me to commune with God and my fellow brothers and sisters in my extended Christian family, whether Protestant, Catholic, Eastern Orthodox, Oriental Orthodox or otherwise. I remember what Christ did and realize that somehow wherever God's grace and human faith touch, Christ is present. I do not claim to understand all that Jesus said or meant or that any one church has it all figured out and knows how to do it right, but I do know the table helps me to be reconciled with God and with others and to see God's desire for the world to be reconciled.

Many Protestants feel hurt when attending a Catholic Mass. They watch some Catholics, nominally committed or not committed at all to Christian faith, given a place at the table, while they, the Protestants of very committed Christian faith, are prohibited from the table. The disparity is often shocking. Likewise, many Catholics feel they are treated as second-class Christians when they are treated a similar way and witness the same thing from the Protestant side.

To be fair, we haven't addressed the other sacraments or ordinances of the Church. Many Protestants will be surprised to find that the Catholic Church customarily accepts the baptism of non-Catholic Christians as valid while many Protestant churches do not accept a Catholic person's baptism as legitimate. There are several other divisive issues as well; however, I start with the table because the table is a place in most cultures where people meet to nourish themselves and to have fellowship with one another.

If we do not attempt to come together at the table for ourselves, then we at least ought to try for the sake of the rest of the world. As Christians, we may distinguish between ourselves based on our denominational or non-denominational cultures and theologies, but the rest of the world does not notice our differences as much as they notice our common sins and mistakes. When many people look at the excesses of the Catholic Church during the Crusades: the killing of Albigensians, Jews, Muslims, and even Orthodox Christians; or the later excesses of the Inquisition, they don't distinguish between Catholic, Orthodox, or Protestant churches. So-called Protestant churches did not even exist back then. However, Protestants later had their excesses too under Oliver Cromwell, Henry VIII, John Calvin, and even Elizabeth Tudor, persecuting or ridiculing Catholics. However, most non-churched people and even many churched people don't understand the differences among the various Protestant denominations or the issues back then. In those days Protestants even martyred other Protestants. These days when law enforcement officials catch a money-grubbing or pedophile priest or pastor, it hardly matters to an ever-growing secular society whether the offender is Catholic or Protestant. Such stereotyping is even greater in the Muslim world where radicals stir up dissention, lumping all Christians into a perceived bad mix of Christendom and Western culture.

Because we have such religious freedom in the United States, it is easier to be with our own kind. However, I have been to other places in the world where such conveniences are not possible. When I was in Iraq and met Christians of Assyrian or Chaldean traditions, their faces lit up when they discovered I was a Christian chaplain. My Baptist uniqueness was no cause for alarm for them. Because Christians of any variety were such a minority in that area, they pushed aside any differences and felt a strong kinship with a Christian of any tradition.

I will stop here, realizing I have given little attention to Eastern and Oriental Orthodox churches and to a host of other Protestant groups and their doctrines on the Eucharist and other issues. Rather, I encourage Christians of all stripes to remember the Apostle Paul's guidance. "There is neither Jew nor Gentile, neither slave nor free, nor is there male and female, you are all one in Christ Jesus." Is there not room here for Catholic and Protestant as well, or for that matter, any number of different varieties of Christian communities?

Paul said in another letter, "Be completely humble and gentle; be patient, bearing with one another in love. Make every effort to keep the unity of the Spirit through the bond of peace. There is one body and one Spirit – just as you were called to one hope when you were called – one Lord, one faith, one baptism; one God and Father of all, who is over all and through all and in all.[83]

Augustine said, "In necessary things unity; in uncertain things freedom; in everything compassion." If you are a Christian, what actions can you and your church (Catholic, Orthodox, Protestant, or otherwise) take to remain true to the orthodox teachings of the Church yet champion the unity of the Church?

In many ways a church service is like a family reunion. At family reunions in the South, someone inevitably brings a plate of deviled eggs. No one in my immediate family likes them. We gag at the sulfur smell. People either love them or hate them. My family often brings collards to such events, and we have discovered that collards fall into that same category as you either "love'em" or "hate'em." Yet just about everybody loves fried chicken and barbeque, and ample supplies of these delicious foods are piled high in the center of a long picnic table. I would not dare mention not liking deviled eggs and risk offending the aunt who brought them. I just skip them and try to move inconspicuously to the next food item. Most everybody goes for the fried chicken and makes several trips to the dessert table.

Such events are opened with prayer. The elderly are honored. Children play and the adults swap stories about the past and brag about their children and grandchildren. While the meal is the major ritual of the reunion, it is not the main reason people come to the reunion. They come for fellowship and for family. They come for communion.

Church is similar. We may squabble over differences in liturgy, worship styles, history, theology, or how we set the table. We can all find something we don't like about any service. However, Church is not about the meal. It's about the fellowship. It's about reconciliation. It's about

---

[83] Ephesians 4:2-6

family. It's about communion and Communion with God and with one another.

Chapter 16

Christianity and Other Religions

Lord, make me an instrument of Your peace.

Where there is hatred, let me sow love;

where there is injury, pardon;

where there is doubt, faith;

where there is despair, hope;

where there is darkness, light;

and where there is sadness, joy.

Francis of Assisi

T he biblical Jewish patriarchs often made concessions to accommodate the pagan practices of neighbors and family members. Even the prophet Micah prophesied a peaceful time when all nations would walk in the names of their own gods.[84]

However, the Bible most often judges the kings of Israel and Judah based on how well they defended the monotheistic faith of Yahweh. The staunch defenders of monotheistic faith are labeled as "good kings" in the Bible and the kings who accommodated pagan practices or

---

[84] Micah 4:8

worshipped the pagan gods are labeled as "bad kings." In the Prophet Elijah's world there were two distinctive theologies: the monotheistic faith of Judaism and the pagan worldview of the Canaanites, and there was not room enough for both of them. To challenge the polytheistic religion, Elijah invited the Israelites and 450 prophets of Baal and 400 prophets of Asherah to Mount Carmel for a contest between Yahweh and Baal to determine whose God was real. In the contest, Yahweh exposed Baal as a fake, and Elijah called on the attending Israelites to kill the 450 prophets of Baal.[85]

Yet Elijah's vengeance on the Baal prophets pales in comparison to that of Antiochus Epiphanes against the Jews a few centuries later. Antiochus Epiphanes pitted Hellenism against Judaism and Zeus against Yahweh. He forced pagan practices at the Jewish temple, denied the Jews the opportunity to practice their holy days and rituals, and killed those who refused to comply. This resulted in the Maccabean Revolt.

By the time of Christ, the Roman government had worked out a way for people of monotheistic beliefs and other worldviews to coexist, though the plan did not last long. We see a glimpse of this pluralism in the New Testament when Paul the Apostle visited Mar's Hill in Athens. Paul, a learned Jewish rabbi and a proud Roman citizen, encountered Stoics and Epicureans at Mar's Hill. Paul was familiar with different groups in Judaism: the Pharisees, the Sadducees, and the Essenes. As a Christian leader, he was well acquainted with Jewish and Gentile forms of Christianity. Paul would have known about Babylonian, Greek, Roman, and Egyptian mythologies and was probably at least familiar with Zoroastrianism, Mithraism, Taoism, Confucianism, Hinduism, and Buddhism. To be sure, Paul did believe his religion was superior and hoped others would follow the Way, but he was respectful of people who held other worldviews, quoting from their poets and affirming them for being religious.[86]

In our age of globalization, there are radicals who want to take us back to the days and ways of Elijah or Antiochus Epiphanes and stamp

---

[85] I Kings 18:1-40
[86] Acts 17:16-34

out opposing worldviews, no matter who gets killed. Then there is Paul's way. Paul's paradigm gives freedom for people to express their own beliefs and at the same time, shows respect for others who believe differently. His methodology is the same used by professional chaplains today. Whatever a chaplain's view regarding other faith traditions, most chaplains use respect and common sense when working with people of different beliefs. In this spirit of Paul, I invite you to look at the major commonalities of Christianity and other religions and then consider the major distinctions between Christianity and other religions.

Values Common to All Religions

According to the Pew Research Center, the following demographics reflect the major religions and worldviews in the world today and the percentage of people that adhere to these particular traditions.[87]

Christianity	31.5%
Islam	23.2%
Unaffiliated	16.3%
Hinduism	15.0%
Buddhism	7.1%
Folk Religions	1.9%
Judaism	0.2%
Other Religions	0.8%

What do most of these people have in common? Over my years of working with people of different faiths, I have discovered two common themes in all the major religions: "let go and let God" and love others.

I am not sure who originally coined the phrase, "Let go and let God," but it certainly expresses a common theme in most all religions. If you come from a non-monotheistic perspective, substitute the word "God" for what best fits your worldview, i.e. "higher power" or an intrinsic value like love. With that said, here is the common theme. To let go and

---

[87] Pew Research Center Demographic Study, "Global Religious Diversity," Size of Major Religious Groups in 2010. April 4, 2014.

let God is to relinquish selfish desire to a power greater than one's self. When we let go of our need to control ideas, things, and relationships and give up our needs and wants to God, we do not become irresponsible. Just the opposite, we accept greater responsibility, cherishing what God has given us. This relinquishing act to God enables us to see the world and others differently and empowers us to use our gifts, talents, and possessions to worship God and love others. The more we let go of everything and let God control us, the more emotionally and spiritually mature we become and the more we are guided by love instead of fear. This is a major theme in all major religions.

The second great commonality is love of others. Admittedly, some religious people extend love and respect only to those within their respective groups, but generally, love of others is a theme in most religions. The following statements show the Golden Rule from various worldviews.

"You shall not take vengeance, or bear any grudge against the sons of your own people, but you shall love your neighbor as yourself. I am the LORD." - Leviticus 19:18

"So in everything, do to others what you would have them do to you, for this sums up the Law and the Prophets." - From Jesus in Matthew 7:12

"Do for one who may do for you, that you may cause him thus to do." - From Ancient Egypt, circa 2,000 BCE

"As you would have people do to you, do to them; and what you dislike to be done to you, don't do to them." - Kitab al-Kafi, vol. 2, p. 146.

"I will be careful for you as I should be for myself in the same need." - Homer

"May I be of a sound mind, and do to others as I would that they should do to me." - Plato

"Do not do to others what you would not want others to do to you." - Confucius

"Hurt not others in ways that you yourself would find hurtful." - From Buddha in Udana Varga 5:18

"We should regard all creatures as we regard our own self." - Jainism, Lord Mahairra, 24th Tirthanhra

"O man, what you do not like, do not do to your fellows." - Ba-Congo saying

"Great Spirit, grant that I may not criticize my neighbor until I have walked a mile in his moccasins." - Lakota (Sioux) saying

In 1893 when Chicago hosted the World Columbian Exposition, the city hosted other conferences as well. One such conference was the Parliament of the World's Religions. A hundred years later in 1993, the Parliament convened again with over 8,000 people from over one hundred religious organizations. This diverse meeting included representatives from Judaism, Christianity, Islam, Hinduism, Buddhism, Confucianism, Taoism, Japanese religions, and various nature and tribal religions. The Parliament also included different sects and denominations within these various religions. The Parliament was not some attempt to create a new world religion, nor was it a meeting for attendees to compromise their sacred dogmas for the rest of the Parliament. The Parliament viewed itself as apolitical. Some participants clarified they were not endorsed by their particular faith groups and could not officially represent their respective organizations. There were no representatives from fundamentalist Christian traditions in attendance.

One of the objectives of the Parliament was to highlight the crucial ethical issues facing the global community. The Parliament has convened four subsequent times since 1993. On the following pages, I show the 1993 Parliament's *Principles of a Global Ethic* as a suggestion of major shared religious values.

The Principles of a Global Ethic[88]

The Declaration of the Parliament Of the World's Religions

I. No new global order without a new global ethic

Common Convictions

- We all have a responsibility for a better global order.
- Our involvement for the sake of human rights, freedom, justice, peace, and the preservation of Earth is absolutely necessary.
- Our different religious and cultural traditions must not prevent our common involvement in opposing all forms of inhumanity and working for a greater humaneness.
- The principles expressed in this global ethic can be affirmed by all persons with ethical convictions, whether religiously grounded or not.

II. The Fundamental Demand

Every human being must be treated humanely

"Do good and avoid evil!"

"What you do not wish done to yourself, do not do to others!"

"What you wish done to yourself, do to others!"

III. Four Irrevocable Demands

First Directive

Commitment to a culture of non-violence and respect for life

a. The Religious and Ethical Tradition: You shall not kill! Have Respect for life!

b. Conflicts should be resolved without violence within a framework of justice.

c. Young people must learn at home and in school that violence may not be a means of settling differences with others.

d. We must cultivate living in harmony with nature and the cosmos. We need to realize our interdependence with the cosmos, earth, plants and animals.

e. To be authentically human in the spirit in our religious and ethical traditions means that in public and private life we must be concerned for others and ready to help.

---

[88] The Global Ethic outlined here is an adaptation from Hans Kung and Karl-Josef Kuschel. *A Global Ethic: The Declaration of the Parliament of the World's Religions* (New York, NY: Continuum Publishing Company, 1993), 17-36.

<u>Second Directive</u>
Commitment to a culture of solidarity and a just economic order
a. The Religious and Ethical Tradition: You shall not steal! Deal honestly and fairly!
b. There is no global peace without global justice! Power and wealth cannot be abused. Rather, they should be used to alleviate poverty, helplessness, despair, and theft.
c. Young people must learn at home and in school that property, limited though it may be, carries with it an obligation, and that its uses should at the same time serve the common good.
d. The world economy must be structured more justly. The participation of all states and the authority of international organizations are needed to build just economic institutions.
e. To be authentically human in the spirit of our great religious and ethical traditions means
- We must utilize economic and political power for service to humanity instead of misusing it for domination.
- We must cultivate mutual respect and consideration instead of thinking only of unlimited power and competitive struggles.
- We must value a sense of moderation and modesty instead of unquenchable greed for money, prestige, and consumption!

<u>Third Directive</u>
Commitment to a culture of tolerance and a life of truthfulness
a. The Religious and Ethical Tradition: You shall not lie! Speak and act truthfully!
b. This is especially true
- For those who work in the mass media
- For artists, writers, and scientists
- For politicians and political parties
- For the representatives of religion
c. Young people must learn at home and in school to think, speak, and act truthfully. They have a right to information and education to be able to make decisions that will form their lives.
d. To be authentically human in the spirit of our religious and ethical traditions means:
- We must not confuse pluralism with indifference to truth.
- We must cultivate truthfulness in all our relationships instead of dishonesty.
- We must constantly seek truth instead of spreading partisan half-truths.

- We must courageously serve the truth and remain constant and trustworthy, instead of yielding to opportunistic accommodation to life.

Fourth Directive
Commitment to a culture of equal rights and partnership between men and women

a. The Religious and Ethical Tradition: You shall not commit sexual immorality! Respect and love one another!
b. We condemn sexual exploitation and sexual discrimination.
c. Young people must learn at home and in school that sexuality is not a negative, destructive, or exploitative force, but creative and affirmative.
d. The relationship between women and men should be characterized by love, partnership, and trustworthiness. Some religious traditions know the ideal of a voluntary renunciation of the full use of sexuality. Celibacy can be an expression of identity and meaningful fulfillment.
e. The social institution of marriage, despite all its cultural and religious variety, is characterized by love, loyalty, and permanence. Marriage should secure the rights of all family members.
f. To be authentically human in the spirit of our religious and ethical traditions means:
- We need mutual respect, partnership and understanding instead of patriarchal domination and degradation.
- We need mutual concern, tolerance readiness for reconciliation and love instead of any form of possessive lust or sexual misuse.

To find out more about the Parliament, consult *A Global Ethic: The Declaration of the Parliament of the World's Religions* by Hans Kung and Karl-Josef Kuschel. In summary the parliament showed common ground for people of various faiths. While the concept of God or a higher power may vary among religious communities, all the major religions insist on devotion to a higher power and loving others.

The Uniqueness of Christianity
What makes Christianity unique from the other religions? Other religions have similar ethical teachings, miracle stories, and in some cases, even a god who dies for a particular group of people and rises from the dead.

From strictly anthropological and psychological viewpoints, Christianity appears to be a synthesis of monotheism and polytheism.

Followers of Christ worship one God; yet experience God through the Father, Son, and Holy Spirit. The Father appeals to the masculine, assertive, and analytical side of our nature. The Spirit appeals to the feminine, nurturing, and feeling side of our nature. The Son, though masculine, is also very nurturing, appealing to both sides of our nature.

However, the real value of Christianity cannot be measured by scientists. It is deeply spiritual and often counter-intuitive. Jesus taught his followers that in order to be rich, one must become poor. To inherit the earth, a person has to become meek. To find mercy, one must show mercy. If slapped on the right cheek, a person must turn the other cheek; and if forced to go one mile, then one must go two miles. Jesus said that persecution was simply part of the experience of following God, but people would be blessed by their sacrificial living. Unfortunately, some institutionalized Christianity does not line up with these radical teachings of Jesus. Gandhi, who was not a Christian, recognized the powerful force of Jesus' teachings and applied them to his non-violent movement in India. Martin Luther King Jr., a Baptist preacher, later used Gandhi's understanding of Jesus' teachings to turn the tide of racism in the United States. True, other religions contain similar elements of Christ's teachings on peace, but rarely have they been used in modern times to transform cultures as they were with Gandhi and King.

And yes, some of the old religions have gods who sacrificed themselves for a particular people and allegedly rose from the dead, but Christianity alone offers an all-powerful God who decided to walk among his creation and to live like them and to die for all of creation. In Christianity God understands what it means to be human because God felt human emotion, suffering, and temptation. When Christ died on the cross, God was sacrificing God's self for the universe. This is Trinitarian faith. The cross experience was more than a Father sacrificing his Son. This was God struggling with God's self to relinquish all control and be executed as a criminal. This stuff is heresy in other religions, but to Christianity, it is the ultimate reconciling story of the universe — that the all-powerful God of creation would stoop this low for us. In giving up his life, God displayed his ultimate redemptive power and empowered those awakened by this radical love to change the world for the greater good. To top it off, the grave could not hold him. The resurrection story is the story of God's ultimate victory over death, illness, tragedy, and all of life's challenges.

So I suggest there are two major distinctions between Christianity and other religions. The most celebrated one is the gospel; that Christ came, died, and rose again for the entire universe. The other is generally unnoticed because the institutions of Christianity often cover it up. This is the radical way self-sacrifice can transform culture.

Chapter 17

Christianity and Islam

To completely trust in God is to be like a child
who knows deeply that even if he does not call for the mother,
the mother is totally aware of his condition
and is looking after him.
Imam Al Ghazali

G rowing up in the Deep South, I did not meet a lot of Muslims. It was not until I was 22 years old that I had a Muslim friend. His name was Ali, a Lebanese American and flight attendant working for Delta Airlines. Ali was a square-jawed handsome man with jet-black hair who followed the fashionable trend of young, macho men in the 1980s and when off-duty, he often wore a wide open-collar shirt, sporting gold chains draped across his dark chest. As opposites often attract, he was smitten by good-looking, blond headed stewardesses.

I was a flight attendant with Delta as well. I shared an apartment in Fort Lauderdale with another flight attendant, a Catholic, young man, and we inevitably invited Ali to come live with us and share the rent. What a motley trio of young friends – three male flight attendants living near the beach, a Muslim, a Baptist, and a Catholic, footloose and fancy-free, traveling around the world.

I teased Ali about his gold medallions and accused him of being a show-off. He told me, "You're the only person I'll let get away with talking to me that way." Ali was also a Golden Gloves boxer. One day I asked Ali to teach me to box, so we put on the gloves and sparred in the front yard. There I discovered the strange phenomena of seeing stars in the middle of the day when his jabs and hooks smacked me upside the head. I am not a natural fighter. I surprised myself when I occasionally snuck in a jab or punch and immediately followed with an apology, "Sorry Ali." He just laughed and countered, "Come on. That's it. Hit me again. You can do it."

Ali grew up in Detroit in a Muslim family. He professed the *shahada* at an early age. The shahada is one of the five pillars of Muslim faith. To officially become a Muslim, one must believe and recite the shahada: "There is no god but God, and Muhammad is his messenger *(Ashadu an la ilaha illa-llah, Wa ashadu anna muhammadan rasulu-llah)."*

Shia Muslims recite this same message, but add one phrase at the end, "and Ali is his friend *(Aliyun wali Allah)."* It is considered heresy by Sunni Muslims to add this phrase to the shahada.

Here are core beliefs in Islam:

- Belief in the Oneness of God *(tawhid)*, that the all-knowing, all-powerful God is the creator of all things, and that it is heresy to associate God with having offspring or human characteristics.
- Belief in the Angels of God who worship and facilitate missions for God.
- Belief in the Books of God as originally given to God's messengers: the Quran to Muhammad, the Gospels to Jesus, the Psalms to David, the Torah to Moses, and the Scrolls to Abraham, but only the Quran remains in its original form, transmitted to Muhammad by the angel Gabriel *(Jibril)* as the Word of God.
- Belief in the prophets and messengers of God, beginning with Adam, then Noah, Abraham, Ishmael, Isaac, Jacob, Moses, Jesus, and ultimately ending in God's final revelation to Muhammad.

- Belief in the Day of Judgment when humans will be judged for their good or bad deeds, ending up in paradise or hell.
- Belief in Divine Predestination (Al-Qadar), but that humans do have the "free will" to make right choices.

These are the five pillars of Islam:
- The *Shahada*: the confession of faith
- *Salat*: the five daily prayers
- Fasting during the month of *Ramadhan*
- *Zakat*: giving to the needy (at least 2.5% of one's income)
- The *Hajj*: a pilgrimage to Mecca

My second Muslim friend was Jamaal, a Muslim chaplain I worked with in the early 1990s at the United States Penitentiary in Lompoc, California. Jamaal, an African American from California, had been raised in a Baptist family. He changed his American name to an Arabic name when he converted to Islam.

My family lived close to Jamaal's family in the staff housing across from the penitentiary. Our children played together, and my wife and I quickly became friends with Jamaal and his wife. In spite of our differences in religion, we connected as children of the 1960s and teens of the 1970s. Jamaal and I were both free spirits, at least for Baptists and Muslims. We were an odd pair when we rode our bikes together to work. I wore a clerical collar and Jamaal wore a *kufi* and *jalabiya*. Donned with our backpacks and unique clerical attire, we rode side by side to the penitentiary to bring our different perspectives of peace to prisoners.

The word *Islam* is similar to the Hebrew word *shalom*. Part of the meaning of *Islam* is peace. One who follows Islam is a Muslim. The simple meaning of the word *Muslim* is one who submits to God.

Jamaal, an African American, reared in Christianity but converting to Islam, was deeply committed to his Muslim faith. Ali, a Lebanese American, reared in Muslim faith, was more secular in his outlook on life. I am not stereotyping Muslims into two simplistic examples based on my two old friends; rather to suggest they represent two different sides of Islam, with plenty of variances in between.

Some Muslims of Arabic descent view new converts to Islam from other faiths as neophytes who do not understand the complexities of Islam, a religion rooted in Arabic culture. Conversely, some passionate new converts may view longstanding Muslims of Arabic descent as arrogant or out of touch with the universality of Islam. Occasionally, Muslim prisoners from countries like Pakistan, Yemen, and Indonesia, upon attending the Muslim services in prison, would come to me unsolicited to say, "This is not the way true Muslims practice Islam." When these men slacked up on their worship attendance because they felt some of the Muslim practices in prison were not genuine, the new converts of the faith in prison often informed me, "Those guys aren't true Muslims."

I realize I am making subjective observations from working in a subculture of Islam in prison, but the argument about what "true" Islam is or what a "true" Muslim is; is not just a debate among outside observers, it is a debate among Muslims in the Muslim world. Followers from other religions have similar debates about their faiths as well.

Islam itself is divided into two large groups: *Sunni* and *Shia*. Sunni Muslims comprise more than 80 percent of Islam in the world. Sunni Muslims view Muhammad as the last and final authoritative prophet and consider it heresy to add subsequent revelation. The word *sunna* refers to the teachings and actions of Muhammad or the orthodox or right way. Most Muslims who are Sunni do no refer to themselves as "Sunni Muslims." They insist a true Muslim is one who submits to Allah and follows the right way. There is no need to clarify the word "Muslim" with an adjective. They only do so to differentiate themselves from Shias.

Shias are so named because they consider themselves to be *Shiat Ali*, the Partisans of Ali. After the death of Muhammad in 632, some Muslims believed that Ali, the cousin and son-in-law of Muhammad, should become the next caliph (leader of the Muslim community) because of his bloodline to Muhammad. Other Muslims preferred the Arabic tradition of selecting the most qualified candidate, regardless of family ties. They believed the elder Abu Bakr, dear friend, father-in-law, and one of first converts of Muhammad, would be a better successor.

Abu Bakr became the successor, so the partisans of Ali waited. As Abu Bakr neared the end of his life, he nominated Umar to succeed him, and so Umar was chosen as the next caliph. Ali waited again. A Persian Christian stabbed Umar in 644. Still conscious on his deathbed, Umar selected a group of six men, including Ali, to choose the next caliph. The group elected Uthman. Ali and his partisans waited yet a third time. During Uthman's tenure as caliph, he was accused of promoting too many of his own relatives to government positions. Incensed Egyptians assassinated him in 656.

Ali claimed to be the rightful successor. A substantial group of Muslims did not accept Ali's leadership because they felt Ali was not passionate enough about hunting down the assassins of Uthman. They declared war on Ali and his supporters. Ali, wanting to reconcile the two groups, asked his group to stand down. Shocked by Ali's willingness to compromise, a dismayed member of the Kharijite sect that had fought to support Ali, killed Ali in 661.

The community selected Mu'awiyah, not related to Ali, to become caliph. Ali's second son, Hussein, took the title *Imam* and like his father before him, agreed not to challenge Mu'awiyah for the caliphate. He would wait his turn. However, Mu'awiyah nominated his own son, Yazid, to succeed him as the caliph.

From that point on, the Muslim world was divided. Those who followed the descendants of Ali were known as Shias, the Partisans of Ali. In the year 680, Yazid's army of approximately 4,000 warriors laid siege at Karbala where Hussein and about 70 of his faithful followers held out. For eight days Yazid's army denied Hussein and his followers access to water, offering Hussein only unconditional surrender. Hussein refused, claiming his position as the rightful caliph. When negotiations failed, Yazid's army killed Hussein and his supporters and took the women and children as prisoners. Hussein's burial place in Karbala became a holy place to subsequent Shias, and to this day, Shias commemorate the martyrdom of Ali every year on the Day of Ashura.

Muslims throughout the world are generally in agreement with all of Muhammad's teaching and generally accept the authority of the four caliphs that succeeded him, but many of the divisions in Islam today are rooted in what took place at Karbala over 1,300 years ago. Generally, Sunni Muslims believe those who follow subsequent beliefs added to the faith after the teachings of Muhammad and the four caliphs are in error. Shias, on the other hand, generally still feel betrayed by what happened at Karbala, and they believe enlightenment came through subsequent notable caliphs and ayatollahs as well. Therefore, Shias venerate certain holy sites, recognize various holy days, and practice various rituals, all considered unorthodox by Sunnis. They also have slightly different ways of practicing communal prayer. The following list shows general differences between Sunnis and Shias. The operative word is "general." There are exceptions.

Sunnis	**Shias**
Believe final revelation ended with Muhammad	Believe revelation continues through ayatollahs and other leaders
Say the *Shahada*: "There is no God but Allah, and Muhammad is his messenger"	Add to the *Shahada*: "and Ali is his friend"
Do not venerate grave sites	Venerate certain grave sites
Do not venerate saints	Venerate certain holy people, i.e. Ali and Hussein
Sharia (Islamic law) is closed to new revelation.	Sharia is open to new revelation
Inclined to a spirituality of seeking Allah's blessings	Inclined to a spirituality of martyrdom and suffering
Accept the Hadith (the collection of sayings and practices of Muhammad) as authoritative	Do not necessarily accept all the Hadith as authoritative
Generally believe in predestination	Believe that Allah knows the future but does not predestine everything

Because Shias see themselves as the oppressed minority, they tend to practice a spirituality of suffering and martyrdom in a similar way that Christians, centuries ago, practiced suffering and martyrdom during the era of Roman persecution. The twelfth imam, Muhammad Al Mahdi, mysteriously disappeared in the ninth century, and Shias still await Al Mahdi to return to redeem his people in a similar way that Jews await the Messiah or Christians await the return of Christ. Some Shias believe the returning Mahdi is Jesus.

In addition to Sunni and Shia Islam, there are various Islamic sects. Sufism is a mystic tradition dedicated to Divine love. Suffis are known among those outside the tradition for their whirling dervishes. Suffis desire to let go of the individual self and unite with the Divine. Most Sunnis and Shias consider Sufism a heretical religion. However, the influence of Sufism on Islam in many parts of the world is undeniable. Many Pakistani Muslims practice Barelvi Islam, a synchronization of Indian Islamic practice and Sufism.

Generally, if Sufis are on the far left of Islam, then Salafists are on the far right. ISIS and Al Qaeda members typically follow a Salafist form of Islam. So do most Muslims in Saudi Arabia, Kuwait, and Qatar. Yet these nations are some of the biggest allies of the United States in the fight/struggle/jihad/Just War against religious terrorism. The word s*alif* in this context is an Arabic word that means "predecessor" or "forefather," a reference to the first three generations of Muslims. Salafists desire to protect the purity of Islam and guard against adding additional religious teaching outside the circle of Prophet Muhammad's companions and the early generations. Of the various schools of Muslim jurisprudence, Salafists ordinarily follow the Hanbali school. In the 13th century, Ibn Taymiyya, one of the most influential proponents of the Hanbali school, advocated a return to the basics of Islam, including a stronger version of jihad and a *fatwa* (an edict by a Muslim religious leader) against apostates, as many Muslims in his day felt squeezed and/or compromised by the Mongols on one side and Crusaders on the other.

In the 18th century, Ibn Abd al-Wahhab, a Hanbali as well, led a Salafist revival to return to the basics. Wahhab preached against idolatry and against the veneration of saints, shrines, and tombs, and declared jihad against Muslims who allegedly practiced polytheism. He also aligned himself with the House of Ibn Saud. As Saudi Arabia grew into a kingdom, Wahhab's style of faith became a part of the fabric of Arabian culture. So that today, this style of faith is the state religion of Saudi Arabia and governs the religious practices in the holy Muslim cities of Mecca and Medina. This Salafist faith is also the dominant form of Islam in the Gulf States. As Saudi Arabia and these states grew in wealth from oil resources, the message of Wahhab was spread to other places around the globe, including the remote mountains of Afghanistan and Waziristan.

Over time the Salifist movement became nuanced, including even a pacifist form of the faith. Most Salafists are good people who respect people of all faiths. While they may believe that a Muslim world will ultimately prevail, they trust Allah to do so in Allah's own timing, and in the meantime will do their part to spread their faith in a peaceful coexistence with people of other faiths and worldviews.

A few other minority groups, however, influenced to some extent by naivety about the history of their own faith, began to focus on Ibn Taymiyya's fatwa against apostates and Wahhab's teachings on jihad, misinterpreting the fatwa and teachings to justify their own escapist, exploitive, and enraged faiths. These groups, including the Taliban, Al Qaeda, Boko Horam, and especially ISIS have created volatile religious cocktails. Many mainstream Muslim scholars are eager to set the record straight and show a proper interpretation and application of Ibn Taymiyya's fatwa. They want the world to know these terrorists are not the true face of Islam, and they ultimately want to convince the terrorists and those who might be attracted to such hostile groups to turn from bad theology back to a more orthodox Islam.[89]

---

[89] Thanks to Imam Iskandar Atajanow (Chaplain, 1LT, USAR) for helping me to see the importance of a proper interpretation of Ibn Taymiyya's "Mardin Fatwa" and the relevance of a proper interpretation of this fatwa in the war on religious terrorism. I also

If you are not Muslim, and even if you are, understanding all the nuances of Islam or for that matter any religion, can be rather daunting. To be sure, Islam is a diverse and complex religion. Just as Judaism and Christianity include many different denominations and sects and extreme left and right interpretations of the Bible, so the Muslim world is very nuanced. We have just skimmed the surface in this chapter. We haven't looked at the various holy days, nor have we addressed the different schools of Sunni or Shia jurisprudence that impacted the historical development of many sects of Islam or the various ways Muslims interpret and apply the Quran, the Hadith, and Sharia. To see the different ends of the continuum, simply read *In the Shade of the Quran* written by Muslim Brotherhood leader Sayyid Qutb. Then read *Reconciliation* written by Pakistan President Benazir Bhutto to see vast differences in worldviews from people who claim the same religion.

Muslim Commonalities with Judaism and Christianity

The Quran refers to Christians and Jews as "people of the book," a reference to Christians and Jews for their belief in the Bible. Many Muslims respect the Bible for its revelations from God, prior to Muhammad, and for the Bible's moral teaching, but they believe the modern-day Bible is filled with errors and cannot be fully trusted.

Islam shares a number of core theological beliefs with Christianity and Judaism. All three religions are considered to be monotheistic Abrahamic faiths.

With the exception of Muhammad, Christians and Muslims generally share the same prophets; generally believe in a Heaven and Hell, a final judgment, angels, demons, and the power of living a righteous and holy

---

want to acknowledge Dr. Muqtedar Khan, Director of the Islamic Studies Program, University of Delaware; and Dr. Sebastian Gorka, professor at the Marine Corps University, instructor affiliated with the Joint Special Operations University, and author of several articles and one book on defeating ISIS. If placed on a continuum, Khan comes from a more "dovish" perspective and Gorka comes from a more "hawkish" perspective, but both are helpful in understanding the motivations behind religious terrorist groups like ISIS.

life. Christianity and Islam share a common belief that Jesus was born of the Virgin Mary and was a great prophet. Both faiths look to the return of Jesus prior to the Great Judgment.

The custom of Muslim community prayers at specific daily times is rooted in earlier Jewish and Christian traditions. Muslims often use *zikr* beads to assist them with prayer, a custom that evolved from the Catholic Rosary.

Generally, Judaism, Christianity, and Islam share many common moral values; among these, a love for God, a love for community, the notion of letting go and letting God, a concern for the oppressed, and the desire to treat all people with fairness and respect. Though admittedly, not all Jews, Christians, and Muslims share the same ideas about fairness and respect.

Differences

We are at an impasse on the Christian doctrine of the Trinity. In orthodox Christianity, the Trinitarian doctrine is viewed as a complex or mystical way to express the unity and oneness of God, but most Muslims and Jews do not see it this way. They view such theology as polytheistic and heretical.

Christians today, and especially American Christians, generally believe religion and state ought to be separated, though they often differ on the amount of separation. Muslims generally believe Islam and state should be joined, though they often differ on how much. The secular government of Turkey and the stringent religious government of Saudi Arabia show the diversity in applying Sharia in the Muslim world.

Christians in the West often judge Muslim governments based on the government's level of democracy. However, even in Muslim nations where democracy is championed, democracy is not supported so that religion might be separate from government. It is generally supported so that Muslims can vote to ensure the principles of Islam are followed. Muhammad united Arab tribes to submit them to the will of Allah. Though Muslims do believe in an unseen spiritual world of jinn and angels, they do not separate the spiritual world from the temporal as many Christians do.

Muslims generally believe the Bible is filled with errors. Since many of the biblical stories were passed along in oral tradition for generations before they were written down, Muslims typically assume the original versions of these stories were lost or diluted. They assert the same thing about alleged mistakes in transcribing the biblical texts over hundreds of years. They believe the subsequent revelations to Muhammad noted in the Quran set the record straight on these stories.

Muslims believe the Quran is the Word of God in a similar way that Christians believe Jesus is the Word of God. For Muslims, every Arabic word in the Quran is a word from God. For this reason it is important for Muslims to learn Arabic so they can read the Quran. Other language versions of the Quran are not considered real Qurans. They are mere translations.

Islam differs from Judaism and Christianity on the story of Abraham's attempt to sacrifice his son. In the Bible, Abraham offers his son Isaac. In the Quran, Abraham offers his son Ishmael.

While both Christianity and Islam are in agreement that Jesus was a great prophet, they differ on the nature of Jesus. In orthodox Christianity, Jesus was and is God. This teaching is anathema to Judaism and Islam. In Islam, it is heresy to attribute any partnership to God. This includes Jesus and the Holy Spirit.

Christians and Muslims also disagree on the story of the cross. In orthodox Christianity, Jesus died on the cross, and three days later he rose from the dead. While Muslim scholars debate exactly what happened to Jesus during the crucifixion, perhaps the most popular Muslim belief is that a substitute man was crucified in place of Jesus and that Jesus never died. Instead, he physically ascended to Heaven.

For both Judaism and Islam, it is heresy to believe the all-powerful God of the Universe would stoop so low as to live among humans and consent to execution as a common criminal. Yet for Christianity, this God-dying-for-us message is the reconciling story of the universe. In orthodox Christianity, it is heresy to discount Christ as God. In Islam, it is heresy to count Christ as God.

While the Quran teaches Muslims to respect Jews and Christians as "the people of the book" and believe God did reveal himself in Judaism and later in Christianity, Muslims believe Allah's ultimate revelation came through Islam. While most Muslims respect Jews and Christians, they wish their Jewish and Christian friends could understand God's revelation through Islam.

Christians vary on their opinions about Islam. Most American Christians know very little about Islam, and what they do know normally comes from the news media. Views on Muhammad are varied. Some see Muhammad as a great leader and prophet who helped to unite people a long time ago and who gave timeless guidance for the world. Still others view him as a charlatan.

Some Christians have a general respect for the Quran as the holy book of Muslims, but they have never read it and do not intend to read it. Some see the Quran as a good book to help Muslims live a good and moral life. A few may even read translations of the Quran and are able to quote various verses from the Quran.

Others see the Quran as a compilation of already existing biblical stories and a few later Gnostic stories not credible enough to make it into the Bible, all mixed together several centuries later with Muhammad's alleged revelations, with the stories often changed to match his revelations. Since the Bible stories are older than the Quran's stories, most Jews and Christians are skeptical about Muhammad's ability to somehow get the stories right some five centuries later.

The Challenge of Reconciliation

In the summer of 2003 I had the privilege to attend a peace-making venture in Baghdad. World Religions for Peace, a peace organization headquartered in New York and endorsed by the United Nations, facilitated a multi-faith meeting in Baghdad. The meeting included important Sunni and Shia clerics, bishops from the Assyrian and Chaldean churches, monks from the St. John of the Baptist Order, Iraqi doctors, leaders of Iraqi charity organizations, a former Baathist Colonel, and two U.S. Army chaplains (my boss Chaplain (COL) Doug Carver, the Command Chaplain of the Combined Joint Task Force in Iraq, and me). The meeting looked like a scene from a *Star Wars* movie with imams, bishops, monks, and chaplains, all dressed in our distinctive clerical garb and uniforms.

The meeting had two purposes: to inspire participating religious organizations to work together to meet basic humanitarian needs in Iraq and to establish healthy dialogue between various religious factions with the indirect goal of influencing peace in all of Iraq.

There were plenty of clinched jaws at the meeting. Having been persecuted and silenced under Saddam's regime, the forum gave Shias the opportunity to vent their anger and grief. This made it difficult for leaders in the meeting to keep the group on task, but their feelings could not be ignored, and the dialogue was helpful in the process of moving the various religious groups toward reconciliation. Chaplain Carver respectfully responded to accusations that the U.S. military was not moving fast enough in fulfilling its promises to help rebuild the Iraqi infrastructure. However, the fact that such a diverse group of Shia and Sunni Muslims and Assyrian, Chaldean, and Protestant Christians were joining forces, just a few weeks after the war began, is a testimony to peace efforts on all sides.

Perhaps because of Christianity's minority position in the country, the various Christian denominations worked well together. Even many Protestants looked to the bishop of the Chaldean Church for leadership in the Church in Iraq. These Christians are to be commended for their hard work at peace in Iraq.

I was struck by a question from an Iraqi medical doctor at the meeting. He asked me, "How many Jews do you have in your Army?" I misunderstood his question, thinking he wanted to know how many rabbis we had in the Chaplain Corps. I began explaining how Catholic priests, Protestant ministers, Muslim imams, and Jewish rabbis work together to meet the religious needs of all our soldiers, but I stopped when I realized he wasn't getting it. He asked again. He simply wanted to know how many Jews we had in the Army. I did not know exactly, but I told him I would be surprised if we had more than one in a hundred. Then he sincerely asked, "Does your country intend to make Iraq a second Israel?" I began to laugh, but stopped myself when I realized I might offend him. I then realized the intent of his questions. This fully educated medical doctor, prominent enough to be included at this peace conference, actually believed the United States was attempting to create a second Israel in Iraq? I thought to myself, "Where did he ever get such an idea?" Christians and Muslims often have atrocious perceptions of each other.

What Christians can do...

If one wants to offer helpful suggestions regarding tensions in the Middle East and solving the Islamist terrorist dilemma, it is important to have at least a general knowledge of the history of Islam. Suffice it to say, Islam is just as complex as Christianity. To better understand Islam, it is important to read the Quran or at least a translation of it, have an understanding of the Hadith, and listen to the testimonies of Muslims. It is also important to remember the historical contributions of the Muslim world. Were it not for Muslims who safeguarded the ancient writings of Plato and Aristotle and advanced systems in mathematics and trade during the European Dark Ages, there may have never been a Western Renaissance.

As recent as the late 19th century and early 20th century, before the Ottoman Empire fell, before the Sykes-Pikot Agreement, before the Balfour Declaration, or before the Suez Canal, we would discover a time in the Middle East when Jews, Christians, and Muslims, or Europeans and Middle Easterners got along far better. Granted, the population was sparser then, and that may have helped to ease close-neighbor tensions, but the point is – religious groups were generally not trying to kill each other. I am not suggesting we go back to those times and ignore the sovereign rights of new nations birthed through the pains of two world wars or lessen the special relationship the United States shares with Israel. However, if we want to contribute to peacemaking and peace building in any of these areas, it is important to know how lands were divided after the fall of the Ottoman Empire, how the Caliphate ended and why many Muslims want to see the Caliphate restored, how shifts in power and politics impacted various cultures and economies in the Middle East, and how subsequent political jockeying impacted Muslim perception of the West. It is vital we understand the differences among Muslims, particularly between Arabs and Iranians, Sunnis and Shias, and the fine line between peaceful and radicalized Islamic theologies, instead of lumping Muslims into one category.

We must also understand the horror of the Holocaust, how it shaped Judaism, and the history of Israel's conflict with its neighbors. Moreover, it is important to understand the theological differences between Orthodox Jews, particularly the Hasidim, and a continuum of other Jewish religious groups and how these various Jewish sects complement or in some cases conflict with Zionist ideology and Israeli politics.

It is also crucial to understand the development and philosophies of various Islamic political organizations; to name a few: Hezbollah, Hamas, The Muslim Brotherhood, Fatah (Palestinian Liberation Movement), the Islamic Party of Kurdistan, the Taliban, Al-Qaeda, and the so-called Islamic State. Just as it would be naïve to reduce the Catholic-Protestant conflict in Northern Ireland down to a line in the sand between Protestants and Catholics, it would be equally naïve to reduce conflict in the Middle East down to differences in religion. These conflicts are highly nuanced with cultural differences, moderate ideologies, radical ideologies, and the desire for power and/or survival. And this is just the Middle East. The religious tensions in Africa, Indonesia, and other parts of the world need our consideration as well.

The Christian world is not guilty of all the alleged sins that Islamist extremists project on Christianity. However, if Christians believe in communal responsibility, then Christians must do their part in accepting appropriate responsibility and trying to change perceptions.

When many Muslims look at Christianity, they do not see Christ. They see a mixture of Western civilization and Christianity blended together. They often fail to see the good that came out of the blending.

Instead, they have a long, often biased memory and choose to focus on the sins of the Crusades, European exploitation in the last 100 years, poor American decisions in the last few decades, and the perception the United States always sides with Israel, whether right or wrong, against Palestinian Muslims. They focus on mistakes Americans made in the wars in Iraq and Afghanistan and point to a permissive Western culture that includes alcohol, pornography, homosexuality, and capitalistic interest rates, all considered taboo in Muslim faith.

This is one of the reasons I encourage Christians not to refer to the United States as a "Christian" nation. I am certainly proud of my country and the strong Christian heritage in the United States, but if Christians wish to call the United States a Christian nation, then Christians must be willing to accept the responsibility of the sins of the nation as well. Christians should also realize that when we call the United States a Christian nation, we infer that American citizens of other faiths and worldviews are not part of the Republic. This only further alienates Muslims and people of other faiths from the authentic message of Christianity.

Nevertheless, Christians can take communal responsibility where responsibility is due. When Christians approach Muslims with a willingness to listen and accept responsibility, Christians might find themselves in a place to defend the whole truth. Christianity, like Islam and Judaism, was born in the Middle East. Jesus and his 12 disciples were Jewish. The disciples, along with Paul, first took the message to Palestine and Asia Minor and then to Africa, Italy, and Asia. The early Christian faith grew by leaps and bounds in Africa before it ever took hold in Northern Europe.

Outside of the Biblical characters, no one helped to shape Christianity more than Augustine, a bishop from northern Africa. Granted, Christianity was shaped for bad and for good later in Europe, but Christianity owes its basic theological principles, not to Europeans but to people of the Middle East and the surrounding areas.

Christians in the United States often jump to conclusions about Muslims. After 9-11 most Americans did not see media reports about

American Muslims taking a strong stance against terrorism. This only confirmed their suspicions that all Muslims must support extremism and that Islam is an angry religion. Some American Muslims really did view the 9-11 attacks as retribution for the past sins of Christians and the West, but Americans forget that even Iranian Muslims turned out in the streets of Tehran to hold an all-night candlelight vigil to show their grief and support to Americans after 9-11.

We rightfully grieve the nearly 3,000 citizens who were murdered by the terrorists, the over 8,000 U.S. military and civilian personnel who have died as a result of the wars in Iraq and Afghanistan, not to mention the countless wounded and the pain and suffering inflicted on American families. But many forget that Muslims are fighting terrorism and extremists too. According to the Inter-Services Public Relations (ISPR), an administrative organization in the Pakistan Defense Force, since 9-11, over 30,000 Pakistanis have been killed or injured as a result of the global war on terror.[90] And that's just in Pakistan. Our Coalition partners have lost an untold number of innocent people who were killed in Iraq and Afghanistan. Every day, Iraqi policemen and soldiers continue to place their lives on the line in the fight against radicalized religious terrorism.

There are three wide-sweeping statements I sometimes hear from Christians about Islam.

1. "Islam is not a merciful religion."
2. "All Muslims believe in holy war."
3. "All Muslims want Sharia to govern the world."

I often hear well-meaning Christians say, "When you compare Islam to Christianity, the difference is mercy. Christianity is a religion of mercy. Islam is not." From my experience, I can honestly say that most of the Muslim people with whom I have met or developed relationships with are merciful. Of the 99 names that Muslims use for Allah, one of the most commonly used names is "Allah, the All-Merciful." Before passing

---

[90] "Global War on Terrorism Claims 30,000 Casualties," Pakistan News Net, 18 February 2010.

judgments on Muslim people, why not develop relationships with them and then judge from experience rather from biased news reports or material published by non-Muslim religious organizations that intentionally discredit Islam?

Yes, *jihad*, or holy war, is a tenet of Islam. According to the Quran, Muslims are obligated to fight a holy war when they must defend themselves, protect innocents, or protect the faith. We have something similar in the West. We call it "Just War Theory." Just as the Quran and Muhammad shaped jihad, so did the Bible and Augustine shape Just War.

Jihad also means holy struggle. Muslims practice jihad when they struggle to lead holy lives. Sound similar? Christians practice this same holy struggle. There is no doubt that radicalized Islamists have hijacked the word jihad to justify mass murder and terror, so it's no wonder many Westerners view jihad as a bad thing. When they hear about any Muslim practicing jihad, people often leap to erroneous conclusions about any Muslim's holy struggle. It should also be noted that many Muslims in the world are practicing jihad against radicalized Islamist terrorists and are asking people from other faiths to join them in this holy struggle.

Sharia is another scary word to many Americans. Sharia is basically the moral and religious code of Islam, and it specifies how Muslims should practice their spiritual disciplines, family life, sexuality, finances, hygiene, diet, politics, and a host of other daily aspects of life. Many Americans forget that many of our own civil and criminal laws have their roots in Mosaic and Christian principles. While we may champion the separation of church and state, we still follow many laws based on biblical principles. Muslims do not separate "mosque and state." A faithful Muslim wants to follow the moral religious code of Islam and wants his or her nation to do the same.

Sharia is not applied the same way in all Muslim nations. Just look at the difference between Turkey and Saudi Arabia. In some Muslim nations, Muslims only apply Sharia to Muslims, and they do not apply it to people of other faiths. Secondly, many modern Muslim scholars understand that Muhammad lived in a different time, and they often apply sacred traditions in light of a modern world. Before passing judgment on Muslims wanting to live by Sharia, fully listen to what the Muslim person is truly seeking. Is it a practical Sharia accommodating the 21st century and respectful of people outside of Muslim faith, or is it a 7th century violent application? Or is it a Sharia somewhere between the two? It is natural for American Muslims to follow Sharia in their personal, family, and Muslim community lives the same way American Christians desire to live by Christian disciplines in their own personal, family, and community lives. Many Christians in fact vote in public elections to ensure Christian disciplines are championed. True, American Christians generally stop short of trying to impose their beliefs on others in a public setting, but there are many who would if they could. And this is a fair question for American Muslims as well. Where do you stop short on imposing Sharia in public life, and if you are trying to proliferate Sharia in public life, to what degree?

To be sure, there are places in the world where Muslims enact Sharia with exactness and cruelty where groups like Al-Qaeda and the so-called Islamic State have radicalized agendas. This should rightly cause Muslims, Christians, Jews, and people of other worldviews to join together to stop these groups and their radicalized, violent application of Sharia.

What Muslims can do...

If Muslims want to build harmony with Christians, they too need to start with accountability and responsibility, regardless of how off-base Christian perceptions may seem to them. If Muslims want to take it all the way back to the Crusades, then it would be helpful to remember the part Muslims played in exploiting Christians who made pilgrimages to Jerusalem and how these acts incited the Crusades. There were noble and evil people on both sides during the Crusades. It would be helpful to remember the loss of Christian culture in the seventh and eighth centuries to Muslim advances, often at the point of a sword, in vast parts of Africa, Asia Minor, and Europe. Muslims also need to know the rich diversity of Christian faith and Christian contributions to the world.

Many Christians, out of their own naivety, still do not know that many Muslims grieve over what happened on 9-11 and are in the struggle against Islamist terrorism as well. Muslims need to let Christians know they are with them on this issue. There is no doubt that organizations like the so-called Islamic State are a grave threat to the West, but they are even a greater threat to the Muslim world. In a similar way that Christianity hemorrhaged in the 16th century in Europe, Islam is now hemorrhaging in the Middle East and many other places in the world. The primary struggle is not with what the West will do with radical Islamist extremists but with what Islam itself will do with them. The rise of radicalism in Islam is symptomatic of struggles among Muslim peoples over theology, culture, power, and economic conditions. Muslim leaders who love Allah and who are merciful must make an inventory of their own failures and responsibilities and address the issues that make young people attracted to radicalized religious violence in the first place, along with perceived issues (whether real or not) that make the West mistrusting of the Muslim world.

Non-Muslims want to know where Muslims stand on the issue of radicalized religious violence, and it appears there are several places along the continuum where Muslims stand. Unfortunately, a growing number of radicalized Islamists stand on the side of terror and practice their understanding of jihad against moderate Muslims and the West. Others may not belong to such radicalized groups but overtly or passively support such groups. Others, standing in the middle, have not made up their minds. Many have made up their minds and disdain radicalized Islamist groups, but they do nothing to stop them. Many others are using their own form of Sharia, the pulpit, and social media to combat Islamist terrorists, and on the far end of the continuum are Muslims who are practicing their own form of jihad to destroy Islamist terrorist groups.

This same continuum could have been applied to Americans a few decades ago regarding the Ku Klux Klan. The Klan hijacked Christianity and concocted its own radical philosophy. The Klan did not behead its victims, but it certainly lynched them. Some Klan members eagerly joined the violence. Others did not pull the rope, but they stood by in support. Other Klan members may have been repulsed by such violence, but they still supported the Klan's overall agenda. An even larger group of

Americans never belonged to the Klan, but the Klan shaped their prejudices. Other Americans disdained the Klan and were repulsed by racism, but they did nothing to change the culture. Others used the pulpit, the media, and the legal system to defeat the Klan. We have come a long way in just a few decades. Today, we could visit any country-cooking restaurant in the South and sit next to the biggest redneck in the restaurant, and if we were to ask him what he thought of the Ku Klux Klan, he would denounce the Klan as a sick joke and consider anyone a fool for joining such an organization.

If Americans and Christians can change within just a few decades, it can be done in the Muslim world as well. The West can send air strikes and boots on the ground, but the West cannot win the war against terror alone. That's part of the challenge. We have learned over the last few decades that when the West kills terrorists, the terror organizations do not go away. One miscalculation, where grave collateral damage is done and innocents are killed, only makes others want to join these radicalized groups to fight the "evil" West. To win the war against religious terrorism, Muslims in general must see this as their war. Muslims need to use their own pulpits, social media, and legal systems (Sharia) to make the likes of the Islamic State look like the Ku Klux Klan where any young person would consider the joining of such an organization as ridiculous. Only then will young people turn away from a hijacked, radicalized faith to a loving and caring faith.

But there is one crucial difference in the Ku Klux Klan and the Islamic State. As bad as the Klan was, even Klan members did not believe in annihilating groups of people. They would have been repulsed by the violence of the Islamic State. The Islamic State belongs in a category with the Nazis of World War II.

Many from the West are wondering. How long will Muslims permit the Islamic State and other radicalized groups to kill Christians, Jews, and Yazidis? But from a strictly Muslim perspective, how long will Muslims permit these radicalized groups to murder other Muslims?

"Killing them all" is not the final solution or the righteous way. We (Muslims, Christians, Jews, and good people of all worldviews) must turn the hearts and minds of young people who are right now sitting behind a computer screen and considering joining a religious terrorist group, Islamist or otherwise. What can we do in social media to turn their hearts and minds to a peaceful worldview? This is where the war on religious radicalized violence will inevitably be won.

Yet many Christians, Jews, and Westerners simply don't feel, whether right or wrong, that Muslims are in the fight against radicalism, and some even believe that main-stream Muslims silently support radical jihads. It would be helpful if both sides checked or challenged the legitimacy of right wing and left wing news media reports that continue to feed hysteria. Nonetheless, moderate Muslims can change the perception.

While Christians and Muslims may never see each other as brothers and sisters in the same faith, it is still possible to see each other as common children of God in the same quest to find purpose and meaning in life. There is great room for friendship, if only we take the time and hard work to understand.

The Nation of Islam and Islam in American Prisons

I was reluctant to include this section in the book because the Nation of Islam is a relatively small group compared to the worldwide Muslim community; however, many Americans are confused about the differences between Islam and the Nation of Islam (NOI), so I decided to include it.

Several religions were birthed in the early 1900s in a movement to empower African Americans and people from other nations of African ancestry to take pride in their African roots. Jamaican political leader Marcus Garvey preached a message to African Americans to look to Africa as their homeland, not the United States.

Rastafarianism originated in Jamaica in the 1930s and is a synthesis of Christian beliefs and reverence for Hali Selassi I, the Emperor of Ethiopia from 1930 to 1974, and the belief that Ethiopia is the original birthplace of humankind and the new Zion.

The Moorish Science Temple of America (MSTA) originated in 1913 in New Jersey under the leadership of Timothy Drew. The MSTA is based on a synchronization of Christianity, Freemasonry, and various eastern religions and the belief that many African Americans are descendants of the Moorish people of Africa. Some claim the *Circle Seven*, the MSTA holy book, is a plagiarized document from *The Aquarian Gospel of Jesus Christ*, written by a rather esoteric preacher and Union Army Chaplain by the name of Levi Dowling.

The Nation of Islam (NOI) originated in 1930 in Detroit under the leadership of Wallace Fard Muhammad and his protégé, Elijah Muhammad. During the 1960s, the Nation of Islam gained national attention from two charismatic leaders, Malcolm X and Louis Farrakhan, as they struggled to defend African Americans against racial injustices.

Prior to taking his pilgrimage to Mecca in 1964, Malcolm X considered Islam an Africentric religion. During the hajj, he witnessed Muslims from many nations and cultures encircling the Kaaba. When he came back to the United States, he preached a more inclusive view of Islam that included all races. A few members of the Nation of Islam subsequently assassinated him.

When Elijah Muhammad died, his son Warith Deen Muhammad succeeded him to lead the NOI, but he too changed his beliefs about black supremacy, departed the NOI, and influenced many other members to follow him back toward mainstream Islam. Louis Farrakhan subsequently became the NOI's new leader.

In an American culture where African Americans were often treated with disrespect, groups like the Rastafarians, the MSTA, and the NOI offered a new cultural identity. These organizations helped African Americans take pride in their African heritage. Of these three groups in prison environments, the NOI tended to have the largest membership.

The Nation of Islam is still highly organized in prison systems, but it has been losing ground over the last few years. The NOI continues to place a strong emphasis on discipline and respect for authority, and it enables men to prioritize their goals with strong emphasis on community and personal responsibility. Of all the religious groups I encountered over my years in the Federal Bureau of Prisons, I generally found NOI members to be the most respectful of my authority, as authority and respect are important NOI core values. Of all the religious groups, the NOI is the most pro-active faith group in promoting multi-faith programs in a prison environment; however, such programs almost always have an ethnic agenda. Conversely, the inmate Muslim community is ordinarily the least likely to participate in any multi-faith program, as most Muslims consider it heretical to associate the name of Allah with other religions.

Along with all the good the Nation of Islam brings, the NOI still maintains a farfetched story about how white people came into existence. In Genesis there is an obscure story about Jacob increasing the size of his herds of sheep and goats. In the NOI version of the story, Jacob creates a hybrid goat, a sort of hairy, human-like creature that crawls around on all fours and prefers to dwell in caves. This hybrid animal, according to the NOI, is the ancient ancestor of European peoples, the blue-eyed devil.

This story is similar to the white, racist trash I heard growing up. Bigoted whites hijacked the biblical stories about the curses on Cain and Ham to show God's alleged curse on blacks. When people feel oppressed, as many poor Southern whites felt following the Civil War or as African Americans felt, particularly during the turbulent segregation days, people often re-interpret history to justify their situation. Such is the stuff of Arthurian legends.

In a prison setting Nation of Islam members and Muslims typically meet in separate places for *Jumah* (the Friday prayer service). From the 1960s through the 1990s, the Nation of Islam had a significant influence on shaping what inmates thought about Islam. Prisoners attending the Nation meetings normally outnumbered those in Muslim services. After 9-11, the trend reversed.

Many Christians, naïve about Islam, do not know the difference between the two groups and often assume they are the same religion. Though many NOI members will tell you they are Muslims, most Sunni and Shia Muslims will tell you differently. They would say about Nation of Islam adherents the same thing an orthodox Christian might say about Jehovah's Witnesses or Mormons: "good folk but a little off-base when it comes to orthodox theology." Likewise, some Nation of Islam members would say about other Muslims the same thing a Jehovah's Witness or Mormon might say about Christians from orthodox traditions, "Too bad they don't know the whole story."

The shift change toward Sunni Islam in prisons is partly due to the tremendous growth rate of Islam in the world and the attention it receives in the media. With the growth of Islam in the outside world, prisoners are catching on. More and more African American prisoners are seeing the Nation of Islam as unorthodox, not just because of NOI theology about the blue-eyed devil but also because of the NOI's unique blending of the New Testament and the Quran, a synthesis considered heretical by both traditional Muslims and Christians. Farrakhan's claims of having traveled in a spaceship have not helped NOI ratings either.

As I retired from the Federal Bureau of Prisons in 2011, there was an uneasy mix in the prison systems with Nation of Islam followers and Muslim inmates. Some got along better than others. From time to time, and at the encouragement of Louis Farrakhan, the two communities came together for combined meetings, but it was almost always understood the meetings would be held in accordance with Sunni, not NOI tradition.

Regardless of the mix, the Nation of Islam still has a subtle effect on Muslim prisoners. When Sunni Muslim prisoners try to recruit converts, they often spin Christianity as the "white man's religion" or European religion. Unfortunately, this perception is also held beyond the prison walls and still fuels debates between Christians and Muslims.

Summary

Christians and Muslims are too complex to be lumped into single stereotypes. The Christian world is not guilty of all the alleged sins that Islamist extremists project on Christianity, nor should the entire Muslim world be blamed for Islamist terrorists. However, if either side believes in communal responsibility, then both Christians and Muslims must do their part to accept appropriate responsibility, change perceptions, work toward a better understanding of the many nuances and histories of both religions, celebrate commonalities, and work together to stop radicalized religious violence.

One of the most important questions for our times is this: What is the difference between Salafists who desire to live an altruistic faith and Salafists who desire to kill their neighbors? Once we know, we (Muslims, Christians, Jews, or otherwise) can influence those teetering between a peaceful Islam and a radical, violent Islam to seek the more peaceful way.

Other Muslim nations, our Coalition Forces, and even some of our enemies on other fronts share the same interests in defeating ISIS. As we grieve our own losses at the hands of Islamist terrorists, from events like 9-11 and San Bernardino, we cannot forget about the thousands of Muslims who have already died at the hands of ISIS and groups like them.

It's complicated. We can win battles with airstrikes and boots on the ground, but we have to remember – whenever innocent people get killed in the crossfire, this only fuels the cause and the recruitment of the religious terrorists. The real war will inevitably be won by pitting ideology against ideology, especially through social media that changes the hearts and minds of young people who are teetering between a bad theology of hate and a mainstream religion of peace.

Chapter 18

Common Ground in Sadr City

You can imprison a man, but not an idea.
You can exile a man, but not an idea.
You can kill a man, but not an idea.

Benazir Bhutto

T wo of the finest men I met on my last deployment to Iraq were Major Dwayne Kelley and Mr. Steven Farley. I met them in Sadr City[91] in the summer of 2008.

Our unit, the 926th Engineer Brigade commanded by Brigadier General Jeffrey Talley, arrived in Iraq as the Battle for Sadr City was ending. The Iraqi Army and the 3rd Brigade Combat Team of the 4th

---

[91] Sadr City is a suburb of Baghdad, named in honor of the Grand Ayatollah Mohammad Mohammad Sadeq al-Sadr, a highly respected leader among Shia Muslims. The majority of Muslims in the world come from the Sunni tradition. The largest minority is from the Shia tradition. The largest concentrations of Shias in Iraq are located in various parts of Baghdad and near the coast. Shia adherents believe that the leadership of Islam descends through Muhammad's family line. They also tend to venerate various holy sites and prophets in Islam. These practices are considered heretical in Sunni tradition. There are also cultural differences in the two traditions. Saddam Hussein, a Sunni Muslim, marginalized and exploited Shia Muslims during his reign.

Infantry Division had driven out most of the insurgents from Sadr City. During the battle, many homes and businesses were completely razed. Others, still standing, were pockmarked from small-arms fire. Main sewer lines were busted and raw sewage ran down the middle of the streets. Trash was everywhere.

The 926th Engineer Brigade was given the mission of Task Force Gold: to make Sadr City safe again, rebuild infrastructure, and improve the economy. With the help of other subordinate engineer battalions, our unit cleared improvised explosive devices from the roads, renovated schools and health clinics, provided clean water and fixed the sewage system, increased electricity on the power grid, removed trash and debris, and led small scale agricultural and beautification projects.

Most of the citizens of Sadr City were torn between the direction of the young militant Imam Muqtada al-Sadr[92] and the older peace-loving Imam Ayatollah Ali al-Sistani.[93] While not every citizen was a big fan of the young hothead, most everyone was loyal to the Sadr family and for good reason. During Saddam Hussein's oppression of the Shia residents, the Sadr family provided the citizens of Sadr City with enduring economic and spiritual support.

The Army Chief of Chaplains encouraged all Army chaplains to facilitate healthy dialogue with local clerics, wherever and whenever possible in Iraq, but with Muqtada's heavyweight influence over local Shia clerics, this was not likely to happen in Sadr City. Every week Muqtada preached a fiery anti-Coalition and disseminated his messages to every imam in the city where they were expected to repeat the same messages from their pulpits.

---

[92] After the fall of Saddam's regime in 2003, Muqtada al-Sadr, the son of the late Grand Ayatollah Sadeq al-Sadr, organized a para-military organization known as the *Jaysh al-Mahdi* (Mahdi Army). Claiming to be the new spiritual leader of Shias in Baghdad, he led his movement in an armed struggle against Sunni Muslims. The relationship between his faction and Coalition forces was stressful.
[93] Ali al-Sistani is the highly respected Shia Ayatollah who called for peace after the fall of Sadaam's regime. He issued a *fatwa* (religious edict from a high official cleric) for Shia Muslims not to use violence against Sunni Muslims and Coalition forces. He also supported democratic elections and voting rights for women.

Staff Sergeant Greg Huff, my chaplain assistant, and I went on our first trip to Sadr City on 28 May 2008. We led a Communion service for our troops at the small base. After the service we left the base and accompanied a civil affairs team to Jamilla Market, the most damaged area in the city. We conducted an atmospheric mission, a glad-handing visit in the community, where we met with shopkeepers, shoppers, and various workers downtown to sense how they felt about our military presence and to do everything within our influence to convince them of a helping presence.

In subsequent visits to Jamillah Market with the civil affairs team and with the aid of interpreters, I talked with contractors, shopkeepers, and townspeople. My goal was to let residents know we respected their religious beliefs and practices. My mantra went something like this, "Do we give your workers the time they need to make their prayers? Do we need to make a place available for workers to have communal prayer? When we work on Fridays, does our work disturb you or distract from worship? Do our soldiers show respect for you?" I always received welcomed responses and never got a negative report.

On one mission with the civil affairs team, I met an Iraqi commander who had led his forces in the Battle of Sadr City. When I asked him about the religious dynamics in Sadr City, he said, "One of the first things I did when I came here was to reopen a Sunni mosque... Shia, Sunni, makes no difference to me. We're the same... all Muslims. There are Christians here too. We're all Iraqis." I reported his comments to my higher leadership in the brigade and the division, noting his desire to foster religious liberty in Iraq. He was the kind of leader we wanted to support.

When Sadr City residents discovered I was a chaplain, their faces lit up and they responded spontaneously with, "Oh, we worship the same God," and they seemed to respect me as a type of Christian imam or sheik.

On the left shoulder of our Army uniforms, we wore the engineer unit patch. This patch became recognizable to Sadr City citizens and gave us instant credibility. The local citizens called us *mohandas* (the Arabic word for engineers). They knew we were there to improve their quality of life, and many benefited financially from the contracts we offered.

Major Dwayne Kelley, 48 years old, was an Army Reserve Civil Affairs Officer and our operation officer for Task Force Gold in Sadr City. Back home in his civilian job, he served as a New Jersey State policeman and served on a homeland security task force with the FBI. He was married and had two daughters. He looked like a linebacker but spoke in a gentle voice. He was learning Arabic on his own time in order to be an effective communicator with Iraqis.[94]

Mr. Steven Farley, 57 years old, was a retired Navy captain and worked for the U.S. State Department in Sadr City to train Sadr City District Council members on modern techniques of city council organization and working together as an effective team. He was married, had three sons and five grandchildren. I met him when he noticed the cross on my patrol cap and introduced himself to me. He wanted me to know he was a Christian and told me about his family and work. Mr. Farley was a visionary. He combined his identities as a Christian, American, and global citizen into a passion to build peace in Sadr City. He loved jazz music and every time I saw him, he had a bright smile.

When Coalition leaders[95] first met with the Sadr City District Council, they were convinced the leader of the council had to go. He was a Mafioso-type leader and had used his position to gain personal wealth and power in the city. The council replaced him with a new leader, Sayyid Shaman. Under new leadership the Council met on 24 June. With the old leader out of the way and Shaman now in the new leadership seat, everyone around the table was looking forward to working together to rebuild the city.

Mr. Farley's interpreter would later tell me Farley was up early that morning, listening to jazz music and polishing his shoes in order to look his best for the meeting. I had wanted to attend the meeting and had been bugging Major Kelley to get me on the roster for such meetings.

---

[94] Major Dwayne Kelley was technically assigned to the 432nd Civil Affairs Battalion but worked in Task Force Gold under the direction of the 926th Engineer Brigade.
[95] Team members came from the 3rd Brigade Combat Team of the 4th Infantry Division, the 432nd Civil Affairs Battalion and the 926th Engineer Brigade.

Instead, I was at Camp Liberty that morning and was trading laughs with a few soldiers in the chow hall when a runner from headquarters barged in on my joke. He leaned in and whispered, "There's been an explosion in Sadr City. We've got KIAs (killed in action). Come on, the general wants you there now." Staff Sergeant Huff and I threw our gear together, climbed into an MRAP, and the Personal Security Detachment escorted us to the Sadr City Forward Operating Base (FOB).

By the time Staff Sergeant Huff and I arrived at the FOB, we had pieced together parts of the story. An assassin had infiltrated the Sadr City District Hall and hidden a bomb under the table where Sadr City council members and Coalition personnel met.

As Major Kelley, Mr. Farley, and other personnel gathered around the table mid-morning, the bomb exploded. Major Kelley survived the initial blast. Others were killed instantly. The dead included Mr. Steven Farley. Also killed were Mrs. Nichole Suveges, a civilian with the Fourth Infantry Division; Chief Robert Hammet, also with the Fourth Infantry, AJ; an Egyptian interpreter; and approximately five other Iraqis. Unfortunately, such events were common in those days, and I have not been able to substantiate the exact number of Iraqis killed or their names. Other U.S. and Iraqi personnel were wounded, including an Iraqi colonel and the intended target of the blast, District Council leader Sayyid Shaman.

As Staff Sergeant Huff and I dismounted the MRAP at the Sadr City FOB, I saw the Air Force photographer assigned to cover the meeting. I listened to his story. He had just stepped out of the meeting room to go to the latrine when the bomb exploded. He immediately rushed back to the explosion site to help other first responders. He helped place Major Kelley into the back of an MRAP, climbed in with him and held on to him as the MRAP sped toward the awaiting medical team back at the FOB. Aware of his mortal wounds, Major Kelley told him, "I don't think I'm going to make it."

After speaking with the photographer and praying with him, I went to every soldier and interpreter involved in the incident and to those who knew our fallen comrades. A number of soldiers were visibly shaken.

Some, experiencing survivor guilt, wondered what they could have done differently. I tried to reassure them and knew they had done everything within their power to ensure a safe meeting, but I realized I would not talk them out of their feelings, at least not on that day. One officer was cussing mad. I walked with him for about an hour around the dusty FOB as he criticized, "Those bleeding hearts... I told them something like this was going to happen, but they wouldn't listen." He was not the only one. I heard a lot of "what-ifs" that day. "What are we doing here? How many more will it take?" A few soldiers and interpreters wanted to tell me every detail of their experience during the crisis. Others had no desire to talk at all, preferring to grieve alone. I sat on the gravel with several soldiers, leaning against a concrete barrier and prayed with them.

In the meantime I had directed Staff Sergeant Huff to invite everyone to an inter-faith prayer service at 1800 hours. All the Iraqi interpreters attended. With Muslims and Christians in the circle, I opened with, "May the words of our mouths and the meditation of our hearts...,"[96] and read from Ecclesiastes, "there is a time and a season for everything on earth... a time for love and a time for hate... a time to embrace and a time to refrain from embracing... a time to gather and a time to cast a way... a time to be born and a time to die... a time to kill and a time to heal.... a time of war and a time of peace."[97]

We honored the names of our fallen comrades and Iraqi citizens, praying for their eternal safekeeping and comfort for their families and friends. I briefly mentioned the different stages of grief, encouraged them to grieve in their own way, and we closed in prayer. As we parted, Muslims and Christians wept and embraced in common grief and a common yearning for God.

Staff Sergeant Huff and I had to leave the next day to attend a meeting with General Talley and the public education superintendents of Baghdad and Sadr City. After the meeting I accompanied General Talley to the Baghdad hospital to visit Sayyid Shaman who had miraculously survived the blast and was recovering from the damage of a broken leg.

---

[96] Psalm 19:14
[97] Ecclesiastes 3:1-8

From there, Huff and I went back to Camp Liberty to support a memorial service. Since most of the personnel at Sadr City could not leave the FOB to attend the official memorial services at Camp Liberty, I returned to the FOB a few days later to lead a memorial service for them.

We met in a trailer that night. It was packed with Muslims and Christians. Sergeant First Class Jeff Bishop read from Psalm 23. "The Lord is my shepherd... Even though I walk through the valley of the shadow of death, I will fear no evil... You prepare a table before me in the presence of my enemies... Surely goodness and love will follow me... and I will dwell in the house of the Lord forever."

I assigned a Muslim interpreter to read an English translation portion of Surah 93, from the Quran.

> By the Glorious Morning Light, And by the Night when it is still, Thy Guardian-Lord hath not forsaken thee, nor is He displeased. And verily the Hereafter will be better for thee than the present. And soon will thy Guardian-Lord give thee (that wherewith) thou shalt be well-pleased. Did He not find thee an orphan and give thee shelter (and care)? And He found thee wandering, and He gave thee guidance. And He found thee in need, and made thee independent.[98]

Captain Darrick Wright, who had taken over Major Kelley's duties, read from the Beatitudes in the Gospel of Matthew. "Blessed are the poor in spirit... Blessed are those who mourn... Blessed are the peacemakers..." Captain Wright also served as my unofficial deacon in Sadr City. When I could not be there, Captain Wright led Christian devotionals, helped coordinate Catholic services, and assessed the religious needs of our Muslim personnel. A few weeks later I would read the Beatitudes in another Memorial Service, this time to honor Captain Wright.

In the days following the explosion, investigators identified the conspirators and the leader of the plot. The ringleader was the ousted Sadr City District Council leader. He was jealous of Shaman's new

---

[98] Surah 93:1-8, Usuf Ali Translation of the Quran

leadership and wanted to kill Shaman and as many others as possible along with him. He had committed the sins of all three Genesis falls. He had rebelled against God, against his brother, and against his community.

While I was in Sadr City over the course of those days, I did not try to talk anyone out of his or her anger or sadness. I did not confirm or deny suspicions on whom to blame, nor did I try to manipulate anyone's faith. I simply listened to stories of those in grief, prayed with those who wanted to pray, and had a sense of what might work in a multi-faith service. We were a diverse crowd at the memorial service in the trailer: Muslims and Christians, civilian and military personnel, Iraqis and Americans. As we embraced and shed tears, we found strength in our common need for God's comfort, our warrior spirit, and our need to ensure our fallen comrades did not die in vain. The conspirators may have succeeded in murdering innocent people, but they failed in their efforts to obstruct reconciliation. If anything, the crisis empowered Mr. Farley's vision for Sadr City.

When I think about the sacrificial deaths of Major Kelley and Mr. Farley and the thousands of others who have given their lives in the war against terror, I am reminded of the sacrificial death of Christ – to die that others might live. When soldiers take the oath of enlistment or oath of office, they make a solemn vow to protect and defend the Constitution of the United States. They understand when making this oath they may be called upon to pay the ultimate sacrifice. Likewise, when people make a commitment to Christ or some other religious faith or worldview, they often make such pledges, willing to die for their cause. Many are called upon by their nation or their God to make exactly such sacrifices, but most of us will never have to die for God or country. Instead, we are called upon to live for God and country – to serve as "living sacrifices."[99] And so I end this book with the two quotes from the beginning of the book.

---

[99] Romans 12:1

It is understanding that gives us an ability to have peace.
When we understand the other fellow's viewpoint, and he understands ours,
then we can sit down and work out our differences.
President Harry Truman

When we become old and look back on life,
we will discover the only things that mattered
were the relationships we had.
Carlton Fisher, Sr.

Author's Faith:

Understanding My Beliefs Without Compromising Yours

This chapter was not in the initial draft of the book because I did not want my worldview to be an influencer or a detractor as you examined the process of how you came to your own worldview. However, I decided that if I was going to ask you to be vulnerable with yourself and perhaps with others, then maybe I owed it to you to be honest in answering the same questions. Here again are the questions we posed:

1. How well do you generally…
   o   Love instead of fear?
   o   Trust instead of despair?
   o   Forgive instead of resent?
   o   Choose right instead of wrong?

2. What kind of faith do you have in your worldview?
   o   No certainty, all mystery
   o   Some certainty, mostly
   o   Mostly certainty, some mystery
   o   All certainty, no mystery

3. How do you approach religious belief systems different than yours?
   o   My religion is the only way.
   o   My religion is closest to the truth.
   o   My religion is more enlightened.
   o   All religions are relative.

4. Which word best describes your current stage of spiritual development?
   o   Disorder
   o   Duty
   o   Doubting
   o   Discovery

5. Which statement best describes the way you love?
   o I love myself for self's sake.
   o I love God for self's sake.
   o I love God for God's sake.
   o I love myself for God's sake.

6. Are you currently struggling with any of these issues?
   o Escapist Faith
   o Exploitive Faith
   o Enraged Faith

7. How well do you generally…
   o Handle your anger?
   o Delay your gratification?
   o Understand your own emotions?
   o Understand the emotions of others?

When it comes to beliefs, you may have guessed it. I'm a wonderer. My general faith tends to lean more toward mystery than certainty. My mind wonders about the demythology of Bultmann, the blind faith of Pascal, the neo-orthodoxy of Barth, the belief of Ladd, and the certainty of Pannenberg. I still struggle with what I understand about scientific methodology versus what I have experienced in my faith and what other Christians and people of other faiths have experienced. I would like to think I primarily live in a spiritual stage of discovery but am often stuck in doubting. As a young person, I felt my doubts were a curse and fervently prayed for God to give me a faith of certainty (the stories are absolutely true), but after a while, doubt itself became a stubborn, old friend who refused to leave. This odd friend helped me to relate with other kindred doubters and to be more accepting of people who have different worldviews than mine, thereby increasing my patience.

Nevertheless, in spite of doubts, I made a commitment to follow Christ when I was 12 years old, and I'm sticking to that commitment and to Christ. The gospel is the reconciling story of my life, and I am still awed that God would make the ultimate sacrifice to woo humanity. Therefore, if I had to pick an approach to other worldviews, I would pick somewhere between "my worldview is closest to the truth" and "my worldview is more enlightened." Admittedly, I am drawn to anything that reconciles people, and I have yet to discover anything that equals the reconciling power of the gospel story. I realize the message of the cross may seem foolish to others,[100] but it has been and continues to be the theme of my life.

Yet I have also been touched by the testimonials of people from other worldviews. I still struggle with reconciling the image of a judging, exclusive God portrayed in some parts of the Bible with the loving, inclusive God in other parts of the Bible and believe that some of our attempts at systematic theology, rather from the left or right, are basically theological gymnastics to defend our own biases. It is difficult to believe this good-news God would condemn others simply because they cannot comprehend the gospel, but it is just as difficult to believe that God would simply ignore the consequences of evil in the world. But as I assess other worldviews, I do not believe all worldviews are relative. Some beliefs are healthier than others, even within my own faith tradition.

And when do we ever grow up? I still struggle with my own capacity to love and seem to continually go up and down Bernard of Clairvaux's stages of love. Folks tell me I'm good at understanding my own emotions and the emotions of others, but I am no saint when it comes to handling anger or delaying gratification. I hardly ever fall prey to the pitfalls of escapist or exploitive faith, but I am vulnerable to self-righteousness and have to watch out for the dangers of enraged faith.

I fancy myself as an existentialist, naturalist Christian. Basically I want to know what it means to exist now – to live in the here and now as a Christian. I figure if I'm living right in the present, the future will work out. I love to garden, study the stars, and observe the natural environment. A naturalist believes if nature can take her natural course, the world will get along fine. I think it's hard to go wrong by taking lessons from nature's signs.

But I need something bigger than nature, bigger than my family, even bigger than my church and my country to count on. So the Bible is my

---

[100] See I Corinthians 1:18-31.

ultimate guide for life. I do not look for literal or allegorical interpretations of the Bible. I want to know the original intent of the Biblical writers or compilers, and in spite of their humanness and frailty, I choose to accept what they said or collected as inspired by God. I believe they used the limits of their human language and knowledge to often explain unexplainable events and experiences, but once understood in the context of their time and culture and how they understood history and the universe, their stories and teachings have universal application for all times and all people. There are a few parts in the Bible that are unclear like the symbolic references in Daniel, Ezekiel, and Revelation. I am leery of theology that allegedly decodes all such revelations, particularly when such theology is the centerpiece of a person's faith. However, as the author of Revelation teaches, I would not add to or change anything in the Bible. I realize that Orthodox, Catholics, and Protestants have slightly different variations of the Bible, there are hundreds of different translations of the Bible, and that none of them were translated from the original texts. However, most of the translations today remarkably reflect the oldest pieces of the Bible thus far discovered.

That said, I appreciate what the fundamentalist does to protect the authority of the Bible, but I also appreciate many of the tools of historical criticism that provide greater clarity about the intent of the authors and compilers of the Bible.

Because I choose the Bible as my ultimate source of authority, I am influenced by the overwhelming number of biblical passages that remind me of humanity's responsibility for the poor and the oppressed. When I look at the Bible, I am inspired by God's mandate to Adam and Eve and their descendants to be responsible for the good earth. I still see the earth as good and am optimistic about her future. I tend to be pro-life and pro-creative in everything: protecting endangered species and the environment; helping the poor when they need to get across a border, providing a decent education for all people; safeguarding our most vulnerable (including the child within the womb and the woman who carries it); promoting restorative justice, peace, and reconciliation;

safeguarding freedom of religion; and advancing the beauty of traditional marriage and family values.

While I am a proud Fisher and American, the Bible and nature remind me to look beyond self, family, culture, community, and country to see my connection with the entire world's communities and our collective need to maintain a good earth.

I have seen too much of war and prison to believe that human beings can become so enlightened as to no longer heed lessons from classical sacred texts or from nature. However, as nature has her exceptions, I wonder how to best help individuals and communities that do not fit neatly into long-held traditions.

Part of my deep desire for reconciliation is based on my own emotional need, and as much as I would like to think I have "arrived," I know I have not. I still make wrong choices, struggle with doubt and fear, and sometimes fall into despair and find it difficult to forgive. But in spite of my challenges, I am absolutely convinced, as John the disciple said, God is love and perfect love drives away fear.

In years to come I may look back on parts of this book and shake my head at some of the things I wrote. Thank you for reading the book. This and another book, entitled *Where Warriors Walk*, are my first attempts, with the help of others, to self-publish. The creating part was easy, but the editing was laborious and took longer than I ever intended. It took so long that at least one of my stories in the book outlived its central character, Carlton Fisher Sr., my father. My Dad passed away on 20 August 2015 at the age of 80. Just a few weeks before his passing, he had asked me again, "Carl, when are you going to publish the book?" He had read the proof and told me the book helped him to understand his faith better and that it helped him to normalize his doubts as just another part of his faith. He also liked the parts that helped him to understand how people from other worldviews believe.

You may recall in this book that I was a nervous wreck when I was twelve years old. My father was the first person to notice my anxiousness and asked me what was wrong. He was the person who gently encouraged me to walk down the aisle of our little Baptist church and give my life to the Lord. After I became a Christian, I turned into a religious fanatic. When other high school students saw me coming, they turned and ran the other way, afraid I was going to whip out my Bible and preach at them. My father, while very proud of my decision to follow Christ, was also concerned about my social development. Not wanting to see his son friendless, he told me, "Son, when we become old and look back on life, we will discover the only things that mattered in life were the relationships we had." I have written this book trying with all my might to convey that message.

While we may disagree on various points in this book, I hope you found the book a useful tool to better understand the beliefs of others and why they believe and act the way they do. I also hope the book helped you gain insights into your own journey. Life is all about relationships. Stay in the good fight. Create beauty wherever you go. Live well. Above all, love well.

Acknowledgements

I owe much of my professional knowledge for this book to Southwestern Baptist Theological Seminary, Columbia Theological Seminary, Air War College, and specialized training from the Army Chaplain Corps and the Federal Bureau of Prisons Chaplaincy. The following professors made a significant impact on my worldview: Dr. Russ Bush, Philosophy; Dr. Leon McBeth, Baptist History; Dr. William Estep, Church History; Dr. Derrell Watkins, Social Ministry; Dr. Walter Breuggemann, Old Testament; and Dr. Amit Gupta, International Relations.

The following supervisors were outstanding mentors: Warden Willie Collins, Warden Chuck DeRosa, Warden Scott Middlebrooks, and Warden Jeff Keller. Great chaplain supervisors included Chaplain (COL) Donald Wilson, Chaplain (COL) Duane Westfield, Chaplain (COL) Tommy Smith, Chaplain (COL) Jerry Robinson, Chaplain (COL) Douglas Carver, Chaplain (LTC) Jay Hartranft, and Chaplain (LTC) James Carter. Hands down, the commander that most influenced my life was and is Lieutenant General Jeffrey Talley. I served as Talley's chaplain when he commanded the 926th Engineer Brigade and later served as one of his trusted advisors when he became commander of the U.S. Army Reserve.

The following individuals made a significant impact on broadening my ecumenical and inter-faith understanding. For Catholicism – Father James Holden and Father Matthew Sindik; for Judaism – Rabbi Scott Kramer, Rabbi Ira Ehrenpreis, and many other rabbis over the years from the Aleph Institute; for Islam – Imam Jamal Abdul Rahim and Imam Marcellus Sallam; for the Nation of Islam – Captain Richard Muhammad; for Rastafarianism – Mr. Sydney North; and for Native American Spirituality – Mr. Tommy Berryhill, Lakota Medicine Man John Funmaker, and Navajo Medicine Man Lenny Foster.

For serving along side me as faithful partners in ministry, I am grateful to all the correctional staff, inmates, and prison volunteers in the Federal Bureau of Prisons and to all the military and civilian personnel who worked with me to spread the gospel and/or champion religious freedom. I remember well the faithful service of three of my associate pastors of Peace Community Church: Rev. Gary Coburn, Mr. Jerome Tellis, and Rev. Chuck Latham. There were many inmates along the way who had tremendous personal courage and stood with me to turn a dream of reconciliation into a reality in a prison. I name the men who stand out as my "armor bearers": Mr. George Mims, Dr. Roy White, Rev. Steve Shaw, Rev. Nelson Fears, Rev. Willie Davis, Mr. Bobby Ray Smart, Mr. Fredel Williamson, and Mr. Al Morton. The Army chaplain assistants who stand out are MSG Al Robbins, SGT Lloyd Penn, SGM Richard England, and SSG Greg Huff. Greg literally put his life on the line for me every time we went "outside the wire."

For loving me well, I must thank my parents; Carlton and Rose Fisher, who raised me in a Baptist culture, led me to Christian faith, and taught me to respect people of all faiths. I thank them also for allowing me to share their stories in this book. I am grateful to my three children, Travis, Hannah, and Chloé. They inspire me with their purity of heart and devotion to family. Next to the Good Lord, no one understands my heart better than my wife, Lisa. She is my partner in ministry, soul mate, playmate, and helpmate. She is the person who encouraged me to write this book.

And lastly, I am grateful for the following family members and friends who were helpful in the editing process: Wynn Warren, Becky Hawkins, MaryBeth Cobble, Kevin Burchardt, Jean Wash, Chloé Fisher, Lisa Fisher, and Kenneth Wash. Mr. Wash, author of *The Final Defense*, played a significant role in designing the cover and leading me through the initial stage of publication process, and Chloé Fisher helped me complete the process.

Sources Consulted

The resources noted below include works cited in the footnotes of this book; however, most of these resources are simply consults and are included here for the reader's further consideration.

Ames, Chaplain (COL) Dan, Power Point Briefing. Religious Leader Liaison: The Army Chief of Chaplain's Policy, #3, for the Brigade Chaplain Function Couse, 22 September 2011.

Ames, Chaplain (COL) Dan, Power Point Briefing. "The Chaplain in Religious Leader Liaison: Suggestions for Success, for the Brigade Chaplain Functional Course," 22 September 2011

Armstrong, Karen. *The Bible – The Biography*. London, England: Atlantic Books, 2007.

Armstrong, Karen. *The Great Transformation: The Beginning of Religious Traditions*. New York, NY: Random House, 2006.

Armstrong, Karen. *The History of Islam*. New York, NY: Modern Library Publishing, 2000.

Armstrong, Karen. *Muhammad: A Man for Our Time*. New York, NY: Harper Collins Publishers, 2006.

Army and Marine Corps Field Manual. *Counterinsurgency Field Manual*: U.S Army Field Manuel No. 2-24, Marine Corps Warfighting Publication No. 3-33.5. Chicago, IL: TheUniversity of Chicago Press, 2007.

Army Regulation 165-1. *Religious Support: Army Chaplain Corps Activities*. Washington, D.C.: Headquarters, Department of the Army, 3 December 2009.

Army Field Manual 1-05. *Religious Support*. Washington, D.C.: Headquarters, Department of the Army, 18 April 2003.

Assyrian International News Agency Books Online. *The Epic of Gilgamesh*. www.aina.org.

Bettneson, Henry, editor. *Documents of the Christian Church*, 2nd ed. London, England: Oxford University Press, 1963.

Bettenson, Henry. *The Early Christian Fathers*, 7th ed. Oxford, England: Oxford University Press, 1984.

Bergh, Albert E. editor. *The Writings of Thomas Jefferson.* Washington D.C.: The Thomas Jefferson Memorial Association, 1905.

Beveridge, Andrew A., Q "Who is Marrying Whom," *New York Times*, January 29, 2011.

Beversluis, Joel, editor. *Sourcebook of the World's Religion: An Interfaith Guide to Religion and Spiriutlaity*, 3rd ed. Navato, CA: New World Library, 2000.

Bhutto, Benazir. *Reconciliation: Islam, Democracy, and the West.* Harper Collins: New York, 2008.

Brands, H. W. *The First American: The Life and Times of Benjamin Franklin.* NewYork, NY: Anchor Books, 2000.

Bush, L. Russ and Tom J. Nettles. *Baptists and the Bible.* Chicago: Moody Press, 1980.

Carter, Jimmy. *The Blood of Abraham: Insights into the Middle East.* Boston, MA: Houghton Mifflin Company, 1985.

Carver, Chaplain (Major General) Douglas L. Subject: Chief of Chaplains' Policy #3 – Religious Leader Liaison. Department of the Army. Office of the Chief of Chaplains. Memorandum, 30 September 2008.

Calvin, John. *Institutes of Christian Religion,* ed. Tony Lane and Hilary Osborne. Grand Rapids, MI,: Baker House, 1986.

Campbell, Joseph, ed. *The Portable Jung.* New York, NY: Penguin Books, 1976

Campbell, Will D. *Brother to a Dragonfly,* 25th anniversary. New York, NY: Continuum, 2000.

Chapman, Gary. *The Five Love Languages: How to Express Heartfelt Commitment to Your Mate.* Chicago, IL: Northfield Publishing, 1995.

Chaves, Mark. *Congregations in America.* London, England: Harvard, 2004.

The Constitution of the United States of America

Cronin, Vincent. *The View from Planet Earth.* New York, NY: Quill, 1983.

"Debate Between the President and Former Vice President Walter F. Mondale in Louisville, Kentucky, October 7, 1984."

Sources Consulted

Department of Justice, Federal Bureau of Prisons Program Statement P5360.09, *Religious Beliefs and Practices* Program Statement, 31 Dec 2004.5360.

Department of Justice, Federal Bureau of Prisons T5360.01, *Practical Guidelines for Administration of Inmate Religious Beliefs and Practices* Technical Reference Manual, 27 March 2002.

Dillenberger, John and Claude Welch. *Protestant Christianity.* New York, NY: Charles Scribner's Sons, 1954.

Drakeford, John W. *Psychology in Search of a Soul.* Nashville, TN: Broadman Press, 1964.

Drazin, Israel and Cecil B. Currey. *For God and Country: The History of a Constitutional Challenge to the Army Chaplaincy.* Hoboken, NJ: KTAV Publishing House, 1995.

Eberle, Gary. *The Geography of Nowhere.* Kansas City, MO: Sheed and Ward, 1994.

Estep, William R. *The Anabaptist Story,* revised ed. Grand Rapids: MI, 1975.

Fisher, Carlton. *Common Ground for God and Country: Enabling Chaplains of Various Faith Groups to Work Together for the Common Good,* Columbia Theological Seminary, Decatur, Georgia, 2002.

Fisher, Chaplain (COL) Carlton Fisher. *The Commonalities of Modern Religious Terrorists,* a research report submitted to the faculty of Air War College, Maxwell AFB, 26 September 2012.

Foster, Richard. *Celebration of Discipline: The Path to Spiritual Growth.* San Francisco, CA: Harper Collins Publishers, 1998.

Frankl, Victor E. *Man's Search for Meaning.* Boston, MA: Beacon Press, 1959.

Fromkin, David. *A Peace to End All Peace: The Fall of the Ottoman Empire and the Creation of the Modern Middle East.* New York, NY: Holt Paperbacks, 20th Anniversary Edition, 2009.

Fowler, James, *Stages of Faith: The Psychology of the Human Development and the Quest for Meaning.* San Francisco: Harper's Publishing Company, 1981.

Gibran, Khalil. *The Prophet.* New York, NY: Quality Paperback Book Club by arrangement with Alfred A. Knopf, Inc., 1995.

Gorka, Katharine. "The Flawed Science Behind America's Counter-Terrorism Strategy." A white paper from the Council on Global Security, 2014.

Guthrie, Shirley. *Christian Doctrine: Teachings of the Christian Church*. Atlanta, GA, John Knox Press, 1968.

Halsall, Paul. Web Editor for *On Loving God* by Bernard of Clairvaux. GrandRapids, MI: The Christian Classics Ethereal Library. http://www.ccel.org/ccel/bernard/loving_god.html.

Hatch, Nathan. *The Democratization of American Christianity*: New Haven: Yale University Press, 1989.

Houck, Chaplain (LTC) Ira C. III, USA. "Strategic Religious Engagement for Peacebuilding," a Civilian Research Project. Carlisle Barracks, PA: Army War College, 17 March 2009.

Hudson, Winthrop S., *Religion in America*, 3rd ed. New York, NY: Charles Scribner's Sons, 1981.

Johnson, Ben Campbell, *Pastoral Spirituality: A Focus for Ministry*. Philadelphia: The Westminster Press, 1988.

Johnston, William, ed. *The Cloud of the Unknowing*. London, England, Image, 1996.

Joint Publication 1-05. *Religious Affairs in Joint Operations*. Washington, D.C.: Joint Chiefs of Staff, 13 November 2009.

Khaled, Hosseini. *Kite Runner*. New York, NY: Riverhead Trade, 2004.

Mansfield, Stephen. *The Faith of the American Soldier*. Lake Mary, FL: Charisma House, 2004.

Keirsey, David. *Please Understand Me II: Temperament, Character, Intelligence*. Del Mar, CA: Prometheus Nemesis Book Company, 1998.

Knauer, Kelly. Editor. *The Middle East: The History, The Cultures, The Conflicts, The Faiths*, Time Books: DesMoines, Iowa, 2006.

Kung, Hans, *Yes to a Global Ethic*. New York, New York: Continuum Publishing Company, 1996.

Kubler-Ross, Elizabeth. *On Death and Dying*. New York, NY: Scribner, 1997.

Kung, Hans, *Global Responsibility: In Search of a New World Ethic*. New York: Continuum Publishing Company, 1993.

Kung, Hans, *A Global Ethic: The Declaration of the Parliament of the World's Religions.* New York: Continuum Publishing Company, 1993.

Larson, Edward J. *Summer for the Gods: The Scopes Trial and America's Continuing Debate over Science and Religion.* NewYork, NY: Edward J. Larson, 1997.

Latourette, Kenneth Scott. *A History of Christianity*, Volume I and II, Revised Editiion. NewYork: Harper and Row Publishers, 1975.

Lee, Chaplain (COL) William, Lt Col Christopher J. Burke and Lt Col Zonna M. Crayne. "Military Chaplains as Peace Builders: Embracing Indigenous Religions in Stability Operations." Research Report. Maxwell Air ForceBase, AL: Air Force Fellows, CADRE/AR, April 2004.

Little, David, *Comparative Religious Ethics.* New York: Harper and Row Publishers, 1978.

Macquarrie, John. *Principles of Christian Theology*, 2nd ed. New York: NY, Charles Scribner's Sons, 1977.

Maier, Paul L., translator. *Eusebius: The Church History,* 4th ed. Grand Rapids, MI: Kregel Academic and Professional, 1999.

Maqsood, Ruqaiyyah Waris, *Teach Yourself Islam.* London: Hodder Headline, 1994.

McBeth, Leon H. *A Sourcebook for Baptist Heritage.* Nashville, TN: B&H Academic, 1990.

McBride, Chaplain (LTC) Terry. Power Point Briefing, "Religious Leader Liaison Operations for First Army Division East," presented circa 2009 [no date was listed on the briefing].

McDevitt, V. Edmund. *The First California's Chaplain.* Fresno, CA: Academy Library Guild, 1956.

McDonald, Lee M. *The Formation of the Christian Biblical Cannon*, Peabody, MA: Hendrickson Publishers, 1995.

McDowell, Josh. *Evidence that Demands a Verdict: Historical Evidences for the Christian Faith.* Campus Crusade for Christ, Inc., 1972.

McGinn, Bernard. *Christian Spirituality: Origins to the Twelfth Century.* New York, NY: The Crossroad Publishing Company, 1997.

Meek, Chaplain (COL) Robert T. and MSG Ron R. Brooks. Power Point Briefing, "Engagements Training for Multi-National Division, North (MND-N) Religious Support Teams," 16 August 2008.

Michael, Chester P. *Arise: A Christian Psychology of Love*. Charlottesville, VA: The Open Door Inc., 1981.

Michael, Chester P. *Prayer and Temperament*. Charlottesville, VA: The Open Door, Inc., 1991.

Michener, James. *The Covenant*. New York, NY: Fawcett, 1987.

Michener, James. *The Source*. Fawcett. New York, NY, 1986.

Mitchell, Stephen. *Tao Te Ching: A New English Version*. Harper Perennial: New York, NY, 1988.

Mortenson, Greg. *Three Cups of Tea*. Penguin Books: New York, New York, 2006.

Niehbuhr, H. Richard. *Christ and Culture*. London, England: Harper and Row Publishers, 1951.

Munsey, Brenda, *Moral Development, Moral Education and Kohlberg: Basic Issues in Philosophy, Psychology Religion, and Education*. Birmingham: Religious Religious Education Press, 1980.

Naipaul, V. S. *Among the Believers: An Islamic Journey*. New York, NY: Random House, 1981.

Naipaul, V.S. *Beyond Belief: Islamic Excursions Among the Converted Peoples*. New York, NY: Random House, 1998.

Nash, Ronald H. *Christian Faith and Historical Understanding*. Dallas: Zondervan Publishing Company, 1984.

Nasr, Vali. *The Shia Revival: How Conflicts within Islam Will Shape the Future*. London, England: W. W. Norton and Company, 2007.

Pagels, Elaine. *The Origen of Satan*. New York, NY: Vintage Books, 1995.

Peck, Chaplain (LTC) Steve, Joint Multinational Training Command Writer Instructor, Power Point Briefing. "Religious Leader Liaison Introduction Class, for USAREUR Combined Arms Training Center National," [no date given].

Peck, M. Scott. *A Different Drum: Community Making and Peace*. Simon and Schuster, 1998.

Peck, M. Scott. *Further Along the Road Less Traveled: The Unending Journey Toward Spiritual Growth*. New York: Simon and Schuster, 1993.

Peck, M. Scott. *The Road Less Traveled: A New Psychology of Love, Traditional Values and Spiritual Growth*. New York: NY: Simon and Schuster, 1978.

Peck, M. Scott. *The People of the Lie*. New York, NY: Simon and Schuster, 1998.

Pew Research Center. "Religious Landscape Study," 2015 report.

Pew Research Center. "A Report on the Size and Distribution of the World's Christian Population," The Pew Forum of Religious and Public Life, Pew Research Center, analysis, December 19, 2011.

Pew Research Center. "Religious Landscape Survey," February 2008.

Proctor, Master John Proctor. "A Short History or Religious Leader Engagement Operations in Operation Iraqi Freedom." http://www.slideshare.net/JWP82/a-short-history-of-religious-leder-engagements-in-operation-iraqi-freedomMS (accessed 30 September 2011).

Qutb, Sayyid. *In the Shade of the Quran*. Nairobi, Kenya: The Islamic Foundation, 1979.

Ratnesar, Romesh. "Madeleine Albright Opens Up," Time U.S. website, 27 April 2006, http://www.tiime.com/timie/nation/article/0,8599,1181 (accessed 28 November 2011).

Religious Ministry Team Handbook, MCRP 6-12A. U.S. Marine Corps. Department of the Navy: Headquarters, U.S. Marine Corps, 16 May 2003.

Richardson, Chaplain (Major General). Subject: "Air Force Chaplain Corps Policy on Religious Leader Engagement." Department of the Air Force. Office of the Chief of Chaplains. Memorandum, 6 October, 2009.

Roberts, J. M. *History of the World*, Third Edition, London: Penguin Books, 1995.

Rushdie, Salman. *Midnight's Children*. New York: Random House, 2006.

Schaick, Chaplain (LT Col) Steven. "Examining the Role of Chaplains as Non Combatants while Involved in Religious Leader Engagement/Liaison." Research Report. Maxwell AFB, AL: Air War College, 17 February 2009.

Sheehy, Gail. *New Passages: Mapping Your Life across Time*. New York, NY: Ballantine Books, 1995.

Sheehy, Gail. *Passages.* New York, NY: Ballantine Books, 1976.

Shelly, Bruce, *Church History in Plain Language.* Nashville, TN: Thomas Nelson, 2008.

Sider, Ronald J. *Rich Christian in an Age of Hunger.* New York: NY: Paulist Press, 1977.

Smalley, Gary. *The Blessing.* New York, NY: Pocket Books, 1990.

Spitz, Lewis W., ed. *The Protestant Reformation.* Englewood Cliffs, NJ: Prentice-Hall, Inc. 1966.

Sullivan, Michael, Executive Producer. *God in America,* PBS Frontline Film Documentary. Boston, MA: WGBH Education Foundation, 2010.

Van der Ven, Johannes, *Formation of the Moral Self.* Grand Rapids: Eerdman's Publishing Company, 1988.

Warren, Rick. *The Purpose Driven Life.* Grand Rapids, MI: Zondervan, 2002.

Watt, W. Montgomery. *Islamic Philosophy and Theology.* Edinburgh: Edinburgh University Press, 1985.

Whiston, William, translator. *The Works of Josephus: Complete and unabridged.* Peadbody, MA: Hendrickson, 1980.

Winter, Donald. Secretary of the Navy. Subject: Chaplain Advisement and Liaison. Memorandum, SECNAVINST 1730.10, 23 January 2009.

Winter, Donald. Secretary of the Navy. Subject: Religious Ministry Within the Department of the Navy. Memorandum, SECNAVINST 1730.D, 8 August 2011.

Wright, Lawrence. *Thirteen Days in September: The Dramatic Story of the Struggle for Peace.* New York, NY: Vintage, 2015.

The following list contains the names of the authors I consulted in my paper entitled "Commonalities of Modern Religious Terrorists."

Armstrong, Karen. *A History of God: The 4000-Year Quest of Judaism, Christianity, and Islam.* New York, NY: Ballantine Books, 1994.

Armstrong, Karen. *Holy War: The Crusades and Their Impact on Today's World.* New York, NY: Anchor Books, 2001.

Sources Consulted

Armstrong, Karen. *The Battle for God: A History of Fundamentalism*. New York, NY: Ballantine Books, 2001.

Berman, Eli. *Radical, Religious and Violent: The New Economics of Terrorism*. London England: The MIT Press, 2009.

Bhutto, Benazir. *Reconciliation: Islam, Democracy, and the West*. New York, NY: Harper Collins Publishers, 2008.

Hoffman, Bruce. *Inside Terrorism*. New York, NY: Columbia University Press, 1998.

Hoffman Joseph R. *The Just War and Jihad*. Amherst, NY: Prometheus Books, 2006.

Juergensmeyer, Mark. *Terror in the Mind of God: The Global Rise of Religious Violence*. Berkeley, CA: University of California Press, 2003.

Lewis, Bernard. *The Crisis of Islam, Holy War and Unholy Terror*. New York, NY: Random House, 2004.

Lifton, Robert Jay. *Destroying the World to Save It: Aum Shinrikyo, Apocalyptic Violence, and the New Global Terrorism*. New York, NY: Metropolitan Books, 1999.

Markusen, Eric and Craig Summers. *Collective Violence: Harmful Behavior in Groups and Governments*. New York, NY: Rowman and Littlefield Publishers, Inc., 1999.

Michael, George. "Adam Gadahn and Al-Qaeda's Internet Strategy," *Middle East Policy*, Vol., XVI, No. 3, Fall 2009.

Michael, George. *The Enemy of My Enemy: The Alarming Convergence of Militant Islam and the Extreme Right*. Lawrence, KS: University Press of Kansas, 2006.

The following list contains sources I consulted on emotional quotient (EQ).

Bar, Rueven. The Bar-On Model of Emotional-Social Intelligence web site. Rueven Bar-On.org (accessed 27 November 2011).

Furnham, Adrian and K.V. Petrides. "On the Dimensional Structure of Emotional Intelligence." London, UK: Department of Psychology, University College, 1999.

Salovey, Peter and John D. Mayer, Susan Lee Goldman, Carolyn Turvey and Tibor P. Palfai. "Emotional Attention, Clarity, and Repair: Exploring Emotional Intelligence Using the Trait Meta-Mood Scale," Emotion, Disclosure, and Health. Washington D.C.: American Psychological Association, 1995.

The 1997 Mayer-Salovey Four Branch Model of Emotional Intelligence. EQI.ORG. http://eqi.org/4bmodel.htm#The 1997 Mayer-Salovey 4 Branch Model of Emotional Intelligence (accessed 27 November 2011).

About the Author

Carlton (Carl) Fisher is a three-time bronze star recipient and the Aleph Institute 2004 Chaplain of the Year. As a dual-career chaplain, he served as a chaplain in the Federal Bureau of Prisons with service in maximum, medium, and minimum-security prisons and still serves in the U.S. Army Reserve in the rank of brigadier general as the senior chaplain for the Army Reserve. His many military assignments include deployments to Afghanistan and Iraq and service as Advisor on Individual Readiness to the Chief of the Army Reserve.

Chaplain Fisher earned a Doctorate of Ministry from Columbia Theological Seminary, a Master of Strategic Studies from the Air War College, a Master of Divinity from Southwestern Baptist Theological Seminary, and a B.A. from Georgia State University. He is a graduate of Command and General Staff College, Airborne School, and an honor graduate from the Federal Law Enforcement Training Academy.

Fisher is married to Lisa Peace Fisher. They have three adult children, Travis, Hannah and Chloé. He is the son of Carlton and Rose Fisher of Wilcox County, Georgia. He is also the author of *Where Warrior's Walk: A Chaplain's Guide on Life, Family and Work.*

Made in the USA
Lexington, KY
03 September 2018